THE ECONOMIES OF
THE BALKAN COUNTRIES

THE BALKANS AFTER 1945

THE ECONOMIES OF THE BALKAN COUNTRIES

Albania, Bulgaria, Greece, Romania, Turkey, and Yugoslavia

Nicholas V. Gianaris

PRAEGER SPECIAL STUDIES • PRAEGER SCIENTIFIC

Library of Congress Cataloging in Publication Data

Gianaris, Nicholas V.
  The economies of the Balkan countries.

  Includes index.
  1. Balkan Peninsula—Economic conditions.
I. Title.
HC401.G5   1982   330.9496   81-10748
ISBN 0-03-060232-7   AACR2

82-10260

Published in 1982 by Praeger Publishers
CBS Educational and Professional Publishing
A Division of CBS, Inc.
521 Fifth Avenue, New York, New York 10175 U.S.A.

© 1982 by Praeger Publishers

23456789   145   987654321

Printed in the United States of America

To the peoples of the Balkans

PREFACE

From antiquity to the present time, the Balkan Peninsula has been the battleground of rival cultures, economic institutions, and peoples (Illyrians, Thracians, Greeks, Persians, Romans, Slavs, Turks). This is so mainly because it is located at the crossroad of three continents—Europe, Asia, and Africa—and thus is affected by and affects developments not only in Europe, but in the whole world.

From an economic point of view, there is an enormous diversity of problems in the Balkan countries, and it is difficult for a book to encompass all of them. There is not a dualistic schema with pure market and pure command economies; rather, there are all kinds of varieties and diversities between the two economic extremes. What is common in all these countries is the acceptance of the extension of industrial civilization, which brings the need for closer cooperation among them. However, it should be recognized that there are so many political, social, and ethnic elements involved that any analysis without regard to noneconomic matters would be narrow and self-defeating.

It is our hope that this survey will suggest, and lead to, more detailed studies of the various phases of the Balkan economies. Such studies might be of major practical value in the coming years, since the Balkan Peninsula is expected to play an important role in facilitating transportation and trade between Europe and the Middle East. Moreover, the trends toward closer cooperation among the Balkan nations, with their diverse economic ideologies, present new areas for further research and exploration not only in economics but also in sociocultural and political developments. However, the weakness of comparative analyses of countries with different economic systems, such as the Balkans, remains a major difficulty and a challenge to economic theory and measurement.

Although a considerable number of studies have been made on the economies of the individual Balkan countries, little or no attention has been given to the Balkan economies as a group. This work attempts to fill this lacuna and to furnish a comprehensive examination of the economic development of this region. Recent visits and personal contacts in all Balkan countries, except Albania, have reinforced the belief of the author that the Balkan peoples desire closer economic and sociocultural cooperation for the improvement of their standards of living.

The purpose of this book is to reveal the main characteristics of the Balkan economies and to review developmental trends toward closer cooperation among them. Such trends may affect the nature of development in larger blocs of countries, particularly between the Common Market group in western Europe and the

Comecon bloc of eastern Europe, or even between market economies and planned economies in general. From that point of view, portions of the book can be used as supplementary material to related graduate or undergraduate courses in comparative economic systems, public policy, and international economic development.

After a brief historical review in Chapters 2 and 3, emphasis is given to the more vital recent phases of the economic and social life of the Balkan peoples. To make this study clearer and more practical, ample statistical data are provided in tabular form. Chapters 4, 5, and 6 deal with human and natural resources, the economic structure, and the sectoral organization and development of the Balkans. Chapters 7 and 8 deal with the foreign sector from the viewpoint of trade, investment, and the possibilities of closer cooperation and eventual integration of the Balkan countries.

I wish to acknowledge my indebtedness to Professors Ernest Bloch, David Connoli, Solomon Fabricant, George Giannaris, Selam Kute, Stergio Mourgo, Gus Papulia, John Roche, Dominick Salvatore, Eva Santis, John Shena, Paul Voura, and Xenophon Zolotas for their stimulating comments during the earlier stages of preparation of this book. I gained significant insights from valuable discussions with Professors John Kenneth Galbraith and Arthur Schlessinger, Jr., during the International Conference on the Future of Democracy (Athens, October 1977), on matters of trade expansion and the possibility of "convergence" in the Balkans. Professors Ilie Ceausescu, Aurel Chibutiu (Romanian Academy), Eleftherios Pournarakis, and Robert Wolf provided useful criticism during a related panel discussion during the Symposium on Southeastern Europe (April 1977, at Columbus, Ohio). Many thanks to all my colleagues, especially Claude Bove, Clive Daniel, Swati Desai, Richard Kjetsaa, and Laura Nowak, for their valuable suggestions for the improvement of the manuscript. My final debt to Felix Batista, Nancy Dudrow, and Jack Harte for their assistance in typing, photocopying, and related technical services.

CONTENTS

LIST OF TABLES AND FIGURES

PART I
Socioeconomic Background

INTRODUCTION TO PART I

Part I of this study presents a brief historical review of the economic problems of the Balkan countries, and attempts to shed light on the underlying demographic factors that have affected the process of development in the area. It also points out that the complex terrain, the struggle against invasions, and the political and economic instability within the region have hindered regional cooperation and racial assimilation of the Balkan peoples, in a way similar to what other countries have experienced throughout history. The strategic position of the peninsula has attracted the intrusion and repeated involvement of the great powers in the affairs of these countries, for the promotion of their own geopolitical and economic interests.

From ancient times to the Roman period, then through Byzantium, the Ottoman occupation, and primarily during the postliberation and interwar years, the Balkan Peninsula had such a turbulent history that some specialists argued that peace in the West could be assured if the Balkans could be sunk beneath the sea. Events there were usually reported to the rest of the world in times of trouble and terror; otherwise they were ignored.

The following review of such a broad history of the Balkans is admittedly very brief and selective, but it was considered necessary for an objective evaluation of the socioeconomic complexities of the countries involved.

1

INTRODUCTION

Geographically, the Balkan Peninsula is located southeast of the Alps and the Carpathian Mountains. It is a mountainous area (the term "Balkans" means "mountains" in Turkish) that includes Albania, Bulgaria, Greece, Romania, Yugoslavia, and part of Turkey. Although all six countries are included in most Balkan studies, at times Turkey is excluded as an Asian country and Romania as a country depending heavily on central Europe.

It is usually argued that the geographical complexity of the area has been a significant factor in the disunity and polyethnicity of the Balkan peoples, who throughout history have repeatedly found themselves in the midst of powerful cultural and economic crosscurrents. In a region with such great diversity, it is difficult to find a unifying force, a center around which a strong state could be created.

Although the Hellenes (Greeks) were not considered the original inhabitants of the peninsula, they were the first to leave a record of themselves and their neighbors. The Illyrians were probably the first inhabitants of the peninsula. They settled mainly on the western coast, opposite the heel of Italy, where the Albanians (who are considered their descendants) live today. In the eastern part of the peninsula were the light-haired and gray-eyed Thracians. The Vlachs or Walachians and present-day Romanians are, in all likelihood, their descendants.

In the southern part of the peninsula—in mainland Greece—were the Achaeans, an Alpine people who had migrated from central Europe. They were descendants of Achaeus, grandson of Hellen, the legendary ancestor of the Hellenes—a branch of the Indo-European race to which Romans, Germans, Slavs, and other Europeans belong.

The Balkan triangle incorporates a sample of different economic systems. Greece and Turkey follow the market (Western) economic model; Albania, Bulgaria, and Romania follow the centrally planned (Eastern) economic model, with some variations; Yugoslavia follows a peculiar mix of market and planned economic systems with worker-managed enterprises. Thus, recent economic and sociopolitical trends in this peninsula are of considerable interest.

The main problems of the economies of Greece, Turkey, and (to some extent) Yugoslavia are those that plague any other market economy: inflation, unemployment, and maldistribution of income and wealth. As these economies waver between the Scylla of unemployment and the Charybdis of inflation, policy makers in these countries may turn away from relying on the market mechanism, and adopt control measures in order to correct undesirable economic trends. Such conditions may lead to more government, despite the fact that "the government is best that governs least," as Thomas Jefferson said.

The centrally planned economies of other Balkan countries face the problems of low production incentives, inadequate consumer choices, and, in many cases, inefficient resource allocation. Production incentives seem to be higher under private ownership than under state or public ownership, especially in agriculture and small-scale industries. As Aristotle once said in criticizing Plato's ideal communist state, "Common ownership means common neglect." The establishment of middle-level corporations, and the encouragement of private farm markets and vertical and regional decentralization of decision making, practiced to a large extent by Balkan planned economies in recent years, are measures intended to stimulate incentives and increase productivity.

Such concurrent trends and reforms bring the Balkan nations closer to each other, and prepare the ground for more economic cooperation and, possibly, common developmental policies. The rapid growth of mutual trade in recent years, and the numerous bilateral and multilateral agreements for joint investment projects, tend to submerge ideological and nationalistic differences and to lead these economies toward eventual convergence by adopting the best of each other's traits. There is always the possibility of recurrence of the regional or political disputes and frictions that these nations have experienced so frequently in the past. However, such frictions would most probably lead to greater economic isolation, restrictions on resource movements, and less socioeconomic development.

The need for hard currencies, the recent inflationary pressures (expressed either in price increases or in commodity shortages), and the gradual transformation from agriculture to industry and services, as well as the need for resource utilization and environmental protection, are common problems that require similar and coordinated policies. Moreover, the fact that the Balkan Peninsula stands as a bridge between Europe and the Middle East makes common efforts for the improvement of the transportation network necessary.

CURRENT PROBLEMS

At present, common problems facing the Balkan region that are expected to continue in the future, are those of reducing inflation, raising labor productivity and satisfying growing demand, cutting down on raw-material and energy consumption, and correcting adverse foreign trade balances. To avoid extensive use of raw materials and increased imports, plans with somewhat lower overall and industrial growth targets are implemented. To increase productivity, reforms are introduced that will stimulate capital investments.

Greece and Turkey have introduced tax incentives and other benefits to encourage investment, particularly in backward regions. The governments of these countries make great efforts to manipulate aggregate demand through public spending and tax programs, so that they can achieve the happy, but perhaps elusive, combination of high employment and low inflation. However, as similar programs in other market economies indicate, the problems of inflation and unemployment require long-term policies committed to greater and more efficient production through capital investment and incentives for higher rates of labor productivity. To fight inflation and reduce unemployment, the governments of Greece, Turkey, and Yugoslavia are trying to reduce bureaucracy, implement fiscal restraints, and boost productive investment.

Bulgaria and Romania have effected a number of measures designed to give greater latitude to large enterprises to manage their own activities. Such measures include greater worker participation in decision making, profit sharing and higher rewards to the workers and managers of efficient enterprises, and bringing management closer to production operations. Moreover, reorganizations in industry and agriculture include the creation of larger production units and delegating more powers to middle management on matters of self-financing and more direct participation in the planning process.

Such reforms, which have been introduced in almost all socialist Balkan countries, emphasize more autonomy and a competitive spirit among enterprises. Reforms in Yugoslavia incorporate the novel concept of workers' self-management as an evolutionary process of transforming capitalism to socialism and "withering away the state," as the supporters of the system argue, not in the distant future but in our time. It would seem that a similar principle is contemplated, and is slowly creeping into, the economic reforms practiced by other countries in the area, in the form of easing statism and decentralizing decision making. The dilemma in such reforms is how to stimulate efficiency through decentralization and, at the same time, avoid antisocialist tendencies.

In all Balkan countries inflation has become a serious problem, especially in Greece, Turkey, and Yugoslavia. Each group or class in these countries seeks a bigger share of the national income that is based on its aspirations and expectations about inflation. In the controlled Balkan economies, inflation, which officially is not recognized, is attributed primarily to structural emphasis on investment and the resulting shortages in consumer goods relative to incomes. Continuous emphasis on the capital-producing sector, at the neglect of the consumer sector, in these countries leads to periodic shortages in needed commodities. This is a form of concealed inflation. Occasionally people complain, not so much of the time wasted lining up to buy necessities as of the food wasted through the urge to buy as much as possible of whatever is available, useful or not, because it may not be available later.

Because of bureaucratic delays, workers sometimes complain of long periods of forced idleness on the job while waiting for raw materials, spare parts, or maintenance. The managers, on the other hand, complain that workers do not take their jobs seriously enough to catch up with projected targets during the stop-go process of production.

Because of regional economic differences inherited from the past, all post-war Balkan governments have emphasized policies of development of backward areas, which include establishment of infrastructural facilities, subsidies, and tax incentives for new investment. However, such policies of lessening regional inequities have had only limited success, and per capita income disparities remain a serious problem for the policy makers.

FOREIGN TRADE AND SOCIO-ECONOMIC RAPPROCHEMENT

A common problem for all Balkan countries is the worsening balance of trade. Year after year they face sizable trade deficits and rapidly growing foreign debts. The ratio of debt service to exports increases; more exports are required to pay for servicing the debt; the value of the currency declines; and the credit position deteriorates. That is why all Balkan countries, except perhaps Albania, have changed their laws to encourage foreign investment. This is particularly true for Bulgaria and Romania. These countries hope to attract foreign firms that will do business on their soil, thereby acquiring new technology, improving their terms of trade, and earning hard currency needed to service their growing debt.

Heavy dependence on foreign trade requires flexibility in foreign transactions and, eventually, structural innovations in the economy. However, bilateral negotiations should remain; otherwise, many opportunities may be lost, since some countries want to make greater concessions than others do. Nevertheless, concessions between the European Economic Community (EEC), or Common Market, of which Greece is a full member and Turkey an associate member, and the Council of Mutual Economic Assistance (CMEA), or Comecon, to which Bulgaria and Romania belong, come in packages and affect all member countries.

Sluggish growth in agricultural production, light industry, and services is forcing the planners of the socialist Balkan economies to further loosen central controls and allow more factory autonomy, and to experiment with a new economic principle in which regulation through planning is combined with regulation of the market. Also, the gradual abandonment of food subsidies is expected to reduce consumption and improve the balance of trade in these countries. Such policies are implemented with caution, however, because they may lead to price increases and, possibly, to unrest among workers.

Gradually, Balkan countries are laying aside ideology and making efforts to generate practical solutions to problems concerning a better livelihood for their peoples through a growing foreign trade and improved relations with other countries. In the past, Western discrimination and a monolithic foreign trade system in the East held back expansion of trade in the area. However, growing dependence on money, both domestically and internationally, an increase in multilateral transactions, and the growing role of interest and prices in socialist Balkan economies show striking similarities with the capitalist economies. Such a paradoxical development and the growing "transideological" monetary cooperation make the economic systems of the Balkan countries increasingly similar, and indicate that some arguments of the convergence thesis may prove to be correct.

Economically, there are state monopolies, national price systems (that fail to reflect relative scarcities), and arbitrary exchange rates and inconvertible currencies that lead to domestic and foreign imbalances. Politically, although power is scarce for most persons in the Balkan planned economies, it is abundant for the few, and this gives politics great control over economics. At the same time it is difficult to accept a trade-off between freedom and equality in these economies, despite arguments that an egalitarian society exists.

It should be recognized that country comparisons on economic performance and factor productivity are difficult in practice because of differences in the process of price determination, consumer tastes, and data gathering and interpretation. Secor-by-sector or industry-by-industry comparisons probably are more reliable.

SCOPE

Historically, various peoples have inhabited the Balkan Peninsula. Even the present composition of population of each of its nations is not homogeneous. Furthermore, each of these countries follows its own economic ideology. Perhaps the Balkan Peninsula is the only area in the world that incorporates such a variety of economic systems.

Long occupations, ethnic conflicts, and constant involvement of "big powers" have been common experiences of the Balkan nations throughout history. The area is strategically vital to the world's power centers, but the people who live in the region are not responsible for others' sensitivity and interests. Like the rest of us, they prefer to put their own needs and aspirations first. They do not like to have their own interests subordinated to those of other countries and to remain under the constant uneasiness of superpowers' rivalries. Thus, it is of great interest to examine the possibilities of closer cooperation among the people of this region.

With respect to natural and human resources of the peninsula, the question may arise as to their effective use to achieve high rates of economic growth (compared with other countries at the same or higher stages of development). Comparisons of labor and capital productivities, differences in inflation rates, and deviations in economic policies will indicate areas of further cooperation and possible joint investment ventures.

An important question related to the structure and organization of production and distribution in the Balkan countries is which economic system can be more effective in achieving the highest rates of growth with the least sacrifice in terms of consumer choice, workers' advantages, pollution, and the like. To what extent and in which sectors of the economy can the price mechanism bring about better results than the system of central controls? Is planning—any form of planning instead of no planning at all—a proper instrument to coordinate all the sectors of the economy so as to achieve the highest levels of output, while avoiding the traps of bureaucracy? Are the Balkan countries in the process of economic convergence by adopting the best of each other's traits?

Economic development, which refers to material improvement and the dissemination of knowledge and technology, is identified with structural transformation of the economy from predominantly subsistence agriculture to industry and services. To what extent has this sectoral transformation been achieved by the Balkan economies?

Increase in intra-Balkan and foreign trade would spread the benefits of development to all the countries concerned through division of labor and specialization. However, questions may be raised about sectoral and regional inequalities that may appear in each country and within the region. Moreover, while the rapid spread of multinational corporations in the area is conducive to the dissemination of technological transformation and managerial know-how, it has also created a fear of foreign domination in some segments of the population.

More economic growth means increased production, which in turn may lead to resource depletion, urbanization, and environmental deterioration. Economic progress eases some problems, such as health, education, and material well-being, but it creates others that affect the quality of life. Thus, closer cooperation among the Balkan nations is desirable not only on economic but also on sociocultural and environmental grounds. The following chapters review all of the aforementioned issues associated with the economic conditions and trends in the Balkan countries.

2

A HISTORICAL PERSPECTIVE

ANCIENT TIMES

From 3400 B.C. to 1100 B.C., the first Greek culture flourished on Crete, a Mediterranean island south of the Balkan Peninsula. This culture was transmitted from the Egyptian and Mesopotamian civilizations, which developed around the Nile, the Tigris, and the Euphrates rivers. Gradually the Cretan (Minoan) culture, radiating over the neighboring areas, influenced the mainlanders of the southern Balkan Peninsula, the Achaeans, who came in successives waves from the Alps and central Europe. The Achaeans, with Mycenae (in Peloponnesus) as their center, adopted the Cretan culture and developed their own civilization, which in turn spread to the Aegean islands, Syria, Asia Minor, and other Mediterranean lands. They developed into a powerful maritime nation, and by 1400 B.C. had overrun Crete. Around 1200 B.C. they started the long Trojan expedition in Asia Minor (recounted by Homer in his *Iliad* and *Odyssey*).

About 1100 B.C. the Dorians, from the same Hellenic race as the Achaeans, appeared. They were considered to be the descendants of Dorus, the son of Hellen. Under pressure from the Thracians and Illyrian barbarians, they infiltrated and finally colonized central Greece, the Aegean islands, southwestern Asia Minor, Sicily, and Crete, gradually destroying the civilizations of the Minoans and the Mycenaeans. Finally the Achaeans were restricted to the northern coast of Peloponnesus, mostly to the area presently known as the province of Achaea. The southern coast of Peloponnesus (Laconia) was considered an important center of the Dorians. The Spartans, a military and disciplined people, were always looked upon as the descendants of the Dorians.

During the sixth century B.C., the Achaeans established a league of ten or twelve towns, which survived until the fourth century B.C., when the area was conquered by the Macedonians. Following the death of Alexander the Great (323 B.C.), the Achaean League was reestablished (in 280 B.C.); between 251 and

229 B.C. it was expanded by the addition of the non-Achaean states of Sicyon, Corinth, Megalopolis, and Argos. Each member of the confederacy retained its independence, but all members participated in a council that met twice a year to formulate a common economic and foreign policy and to enact legislation involving common coinage and related matters. Aratus of Sicyon and Philopoemen of Megalopolis were among the prominent statesmen of this Achaean League, which resembled modern federal systems and economic unions similar to the present European economic communities (EEC, EFTA, Comecon).

From the Homeric Age (around 1200 B.C.) to the Classical Age (beginning in the fifth century B.C.), the society of the early Hellenes was primarily agricultural and pastoral. By now the city-state (*polis*) as an independent political and economic unit had been created. Athens was the main center of civilization at that time. The expansion of city-states brought about the development of trade and commerce in the coastal areas of the Balkan Peninsula and the eastern Mediterranean. It was during that time that the first coins appeared in Lydia and Aegina. Banking services, shipbuilding, and agriculture flourished and markets expanded. Trade and commerce not only were carried out in the coastal areas of the Aegean, Adriatic, and Black seas but also were expanded to Phoenicia, Egypt, Sicily, and other Mediterranean lands.[1] All this was accomplished despite opposition from the Greek philosophers and writers (mainly Plato, Aristotle, and Xenophon) who regarded trade as a dishonest occupation and the charging of interest as immoral and unnatural.[2]

As early as the seventh century B.C., the Ionians, from the western islands of Greece, moved eastward and established a number of colonies, including Byzantium (later renamed Constantinople).

During the Golden Age (fifth century B.C.) Athens reached its acme not only in terms of economic prosperity but also in terms of theories and philosophies that are still part of basic scientific concepts. Together with its nearby port of Piraeus, and under the leadership of Themistocles and Pericles, the area thrived in trade, shipping, industry, and the arts. A number of arcades, the most famous called Degma, were used for exhibitions and exchanges of commodities from all the commercial centers of the Balkan Peninsula and the eastern Mediterranean. Merchants and adventurers sailed eastward to the Indian Ocean and westward to Gibraltar, which ancient Greeks called the Pillars of Hercules to explore new markets and sources of supply. These adventurers were the first to support the notion of a direct canal in the Suez[3] for the purpose of facilitating the flow of trade from the Indian Ocean, through Aden, to the Mediterranean ports and vice versa.

Despite arguments presented by Plato, Herodotus, and Aristotle against tariffs and in favor of direct taxes, ad valorem taxes of 1 to 2 percent were imposed on imports and exports. Later, however, a tax system similar to the modern progressive system, referred to as "contribution," was introduced to finance shipbuilding and other state expenditures. Regulations similar to antitrust laws were enacted to prevent price fixing and to discourage monopolization of the market.

Monopolies were permitted only when they supported state policies or offered free meals to the poor. At that time the systematic study of economics or *oikonomia* (estate management and public administration) was introduced. Much later, prominent economists and theoreticians such as Thomas Aquinas, Adam Smith, Karl Marx, and Joseph Schumpeter based their theories of just prices, division of labor, and welfarism ("the good life"), and their economic ideologies upon such philosophies.[4]

However, the non-Hellenic people who inhabited the interior of the Balkan Peninsula did not share very much in the stimulating experience of the commercial and seafaring Greeks, and remained mostly agricultural and pastoral. The penetration of Greek civilization to the interior plateau and the hellenization of the Balkan Peninsula were difficult, mainly because of mountainous and rough terrain. Nevertheless, Greek colonies were established along the coasts of Dalmatia and the Black Sea, along the banks of the Danube (for instance, Vachia, ten miles from Belgrade, and Histria and Callatis on the Lower Danube).

In the colonies of Dalmatia, metallurgical and other craft works were established, and manufactured goods were exchanged for raw materials produced in the interior by the Illyrian tribes. Similar colonies along the eastern section of the peninsula, where the more tolerant and less ferocious Thracians lived, were more successful in trade and shipping.

The independent and jealous Greek city-states, which once had fought each other, were forced to form alliances and leagues in order to defend their land and civilization from Persian invaders (mainly King Cyrus, Darius, and Xerxes) at Marathon, Salamis, and Plataea. It was Philip II, king of Macedonia (395-336 B.C.) and his son Alexander the Great (a student of Aristotle) who subdued and unified the Greek city-states to finally dispel the Persian danger once and for all. The Macedonians marched northward to the Danube and southward to the rest of Greece; and, under the command of Alexander, they marched eastward through Asia Minor and the Middle East, up to Persia and the Far East. After the death of Alexander, a Greco-Macedonian state, incorporating the Balkans as well as other eastern Mediterranean regions, survived until the area fell under the control of Roman conquerors. Throughout this Hellenistic period (395-106 B.C.) the Macedonians, who claimed to be descendants of Heracles, were thoroughly hellenized and Greek culture was extended within the interior of the Balkan Peninsula. It was also diffused along the eastern Mediterranean coast and even into Asia. As a consequence the Balkan Peninsula lost its economic and social supremacy to other commercial centers of the eastern Mediterranean.[5]

THE ROMAN PERIOD

The Romans first conquered the Adriatic coast, then Macedonia and its environs, and finally southern Greece, when the Achaean League of the Greek states was defeated during the second century B.C. As a result the whole Balkan Peninsula was brought under a single rule for the first time. The Illyrian lands flourished under the Romans, but the rest of the Balkans, especially Greece, suffered a steady economic decline. However, the construction of a well-organized network of paved highways, particularly the one stretching from the Adriatic coast at Dyrrhachium (Durazzo) to Salonika, via Egnatia, provided the basis for the development of trade to the interior. This brought into existence local industries: weaving, marble quarrying, mining, lumbering, production of wine and table delicacies, and the like. Also, military camps in Singidinum (Belgrade), Naissus (Nis), Sardica (Sofia), Philippopolis (Plovdiv), and Adrianople (Edivne) were swiftly expanded into trade centers.

The Latin language was spread throughout Balkania, especially among the Illyrians, to the extent that many people thought that they belonged to the same Roman race, the *Romiosine*. This name was later used as a unifying force against the Ottoman yoke, and even in more recent times. However, Greek culture and civilization also exerted a great influence over the Romans, particularly the upper classes, to the extent that many historians and social scientists call this era the Greco-Roman period.[6] The gradual intrusion of Christianity changed, and sometimes destroyed, the ancient Greek culture, including many valuable monuments.

In the north the Romans used the Danube River as their frontier. However, in A.D. 106, Emperor Trajan crossed the river and conquered the area known as Dacia. Although little is known about the first inhabitants of Romania, it is generally accepted that at that time Dacia was inhabited by Thracians, who engaged mainly in agriculture, cattle raising, mining (gold and silver), and domestic and foreign trade. The Romans, with their efficient administration and the highways they built during the occupation (106-275), brought in people from other areas, mainly Italy, to work the rich lands of Dacia and the mines of Transylvania. Moreover, the excellent administration of justice and the security of life and property under the Roman system stimulated the permanent establishment of peddlers, soldiers, and workers from Italy and other Mediterranean areas in Balkania, especially in Romania.

When the Romans withdrew, under pressure from the Goths, they left behind the name of the state as well as the fundamentals for the Romanian language. They managed to latinize the country to a considerable extent. (Even present-day Romanians take pride in the fact that they are the offspring of the ancient Dacians and Romans. Recently they even changed the spelling of the country's name from Rumania to Romania.) After the Romans a number of invaders—the Avars, Slavs, Getae, Huns, Bulgarians, Hungarians, Kumans, and Tatars—succeeded one another. To secure protection, most of the native inhabitants fled to the Carpathian Mountains. After the string of invasions and disturbances, which lasted for about a thousand years, the Romanian population settled (around the thirteenth century) in the provinces of Moldavia, Wallachia, Transylvania, Bukovina, Bessarabia, and the Banat of Temesvar.

In the south, Roman merchants used the Aegean islands for their shipping and trading activities. During that period the island of Delos became an important junction for the transport and exchange of commodities and slaves from east to west. One authority states that some 10,000 slaves were sold in a single day in this market.[7] A similar prosperous market was developed on the Adriatic coast, where thousands of slaves from the Balkan countries were sold. At that time the term "Slav" meant slave. More than a million slaves from Macedonia, Thrace, and the rest of Greece were sold to Italy and Sicily at a relatively high price, because of the variety in their skills.

The Romans were efficient administrators and organizers. They managed to bring together the diverse Balkan and other Mediterranean peoples, and keep them under their control for centuries. Emperor Augustus is credited with bringing the whole Balkan Peninsula within the Mediterranean civilization. However, it was the Roman Emperor Constantine who broke with Western tradition by enthroning himself in the Greek trading post of Byzantium (later Constantinople). This was where merchants from the Aegean and Black seas met with those from Asia and the Balkan interior, developing the city into an important economic and cultural center.

Although wealth was concentrated with limited numbers of people and the breach between the classes widened, commerce and cottage industries flourished in Balkan cities during the Roman period. The Illyrian lands provided valuable raw materials used by the growing commercial cities. Illyrian peasants provided brave soldiers for the Roman legions, and some became famous emperors, such as Claudius II, Aurelian, and Diocletian. The excellent administration of justice, the good roads, the comforts of the towns (with their theaters and baths), and the granting of Roman citizenship to all freemen of the empire by Emperor Caracalla in 212, facilitated business travel and enhanced the economic and cultural development of the area. However, a number of tribes, mainly of German and Slavic origin, started to move toward the south, using the Danube River as their main route, and gradually weakened the Roman military and administrative structure in the Balkan Peninsula.

BYZANTIUM

The overexpansion of the Roman Empire and the pressures of invaders from the north, mainly Goths, weakened its administration, paralyzed the processes of production and exchange, and led to the rivalries of emperors and armies. At that time (326) Emperor Constantine moved the capital of the empire to New Rome (Constantinople). Because of destructive raids carried out by the Goths, the western section of the empire collapsed and Rome came under the control of Alaric I in 410. However, the eastern part of the empire, known as Byzantium, held its ground for about ten centuries, despite raids by Goths, Slavs, and Mongolians.

Administrative reforms, stimulation of trade (by reducing taxes on commerce), the strengthening of a common Hellenic language, and the introduction of the Christian religion through the efforts of the emperors of Byzantium were primarily responsible for the unity maintained in the East. Moreover, the geographical position of the Balkan Peninsula, with its mountainous area and the protection given by the Danube to the north, enhanced the prospects for the survival of Byzantium. As a result, the reputation of Constantinople as a commercial and industrial center was furthered. Jewelry, pottery, weaponry, shipping, and textiles (mainly silk goods) were its main industries.

Nevertheless, attacks from the north continued against the Byzantine Empire. During the fourth century hordes of Slavs crossed the Danube and pushed the native Illyrians and Thracians southward. The influx of the Slavs into the Balkan Peninsula began as a gradual infiltration. Although other peoples, primarily Mongolian Huns (with Attila as their main leader) and Avars from Asia, crossed the area, they did not settle, as the Slavs did. By the seventh century the Slavs were recognized by Byzantium (mainly by Emperor Heraclius I) as permanent settlers, and started forming the different ethnic groups of later times (Slovenes, Croatians, Serbs, and the groups in Bulgaria). At times Avars attacked the Slavs, and Slav tribes began fighting among themselves. While the Mongolians were nomads, dropping no roots in Balkania, the Slavs kept advancing slowly to the south, creating agricultural settlements.

Near the end of the seventh century a Finno-Tatar race, related to the Huns from Asia and later known as Bulgarians, moved from the Volga valley to the south of the Danube, where they settled. Soon they were assimilated into the Slavic majority, which was primarily engaged in agricultural and pastoral pursuits.[8] During the ninth and tenth centuries this population mix created its own (Bulgarian) ethnicity, and once even threatened to overrun Constantinople. In the ninth and tenth centuries, under Khan Boris and his son Simeon, the Bulgarians reached the peak of their political and economic power. At that time they accepted Christianity from Constantinople and were influenced by Greek culture. In 1054 the Roman Catholic and the Eastern Orthodox churches split over doctrine, ritual, and the infallibility of the pope. The main agents associated with this religious and cultural transformation were the brothers Methodius and Cyril; Methodius introduced what is known as the Cyrillic alphabet which is based on the Greek. With the decline of the Bulgarian state, the development and expansion of the Serbian state occurred in the central Balkans, mainly during the reigns of Ivan II (Ivan Asen) and Stephen Dushan in the thirteenth and fourteenth centuries.

On the western side of the peninsula, the Slavs, coming mainly from the northwestern parts of the Carpathian Mountains during the great migration of the sixth century, pushed the Illyrians southward. Occasionally Slav tribes penetrated and settled in Thessaly and even Peloponnesus. However, the coastal cities and the islands remained Greek and kept their traditional Hellenic character.

In a number of ways the Slavic economic and political system could be characterized as a close partnership of goods, some early form of village cooperative, or an early type of communism. Each member of the village was assigned a task, and for performing it would share equally in the total labor product with all the other community members.[9] As late as the nineteenth century, this type of institution (the *zadruga*) was still found in various parts of the peninsula.

Under pressure from the Slavs coming into western Balkania, the native Illyrians were pushed into the mountainous area of present-day Albania. Despite the Slavic admixture and the influence exerted by the Greeks, Romans, Venetians, and Turks, the Albanian people retained their predominantly pastoral activities and their language. They called their land Skiperia (the nest of the eagles) and considered themselves Skipetars (children of the eagles). It seems that modern Albanians are the descendants of the ancient Illyrians.

In addition to the pressures from the north, the west, and especially the east, the economy of Byzantium experienced a continuous decline. Commercially minded Venetians, who were better organized in shipping and foreign trade, managed to settle in a number of ports and other strategic areas around the Balkan Peninsula. With the Crusaders they captured Constantinople in 1204 and annexed many islands and coastal areas, where they established a feudal system. Although they fled from Constantinople in 1261 under pressure from Michael VIII Palaeologus, the Nicaean emperor, they continued to drain the financial resources of Byzantium by collecting customs revenues and controlling banking activities. Being relieved of imperial taxes, the Venetians could undersell the Greek and other merchants in the lucrative Balkan and Mediterranean markets. Moreover, the Genoese, another commercial people, competed with the Venetians for the possession of the Golden Horn and the lucrative trade of the Black Sea.

In the southern part of the peninsula the land of Hellas was divided up and distributed, mostly to the Latin barons. These fiefs, the largest of which were the duchy of Athens and the principality of Achaia (Morea), were established after the Fourth Crusade (1202-04), and existed for many years.

Within domains under their control, the emperors debased the currencies, increased taxes, spent on luxurious living, and pawned their crown jewels with Venetian financiers. This economic mismanagement, on top of social and religious strife and military weakness, led the empire to the point of bankruptcy, and finally it collapsed.[10] However, the spread of Byzantine religious concepts and educational and legal ideas throughout the Balkan countries influenced all the peoples of the peninsula's interior, who until then had been considered barbarians.

In later periods the East Roman or Byzantine Empire faced a still more serious and untiring enemy from the east, the Mongols. Roaming the plateau of western Asia, they approached and finally swept through the Balkan Peninsula, like waves from an inrushing sea. The struggle went on until the last of the medieval invaders, the Ottoman Turks, occupied Constantinople in 1453.

OTTOMAN OCCUPATION

From the eighth century on, Turkish tribes, mainly Mongolians, moved westward and overwhelmed the Islamic and Byzantine empires. While the Byzantine rulers were preoccupied with political, economic, and religious matters at home, they neglected the incursions of the Turkish horsemen into Asia Minor. Emperor Romanus IV finally decided to come to grips with the Seljuk Turks, but it was too late. He was badly defeated at Manzikert, in distant Armenia, in 1071. Asia Minor, except for the coastal areas, gradually fell into the hands of the Turks.

As mentioned earlier, other factors weakening the aging state of Byzantium were the advances of the Crusades and economic pressures exerted by the Venetians. While the Byzantines lamented the losses and prayed for the recapture of occupied territories, they failed to pay proper attention to their defense. In 1354 the Turks advanced on the Dardanelles and gradually moved into the Balkan Peninsula. Following their usual practice, they distributed conquered lands to their warriors. This policy, together with the toleration of the Christian religion and the forceful recruitment of infant Christian males (janissaries), helped them establish Islam in the Christian Balkans. In 1393, Bulgaria came under the heel of the oppressor, as did other Balkan areas during the following years. In 1453, Constantinople, the political and economic center of Byzantium and the symbol of Christianity in Balkania, fell to Moslems under Sultan Mohammed II.

After a bitter struggle (1444-66) Albania was conquered by the Turks. George Castriota, better known as Scanderbeg under the Turk designation, was an Albanian hero during the struggle against Ottoman occupation. Young Castriota, who escaped from Turkish bondage, organized the Albanians and used guerrilla tactics to defeat the Ottoman armies of Murad II and his son Mohammed II. Because of his successes Scanderbeg was acclaimed the prince of his tribe and hailed by Balkania and the West as the "athlete of Christendom." After his death in 1468, Albania, along with other Balkan states, came under the control of the Turks.

In order to promote the economic well-being of the Balkans, Mohammed recognized the value of trade and industry, and even wanted to repopulate the peninsula with merchants, preferably Greeks. Also, trading privileges that Venice enjoyed under Byzantium were renewed.

Within a few decades after the fall of Constantinople, the whole Balkan Peninsula and its assortment of ethnic groups (Albanians, Bulgarians, Greeks, Romanians, Slavs) were under the Ottoman yoke. For four centuries the Balkan peoples were subjected to ruthless exploitation. But, "far worse than the material injuries were the spiritual wounds, the traces of which it will require generations of educational effort and moral reconstruction to obliterate."[17]

Administratively the Turkish government, called Porte, was concentrated in the *serai* (the sultan's palace), while the counselors (viziers) operated as civil chiefs and army heads. Pashas and *sandjakbegs* were the main regional or provincial chiefs, while *cadis* and muftis acted as judges and jurists. The spahis (landlords and warriors) and janissaries (Christian boys violently recruited and converted to Islam) were part of the Ottoman troops. The sultans rewarded their followers (mainly the spahis) with gifts of land (*ziamets* or smaller *timars*) after each military victory, and trained the most promising janissaries for high positions in administration. The empire was ruled by the sultan and his family for the benefit of Moslems, who monopolized the professions and exploited their Balkan Christian subjects (the *rayahs*). Under the laws of Islam, polygamy was permitted and harems (where women were treated as inferior beings) were common.

The establishment of a common Ottoman system put an end to internal Balkan strife, and perhaps brought the peninsula and the lands of the east Mediterranean some economic improvement; but, if so, it was most likely accomplished with some sacrifice of the liberty of the people and their cultural improvement. Periodically outside powers such as Spain, Venice, Hungary, Poland, Austria, and Russia engaged the Turks in wars, but with limited success.

The Venetian fleet attacked Turkish army and naval forces, and established a number of colonies in Dalmatia and other coastal areas of the Balkan peninsula, as well as on a number of islands, where Venetian-style buildings and fortresses can still be seen. One of the more serious attacks by the Venetians occurred in 1687, when an army commanded by General Francesco Morosini marched from Morea and captured Athens. During the siege of Athens, the Venetians bombarded the Acropolis, which was used as a powder magazine by the Moslems, causing a partial destruction of the Parthenon.[12] Morea was recaptured by the Turks in 1715-18. However, the Ionian islands remained under the control of Venice from 1386 to 1797 and, for a few years (1797-99 and 1804-14), of France.

In Romania, after a short period of independence for Walachia in the thirteenth century and Moldavia in the fourteenth century, the area came under Ottoman domination in the fifteenth century. Prince Vlad III of Walachia, otherwise known as Dracula, strongly resisted the Ottoman occupation, in his peculiar way, by nailing his victims to the ground after the battles in the Romanian plains or nailing fezzes of the Turkish envoys to their heads in order to demonstrate his disdain for the sultan. Around 1600, Prince Michael the Brave managed to assert the independence of Walachia, Moldavia, and Transylvania, but for only a short period.

Economically, before the establishment of the independent principalities of Walachia and Moldavia with a central authority, the Romanian peasants had common ownership of the land in each village (similar to the present cooperatives), giving one-tenth of their produce and three days of labor per year to the village heads (boyars).

During the Ottoman occupation all these principalities were vassal states with some degree of independence. The Turks were more interested in economic exploitation and shipments of grain and sheep to Constantinople than in political domination. As a result, the Romanians enjoyed some degree of autonomy, and the boyars elected their own princes (the *hospodars*). Later the country was split between the main neighboring powers. Austria acquired Transylvania (1699) and Bukovina (1775), Russia obtained Bessarabia (1812), and the rest of Romania remained under Ottoman control. In 1848, Romania and the other subject Balkan states rebelled, seeking national independence.

Toward the end of the Turkish occupation, the boyars and the monasteries controlled a large proportion of land while the peasants worked as serfs. The Greek Phanariots moved into the area as merchants and money lenders, and even achieved political power. The Mavrokordatos family, for instance, furnished five *hospodars* to Moldavia and two to Walachia, where they abolished serfdom in the 1740s.[13] By that time the agricultural sector had been largely commercialized, productivity had increased, and large amounts of grain produced on the plains of Romania were being exported via the Danube and the Black Sea to Austria, Turkey, and Russia. After the introduction of the "Organic Statutes" (1831-32) and the land reforms, large estates were distributed among the poor farmers. Two-thirds of each large estate was given to the tilling peasants and one-third to the local boyar. The boyar also had the authority to distribute the land after the death of the peasant owners. However, he imposed heavy labor obligations in return, or kept the land for himself. The result was the creation in Romania of large latifundia owned mainly by the boyars. In addition to large payments in kind, every Walachian peasant owed the boyar some 14 days of labor a year, set in such terms of production that not even the mythological Cyclopes could have achieved.

The border wars and the heavy taxation and oppression practiced by Moslems and janissaries helped the Balkan *rayahs* to rise and to start a long and difficult war of liberation. Moreover, separate authorities, independent of the sultan, were created primarily by Pasvan Oglu in a large part of Bulgaria and by Ali Pasha in Epirus and Albania during the early 1800s. About that time the Greeks of the Morea and archipelago, influenced by the promise of support from Empress Catherine of Russia, rose up against their Ottoman masters. Although the revolts of the *rayahs* in Morea and other Balkan areas were put down with massacres, the stubbornness of the Greek *klefts* and Serbian *heyduks*, supported by popular ballad literature praising them, gave new impetus to the struggle against the Turkish rule. George Petrovich, called Karageorge (Black George), proved to be a magnetic leader of the Serbian *heyduks*. After Karageorge, having suffered a nervous breakdown, deserted to Austria, Milosh Obrenovich combined revolution and diplomacy to achieve autonomy for Serbia during 1830-34. The insurrection of the Greeks in 1821, combined with Russian pressures, helped speed autonomy for the Serbians.

The rebellion of the *rayahs* was not supported by the behavior of the high Christian clergy and the educated Greek elite in the Phanar quarter of Constantinople. On many occasions Phanariots collaborated with the sultan, and were called upon to serve as administrators and civil servants, especially in Romania, where they appeared as the new masters. They even reached such high positions as dragomans of the Porte and of the fleet. A number of them, however, played an important role in supporting the resistance of Christian *rayahs* by organizing a revolutionary society, the Philike Hetairia (Society of Friends), in 1810, although it was carried out at a price of a demoralizing servility to their Ottoman masters. Alexander Ypsilanti, a Russian officer of Greek parentage, was the head of this society, which, as a conspiratorial group with idealistic aims, began to spread through the Balkan Peninsula, primarily in Greece. This movement preached liberty and equality, ideals that sprang from the French Revolution.

The Greeks of Morea raised the banner of revolution at Kalavrita on March 21, 1821, beginning their struggle for liberation, gradually wiping out the regional Turkish garrisons. Under Theodore Kolokotrones, an experienced and clever leader (born of *kleft* parents and a former officer in the British army in the Ionian Islands), the Greeks managed to besiege and take Tripolis, Navarino, and other towns of Morea. The fighting quickly spread to Sterea Hellas, Thessaly, Epirus, and the islands, despite massacres on the island of Chios (by Sultan Mahmud II), in Missolonghi, and in Morea (by Imbrahim Pasha with his Turco-Egyptian forces). With the help of the philhellenic societies in Europe and the romantic supporters of the Greek liberation struggle, such as Lord Byron, the Greeks achieved their independence.[14] The pressure by the Russians against the Ottomans in the Caucasus and in Balkania, and the help of the European fleet at Navarino in 1827, were additional factors affecting the progress of liberation in Greece and the establishment of a free Greek state with its borders at Thessaly, the Arta-Volos line.[15] From then on, Greece remained under Western influence.

Throughout the Ottoman years, trade among the Balkan countries was conducted primarily by Greek merchants and, to a lesser extent, by Armenians, Jews, and Macedonian Slavs.[16] The Aegean merchants, mainly from the islands of Hydra, Psara, and Spetsai, as well as Macedonian and Vlachian merchants living in northern Greece and Thessaly, became the main traders and artisans of the Balkans. Greek culture, which was influenced by the West, and the Greek language had gradually diffused throughout the commercial centers of the area, especially in the ports of the Black Sea. Other nationalities, primarily Bulgarians, sent their children to Greek schools in Athens, Salonika, Ioannina, Smyrna, and the islands. Greek merchants were regarded as the elite class of the Danube principalities, and they were instrumental in the wars of liberation against the Ottoman Empire. However, within Bulgaria, Serbia, Bosnia, and Vlachia, where people of mainly Slavic extraction lived, trade and entrepreneurial leadership had not expanded very much because of the autarkic family system (the *zadruga*) and the production of primarily competitive goods that were mostly consumed by the producers.[17] This may explain the accumulation of less wealth and the existence of less inequality in the northern Balkan countries compared with Greece and Turkey.

Raw materials from the Balkans were transported to central Europe and shipped from the ports of the Black Sea, mostly by Greeks who had established prosperous communities in Vienna, Bucharest, Trieste, Odessa, and Taganrog. After permission was granted to have Greek ships fly the Russian flag, in accordance with the terms of the Russo-Turkish treaty of Jassy (1792), and also as a result of the French Revolution (1789) and the Anglo-French wars, Greek merchants and mariners were able to expand their operations to ports of Spain and France. Some 615 Greek ships carrying 5,878 cannons (useful during the struggle for liberation) were by 1813 plying the Mediterranean.[18] This expansion of trade helped to develop handicraft industries and to create production cooperatives, such as the Ambelakia enterprise in Thessaly (1795), which manufactured and distributed dyed cotton thread, despite growing English competition.

Toward the end of the Ottoman Empire, the influence of the industrial revolution in western Europe was felt in the Balkans, particularly in Romania and Yugoslavia.[19] New handicraft and manufacturing units were created with the help of capital and know-how from capitalist Europe, and even the educational system was affected. This trend of modernization also spread in agriculture and finance, despite the Turkish bureaucracy. Exports of cotton and thread increased considerably during the second half of the eighteenth century, in spite of the existence of export tariffs.[20]

As a result of Europeanization, the administrative structure of the Porte changed and the units of janissaries were dissolved in 1826. Extensive training of army officers and civil servants took place domestically and abroad, and the bureaucratic centralism of the Ottoman Empire started to change. Even high-ranking administrators and army generals suggested that "Either we follow the European trend, or we have to return to Asia."

THE POST-LIBERATION YEARS

Having been under long periods of occupation and economic exploitation, the newly liberated *rayahs* of Balkania were by and large uneducated and not anxious to establish their own governments and manage their own economic affairs. Thus, during the struggle for liberation and afterward, the Greek ex-*rayahs* appeared as courageous individualists with characteristics similar to those of their ancestors. However, the violent and fatal quarrels among the Greek *klefts* and among the sea captains over personal or territorial interests (similar to the ones among the ancient city-states) reappeared. With the economic and educational improvement of the newly created Greek state came the mystic fervor to expand the state to engulf the Greek "brothers" of Crete, Thessaly, Epirus, Macedonia, and the coast of Asia Minor.

In the meantime, Great Britain, in alliance with France, Austria, and Prussia, supported the preservation of the Ottoman Empire in order to oppose Russian expansion. Russia was forced to recross the Prut and give up Moldavia, Walachia, and Bessarabia in 1854–56, while the Ottomans were strengthening their hold on large portions of Balkania. In 1859 the assemblies of Moldavia and Walachia jointly elected Prince Alexander Cuza (a native boyar) as their common leader. With his minister Michael Kogalniceanu, Cuza introduced laws to confiscate the property of monasteries (which controlled about one-third of the arable land), and implemented agricultural reforms favoring the poverty-stricken peasants. However, Cuza was opposed by the great landlords, and since he was not effectively supported by the uneducated peasants, he was forced to abdicate in 1866. In the meantime many schools, from the elementary to the university level, were established, the judicial system was modified, and tax collection was improved.

Then, Charles Hohenzollern, a member of the ruling dynasty of Prussia, was offered the throne of Romania, which he occupied until 1914. The long period of sociopolitical stability provided the proper conditions for the modernization and economic development of the country. The construction of railways, roads, and ports, and the use of the Danubian waterway, increased the volume of mercantile traffic and stimulated domestic and foreign trade. Bucharest grew rapidly, and became an intellectual and artistic center, while Braila, Galati, and Sulina developed as important ports facilitating the steadily growing exports and imports. The fertile plains of the country helped to increase productivity in wheat and corn, and Romania became a great grain-producing and grain-exporting country. Toward the end of the century, petroleum was discovered in the foothills and the Carpathians, and this new source of wealth increased the industrial and commercial potential of the country.

However, the bulk of the rich Romanian lands belonged to a few landlords, while the peasant masses owned small pieces of land burdened with heavy debts that forced them to work as laborers on the large estates, barely earning a living. This undesirable situation led to economic unrest among the peasants.[21] Five peasant uprisings took place, the most severe occurring in 1907 (some 10,000 peasants were killed); all of them were suppressed by troops, and resulted in unfulfilled promises. Most severely repressed were the Romanian peasants of Transylvania, by the Magyars (Hungarian landlords). As a result some 77,000 of them had emigrated to the United States by 1910.

Roughly the same conditions prevailed in many other Balkan areas, especially Serbia, where the peasants cultivated the fields for a bare livelihood while the mainly Moslem lords (*beys*) extracted a large share of crops as well as personal services from the working peasants. The heavily taxed peasants were pressed to the point of revolt in 1875, particularly in Bosnia and Herzegovina.

On the other hand, the *rayah* group living between the Danube and the Rhodope Mountains—the Bulgarians—were gradually absorbed into the Ottoman system after the occupation of their lands in 1393, and were more completely subjugated by the Turks than the other Balkan people. Only after 1835, when they heard about the Serb and Greek rebellions, did they begin organizing for their own resistance, which lasted until their liberation was achieved in 1878. A Bulgarian uprising in 1876 was crushed by Turkish militia, who were well-known for their terror tactics, and more than 10,000 Bulgarians were slaughtered. The Albanians, on the other side of the peninsula, were the only people in Balkania who did not revolt against the sultan, mainly because the Turks were unable to keep these mountain people under their domination. Also, many of them had turned to Islam by the time of their liberation in 1912.

After the victory of Russia over the Turks in 1877–78, when the Russians reached Adrianople and supported the creation of an enlarged Bulgaria with an outlet to the Aegean Sea, in accordance with the terms of the treaty of San Stefano, the west European powers, especially Great Britain, were jealous and suspicious of the expansion of control by the "northern bear," and wanted to revise the Treaty of Paris (1856). The Treaty of Berlin was concluded in June 1878. It permitted Russia to retake southern Bessarabia from Romania (lost in 1856), and allowed Austria to take Bosnia and Herzegovina; Britain would take over Cyprus. Romania, Serbia, and Montenegro were declared independent from the Ottoman Empire; and Greece, after negotiations, gained Thessaly and a part of Epirus in 1881. The Treaty of Berlin sanctioned the gradual replacement of Turkey in Europe by the new Balkan states; Serbia, Montenegro, Romania, and Greece were enlarged territorially.

Bulgaria elected young Alexander of Battenberg, German by birth, as ruler in 1879. But the influence of Russia upon him was so great that he was considered its agent, despite his efforts to serve the people. In 1885 a revolution took place in East Rumelia, which was united with Bulgaria. This increased the jealousy of other neighboring countries, particularly Serbia (which invaded Bulgaria unsuccessfully) and Greece; as a result a new doctrine of a Balkan balance of power emerged. In 1887, Prince Ferdinand was crowned ruler of Bulgaria, and a few years later he supported agitation and underground activities in Macedonia— an action that stimulated similar activities and speeded up invasions by Serbia and Greece. Economically, notable progress took place in Bulgaria after liberation. Highways and railroads, connecting the interior with Varna on the Black Sea and Ruse and other ports on the Danube, helped improve internal communications and exports of cattle, wheat, and other agricultural products in exchange for manufactured goods. Similar developments occurred in education and culture.

In the Treaty of Berlin the European powers designated Crete, Macedonia, and Armenia as objects of their concern. The Turkish Sultan Abdul Hamid II, who had been associated with the Bulgarian massacres of 1876, resorted to organized genocide of the Armenians. Utilizing religious passions for political ends, he extended the slaughter of Armenian Christians not only to the mountains of Armenia bordering Russia but also to the streets of Constantinople (1894–96, 1909). By the end of 1898 the sultan, under pressure from the world powers and the rebels, withdrew his troops and administrators from Crete, which voted to join Greece in 1908. By that time disturbances had broken out in Macedonia, which later became an important area of interest in Balkan politics because of its geographical location (including the three Turkish *vilayets* of Kosovo, Monastir, and Salonika) and the variety of races and nationalities (mainly Greeks, Serbs, and Bulgarians). Other people in the area, besides the handful of Turks (landlords or beys), were the Albanians of western Macedonia, the Kutzo-Vlachs (related to the Romanians) in scattered highland villages, and the less numerous Jewish merchants exiled from Spain (called Spanioles), who lived mainly in Salonika. Propaganda and secret groups, used primarily by Bulgarians and other ethnic groups against the Turkish garrisons, later experienced serious animosities among themselves. From 1908 on, military uprisings were carried out by the Young Turks in Macedonia, and later spread to other Turkish areas. For a short period of time, this Young Turks movement, which started with democratic appeals, unified the ethnic groups in Balkania, but it later proved to be as nationalistic as the Ottoman expansionary movement.

Throughout the last years of the nineteenth and the beginning of the twentieth centuries, the industrial revolution in western Europe brought the need for new markets as well as new resources. Fired by commercial ambitions and the promise of good returns from investing in backward Balkan countries and other areas, the European powers increased their imperialist desires. Thus, France occupied Algiers and Tunis, England took over Egypt and Cyprus, and German enterprises moved into the Balkans and Asia Minor. The opening of the Suez Canal in 1869 gave new impetus to commercial and industrial development of the eastern Mediterranean. In the early 1890s German companies built railroads in Asia Minor, including the important line from Haidar Pasha, opposite Constantinople, to Angora, the old Seljuk capital of Konya, and as far south as Baghdad. This railway opened up trade between Europe and Asia, carrying passengers and goods from Hamburg to the Middle East. The German economic and military influence in the area alarmed not only England and France, but also Russia, because of its possibility of blocking the Black Sea outlet at the Dardanelles.

In the south, as a result of the Turco-Italian war of 1912, Italy occupied Rhodes and the Dodecanese Islands, while almost all other Aegean islands, which had been considered as the historic home of the Hellenic race, were evacuated by Turkey and handed over to Greece. In the meantime, an alliance of the four Christian Balkan states (Serbia, Bulgaria, Greece, and Montenegro) was formed against the Ottomans. They defeated the Turkish army and annexed neighboring territories. The Serbs occupied Üsküb (Skopje) and moved as far south as Monastir, the Greeks moved northward into Epirus and Macedonia, the Bulgars moved south through the Maritsa River valley to the Aegean, and the Montenegrans moved into northern Albania; these changes were later incorporated into the Treaty of London on May 30, 1913. Just a month later, however, war among the Balkan allies led to the defeat of Bulgaria and the signing of the Treaty of Bucharest. Greece acquired Epirus, Serbia acquired Kosova and eastern Novi Pazar, and western Novi Pazar was given to Montenegro.

During World War I, the Ottoman Empire and Bulgaria took the side of Germany and Austria-Hungary (the Central Powers) against France, Great Britain, and Russia (the Allies). Serbia, and later Greece and Romania, joined the Allies. Germany, Austria, and Bulgaria attacked Serbia and drove its army to the Adriatic coast, from which it was transported to Corfu by the Allies (1915).

In the meantime, an Allied attack on the Dardanelles failed, but a new front was created in Salonika. In 1916, Russia attacked Austria and pushed into Bukovina. Romania was badly defeated by Austria, and driven not only out of Bucharest but also out of the province of Walachia.[22] On the other hand, the British army, helped by the Arabs, pushed the Turks north from the Persian Gulf and Suez, and occupied Baghdad, Jerusalem, and Aleppo, cutting off the Baghdad Railway (1917). In Greece, despite the refusal of King Constantine to enter the war on the side of the Allies (because of his family connection with Germany), the army in Salonika started an attack against Bulgaria in September 1918, and advanced north through the Vardar valley, threatening Sofia. In the meantime, the United States entered the struggle (1917), filling the gap that had been created by the withdrawal of Russia from the Allied ranks after the Bolshevik Revolution. As a result, the balance of power turned in favor of the Allies. President Woodrow Wilson was instrumental in drafting the Treaty of Versailles (1919) and of other treaties drawn up by the Allies (including Italy and Japan), all of which gave territorial advantages to the Balkan Allies (Serbia, Greece, and Romania).

By the Treaty of Neuilly, Bulgaria was required to pay heavy reparations to Greece, Romania, and Serbia in the form of money, cattle, and coal. This led to the abdication of King Ferdinand in favor of his son Boris III and the accession of Stambuliski to the premiership (1919-23). As leader of the Peasants' Party, Alexander Stambuliski introduced compulsory labor and land expropriation laws. Crown and church lands, as well as private lands above 75 acres were confiscated, with small compensation. These lands were distributed to the poor peasants.

After the establishment of borders in 1919, territorial grievances cropped up between Bulgaria and Greece, Romania, and (mainly) Serbia. Bulgarian border bands (*komitadjis*) resorted to massacres, kidnappings, and assassinations, especially on the Macedonian frontier. Stambuliski's policy of Balkan cooperation and friendship led to the suppression of the *komitadjis* and the voluntary exchange of populations. In 1922 large numbers of Bulgarians had to be dispossessed from Macedonia and Thrace to make room for thousands of Greek refugees from Asia Minor. As a result of these difficult economic problems, heavy taxation and hard collective labor remained the lot of the Bulgarian people for decades.

After World War I, Romania was rewarded by the Allies, receiving Transylvania from Hungary, Bukovina from Austria, and Bessarabia from Russia, and the Dobruja boundaries with Bulgaria were reestablished. However, Bessarabia, with a large number of Ukraianians living in the south and the severe russification carried out by the tsars, remained as the sword of Damocles over Romania.

Agricultural reforms similar to those carried out in Bulgaria were enacted in Romania between 1918 and 1921. Lands belonging to the crown, the state, foreigners, and absentee owners, as well as to landlords with large estates (above 100 hectares), were expropriated and distributed among the peasants having small farms. Compensation was granted to the owners in the form of state bonds with 50-year maturity and 5 percent interest. However, a large number of peasants with small farms still remained. After Julius Mania, the leader of the National Peasant Party, became premier in 1928, export taxes were gradually abolished, rural banks were created to help provide credit to the peasants, state enterprises were improved, tariffs were reduced, and foreign investments were encouraged. Among other foreign commitments, a British firm agreed to build a canal connecting Bucharest with the Danube.

In the post-liberation years the death rate in the Balkan countries, as in the rest of Europe, declined because of medical advances and improved nutrition. However, the birth rate did not drop as much as it did in other European countries, resulting in a sharp increase in population. Immigration was curtailed by the United States and by some areas of the British Empire that either closed or drastically reduced their quotas during the interwar period. At the same time, industrialization in the cities, which could have absorbed some of the underemployed peasants, proceeded at a very slow pace if at all. Therefore, the pressure of overpopulation upon agricultural areas was obviously great all over Balkania. It was estimated that the rural surplus population in 1930 was 50.3 percent in Greece, 51.4 percent in Romania, 53 percent in Bulgaria, and 61.5 percent in Yugoslavia.[23]

The rapid increase in population and the distribution of large estates that belonged primarily to the Magyars in Transylvania, the Russians in Bessarabia, and the Moslem beys in the other Balkan areas led to the subdivision and redivision of land into small, scattered plots given to the peasantry. This parcelization, which wasted much of the land in the formation of boundaries and paths, reduced the productivity of the land by making it difficult to apply mass-production techniques. Credit availability to the farmers was also limited, and the costs of fertilizers, farm equipment, and agricultural machinery were high enough to make them inaccessible to the peasants. For example, agricultural machinery cost three times or more, and fertilizers two and a half times more, in Yugoslavia than in western Europe. In every Balkan country agricultural production per hectare was far less than that in western Europe. Likewise, production and income per person in the rural sector were as low as one-fourth or less than in France, Germany, or England. Low income left little surplus for investment, causing a pervasive low productivity and thus perpetuating the vicious circle of poverty in Balkania.

The lucrative concessions given to foreign investors also helped to maintain semicolonial economic conditions. Foreign investment concentrated on low-risk and high-profit ventures concerned with production of raw materials and semi-finished products, neglecting formation of long-term capital so badly needed for self-sustained growth. Moreover, large amounts of the extremely high profits from the generous concessions were siphoned off to foreign shareholders, draining the financial resources of the Balkan nations still further. On the other hand, domestic investors concentrated on protected industries in which they could establish monopolies. All these factors were responsible for the misallocation of of resources, low level of industrialization, and inadequate absorption of surplus urban population by the cities, and the perpetuation of low land and labor productivity.

During World War II, Albania, Greece, and Yugoslavia waged bloody struggles against the Axis and suffered from internecine fighting between rival groups; Bulgaria and Romania, having allied themselves with the Axis, avoided a similar ordeal. As liberation approached, the Allies, mainly Britain and Russia, increased their influence to the point of shaping postwar trends in the Balkan Peninsula. By November 1943, when the Teheran Conference took place, the British had about 80 separate missions working with the partisans in the region, sometimes supporting and coordinating them, and at other times dividing them. The main goal of the British, inferred from the statements of Prime Minister Winston Churchill, was to restore (more or less) the prewar status quo with kings and governments sympathetic to Britain. However, the rapid advance of the Allied forces on all fronts and that of the Red Army toward Balkania led to the Moscow Conference in October 1944, at which Churchill proposed, and Stalin accepted, that Russia would "have ninety per cent pre-dominance in Rumania, for us [Britain] to have ninety per cent of the say in Greece, and go fifty-fifty about Yugoslavia."[24] Russia also would have 75 percent predominance in Bulgaria and 50 percent in Hungary. This arrangement was accepted by Churchill, Franklin Roosevelt, and Josif Stalin at the Yalta Conference in February 1945.

The peace treaties signed at Paris during February 1947 gave Yugoslavia the port of Pola, the Isonzo valley, and Istria, while Trieste was placed under international control. Moreover, Italy surrendered the Dodecanese Islands to Greece and Saseno (Sazan) Island to Albania. Bulgaria restored the Greek and Yugoslav territories and acquired southern Dobruja from Romania, while Romania acquired Transylvania from Hungary and confirmed the cession of Bessarabia and northern Bukovina to Russia. As a result of the Churchill/Stalin division of the area, the northern Balkans were dominated by Communist governments, while Greece and Turkey remained under Western influence.

NOTES

1. There were regular routes and established freight and passenger rates between Athens and other Balkan cities. "For example, one could go from Athens . . . to the Black Sea for two drachmas, that is for four days' pay for a rower, which seems convenient." C. Stanley, *Roots of the Tree* (London: Oxford University Press, 1936), p. 24.

2. Loans for shipping trips from Piraeus to the Black Sea, mainly carrying wheat, were granted with an interest rate of 3 percent per round trip. T. Glover, *The Challenge of the Greek and Other Essays* (New York: Macmillan, 1942), p. 59.

3. H. Schonfield, *The Suez Canal in Peace and War, 1869-1969* (Florida: University of Miami Press, 1969), p. 4.

4. For comments on Plato's and Xenophon's writings on the division of labor and productivity, see T. Lowry, "Recent Literature on Ancient Greek Economic Thought," *Journal of Economic Literature*, March 1979, pp. 65-86.

5. W. Tarn and G. Griffith, *Hellenistic Civilization*, 3rd ed., rev. (London: Edward Arnold, 1952), chs. 4, 7.

6. For a penetrating and well-documented historical review, see L. S. Stavrianos,*The Balkans Since 1453* (New York: Holt, Rinehart and Winston, 1958), pt. I; and F. Schevill, *The History of the Balkan Peninsula*, rev. ed. (New York: Harcourt, Brace, 1933), chs. 1, 3.

7. J. Toutain, *The Economic Life of the Ancient World* (New York: A. Knopf, 1930), p. 232.

8. A thorough review of the early history of Slavs is provided by B. Grekov, *Kiev Rus* (Moscow: Foreign Languages Publishing House, 1959), chs. 2, 8.

9. This primitive communistic system of the early Slavs maintained a substantial economic and political equality among the pastoral and agricultural people who produced "an abundance of cattle and grain, chiefly millet and rye," as Emperor Maurice said. Schevill, op. cit., pp. 74–75. It is also argued that Romanian society, with its communal villages, did not pass through a feudal stage, but moved from something like egalitarian communalism to capitalism. H. Stahl, *Traditional Romanian Village Communities*, D. Chirot and H. Chirot, trans. (New York: Cambridge University Press, 1980).

10. For more on the administrative problems of Byzantium, see R. Wolff, *The Balkans in Our Time* (New York: W. W. Norton, 1967), ch. 4.

11. Schevill, op. cit., p. 10. For more detailed accounts, see L. Kirnoss, *The Ottoman Centuries. The Rise and Fall of the Turkish Empire* (New York: Morrow, 1977); S. Shaw, *History of the Ottoman Empire and Modern Turkey* (London: Cambridge University Press, 1976).

12. K. Paparrhegopoulos, *Historia ton Hellinikou Ethnais: Apo ton Achaiotatou Chronon mechri ton Neoteron* (History of the Greek Nation: From the Ancient Years until the Recent Years) (Athens: S. Pavlidsu, 1874), pt. A, p. 538.

13. The Ottoman Empire established the Phanariot regime in Moldavia (1711) and in Walachia (1716). The Phanariot rulers, chosen by the Porte from among the Greek aristocracy in Constantinople, used political oppression and economic exploitation until 1821. *Romania: Yearbook, 1976* (Bucharest: Scientific and Encyclopedic Publishing House, 1976).

14. For a short survey see E. Foster, *A Short History of Modern Greece, 1821-1956* (New York: Praeger, 1957), ch. 1.

15. From 1833 to 1863, Prince Otto of Bavaria ruled Greece. From then until 1967, Prince George of the Danish Glücksberg dynasty and his descendants were enthroned with a few interruptions (mainly 1924–35 and 1941–46).

16. For further details see G. Hoffman, *The Balkans in Transition* (Princeton, N.J.: Van Nostrand, 1963), p. 52; A. Pepelasis, "The Legal System and Economic Development of Greece," *Journal of Economic History* 19, no. 2 (June 1959): 174–76.

17. Leadership was feeble among the Slavs in the centuries of their unchanging and relatively protected life. J. Schumpeter, *The Theory of Economic Development* (New York: Oxford University Press, 1961), p. 88.

18. Stavrianos, op. cit., 275.

19. For an extensive review of the contribution of western Europe, see Herman Gross, "E Symvole tes Dytekes Evropes sten Ekonomeke kai Kenoneke Anaptyxe ton Valkanikon Horon" (The Contribution of Western Europe in the Economic and Social Development of the Balkan Countries), in *Eksyhronismos kai Viomihaniki Epanastasi sta Valkania ton 19^{on} Eona*, papers presented at the Symposium for the Industrial Revolution in Balkania, Hamburg, March 1976 (Athens: Themelio, 1980), pp. 43–53.

20. Ottoman exports of cotton and thread increased from 2.8 million *okas* in 1750 to 8.1 million *okas* in 1787 (one *oka* equals 1.28 kilograms or 2.82 pounds), while export tariffs declined from 5 percent to around 1 percent of the value of exports. Ibid., pp. 286–88. The pattern of production of silk, cotton and raw material was dictated by European economic conditions. M. Czakca, "Price History and the Bursa Silk Industry: A Study in Ottoman Industrial Decline, 1550-1650," *Journal of Economic History*, September 1980, pp. 533–50.

21. For further information see W. Gewehr, *The Rise of Nationalism in the Balkans, 1800-1930* (Hamden, Conn.: Archon Books, 1967), ch. 2.

22. For an extensive bibliography see G. Torrey, "Some Recent Literature on Romania's Role in the First World War," *East European Quarterly* 14, no. 2 (Summer 1980): 189-206.

23. For these estimates, see W. E. Moore, *Economic Demography of Eastern and Southern Europe* (Geneva: League of Nations, 1945), p. 26; D. Kirk, *Europe's Population in the Interwar Years* (Geneva: League of Nations, 1946), pp. 263 ff.

24. Winston Churchill, *Memoirs of the Second World War* (Boston: Houghton Mifflin, 1959), pp. 885-86.

3

ESTABLISHMENT OF
THE BALKAN STATES
AND THEIR EXPANSION

ALBANIA

The Albanians were late in showing signs of national consciousness, and the independence movement started primarily abroad. This was due mainly to the degree of autonomy they enjoyed under the Ottoman rule. However, in 1881 they organized the Albanian League to unite the isolated regions of the country and to counter the interest of neighboring countries in territorial claims or domination, mainly because of its strategic position on the Adriatic Sea. For this reason Albanians at times supported the Turks, and even joined the Young Turks movement.

Albania was born through the Treaty of London signed by the six great European powers in 1913. However, Greek troops occupied southern Albania, including Koritsa and Argyrokastron (1914-16). Montenegrins entered Scutari in the north, Serbians occupied Elbasan and Tirana (1915), and Italians occupied Valona and (later) Argyrokastron, and even Ioannina in Greece (1916). The French, who commanded the Salonika front, extended their position and occupied Koritsa. In 1920, Albania, supported by the British and by American President Woodrow Wilson, became a member of the League of Nations; in 1921 its boundaries were confirmed by the great powers, in spite of protests from Yugoslavia and Greece. By 1926, Yugoslavia, Britain, France, and Italy had signed the final agreement determining the present frontiers of Albania. In 1922, Ahmed Zogu became premier, and after a brief (1924-25) term as premier by Fan Noli (a bishop from Egypt who had been educated in Greek schools and at Harvard, and was the head of the Albanian Autocephalous Orthodox Church in the United States), he regained power and remained premier until 1939.

Zogu, following the example of the other Balkan countries, introduced land reforms and expropriated large estates from Moslem beys and the Church, and distributed them to the poor peasants. Except for some small handicrafts processing local materials, the country's economy was based primarily on agriculture, in which more than 80 percent of the population was engaged. Albania, with 85 percent of the population illiterate before World War II, was regarded as the most backward state of Balkania and the whole of Europe.

After 1925, Italy penetrated Albania and concluded a number of military and economic agreements with Zogu, who in 1928 became King Zog. Through the Company for Economic Development of Albania, Italian engineers and financiers built roads, ports, agricultural projects, and other public works. They also drilled for oil and discovered two fields, one near Berat and one near Valona. Italian engineers later helped Albania increase oil production from 7,000 barrels in 1926 to 1,659,000 barrels in 1940.[1] The crude oil and asphalt produced, together with other raw materials (hides, wool, livestock, olive oil, wine, spirits [raki], and lumber), were exported mainly to Italy. The Italian protectorate and the established controls continued until 1939, when Zog was compelled to flee to Greece before the Italian invasion.

After the occupation of Albania in April 1939, Italy attacked Greece in October 1940, using Albania as an army base for a projected gradual expansion into other Balkan areas. However, the Greeks resisted the invasion, pushing the Italians back to the Albanian mountains and ultimately occupying the major cities of Koritsa and Argyrokastron, and the naval base of Santi Quaranta. However, Hitler's attack against Greece on April 6, 1941, helped the Italians to recapture the Albanian areas and to occupy Greece together with the Germans and Bulgarians.

Resistance against the Italian, and later the German, forces of occupation began in 1942, primarily through the efforts of the National Liberation Front (NLF). The NLF was headed by Enver Hoxha (Hoja), a teacher by profession and later the president of the country. Landless peasants, ready to revolt against their Moslem landlords, and intellectual idealists joined forces with the Front in the cause of liberation and social reforms. Despite the efforts of British and American agents to unite the NLF with another group of Albanian nationalists (the Ballists), the stronger NLF Communist group prevailed. Most of the Ballists collaborated with the Nazis. This practice, which was followed in Yugoslavia and more so in Greece, was intensified after Italy's collapse in September 1943 and the consequent control of the country by the Germans. Following the example of Tito, the Albanian NLF assembled a National Congress. The Congress forbade Zog to return to Albania, and formed a provisional government by December 1944, when the Nazis were driven out of Albania.

During World War II, some 28,000 Albanians were killed and 800,000 cattle were destroyed by the Nazis; 100,000 buildings were leveled to the ground. Albania claimed, and continues to claim, $4.5 billion for these damages. Another $20 million was claimed from Britain for gold seized at the end of the war. Britain claimed about $2 million in compensation for two British destroyers sunk by Albania in the Corfu Channel in 1946.[2]

After the war small Albania, under President Hoxha, followed the Soviet economic model. In 1961, however, the leadership changed its mind, and until 1975 came under the ideological influence of the People's Republic of China.[3] At present the country follows an independent policy that retains many characteristics of Stalin's economic system, which involved strict central planning and detailed controls.

Under the previous occupations and pressures, a large number of Albanians had emigrated to other countries, mainly Greece and Italy, where they advanced culturally and economically. Some 200,000 Albanians had settled in Italy at the beginning of the twentieth century.[4] Francesco Crispi, twice premier of Italy, was a descendant of Albanian emigrants, as is Mother Teresa, the nun who won the 1979 Nobel Price for peace as a result of the valuable social services that the order she founded offers to the very poorest people of India. At present northern Albania is inhabited mostly by the rough and individualistic Ghegs, among whom the law of the vendetta prevails, while in the south, below the Shkumbi River, live the milder Tosks.

Albania is perhaps the only country in eastern Europe that has not deviated from the initial course of strict state control over the economy. The Albanian Labor Party (ALP), in control of the country since World War II, preaches that rapid progress can be achieved through a centralist system that supervises all economic and social activities. As a "true believer" in the Marxist-Leninist-Stalinist dogma, Albania considers the Soviet Union and its faithful ally, Bulgaria, "revisionists." The same thing can be said for Yugoslavia and Romania, which are further removed from the Stalinist system, while Greece and Turkey are considered as capitalist agents in Balkania. From that point of view, Albanian leaders (primarily President Hoxha and Prime Minister Mehmed Shahu), fearing that their country may fall victim to its neighbors—Yugoslavia and Greece—use extreme caution in dealing with other Balkan countries. However, under pressure from the people for better economic conditions, they do conclude treaties for trade and cultural exchanges, predominantly on a bilateral basis.

Thus, for the first time since World War II, during which Albanian and Yugoslav partisans fought together against fascism, diplomatic and economic relations have begun to warm up between Albania and Yugoslavia. Being isolated from the outside world, Albania has felt the need for closer trade relations with its neighbors, particularly with Yugoslavia. As a result, the first railway and air connections between the two countries have materialized, and their foreign trade increased from $30 million in 1978 to more than $80 million in 1980.

The winds of reform that blow throughout eastern Europe affect Albania, although to a lesser extent.[5] More investment emphasis is given to the less industrialized regions of Gramsh, Kukës, Librazhd, Mat, Përmet, and Tepelenë, and less emphasis to the industrial areas of Karja, Shkodër, Tirana, Berat, and Durrës. Western enterprises with oil-drilling equipment are invited to increase oil production. Albania is self-sufficient in oil, producing an estimated 20 million barrels a year, small quantities of which are exported to Greece and Italy. It is also the world's third largest producer of chrome, behind South Africa and the

Soviet Union, and second in the export of this strategically important product (more than 350,000 tons a year). Other major exports are olives, oranges, and dried fruits, primarily to Italy.[6]

BULGARIA

Because Bulgaria was close to Constantinople, the center of the Ottoman Empire, it was the first Balkan country to be occupied by, and the last to be liberated from, the Turks. There were some uprisings, such as that conducted by Michael the Brave in 1598, but they had limited or no success. Only after the establishment of the Autocephalous Exarchate Church in 1870 were serious efforts made to organize the Bulgarian people to seek independence. In addition to the Turkish occupation, the Bulgarians suffered looting by armed bandits (*kirjalis*), exploitation by *chiflik* (large estate) owners and tax collectors (*chorbajis*, similar to the Greek *kodjabashis*), and the economic and cultural influence (at times oppression) exercised by the Greek bishops. That is why a number of people fled the country, going mainly to Odessa and Bucharest, where they made fortunes.

A number of revolutionaries, outstanding among whom were George Rakovski, Lyuben Karavelov, Khristo Botev, and George Benkovski, were educated primarily in Moscow. They set out from Bucharest, together with the *haiduk* outlaws (the equivalents of the Greek *klephts*), to attempt a number of unsuccessful revolts, the last occurring in 1876, when the *bashi-bazouk* irregulars and the Turkish regulars massacred thousands of people. This helped contribute to intervention by the world powers, especially Russia, which resulted in the liberation of Bulgaria in 1878.

During the post-liberation period, the country's economy remained for the most part agrarian, with a gradual transformation toward market-oriented agricultural and industrial development. From a political point of view, the Russian influence was great, despite the fact that Prince Alexander Dondukov-Korsakov (1879–86) tried hard to maintain an independent position. By 1885, East Rumelia was incorporated into Bulgaria. Under the rule of Premier Stefan Stambulov (1887–94) and King Ferdinand (1887–1918), the country experienced considerable stability. Ferdinand, however, secretly permitted the *komitadjis* to raid Macedonia, and committed his dynasty to two disastrous wars (1913 and 1915), while his policy of rapprochement with Russia was not very fruitful.

Representatives of the Ottoman authority (the pashas, the agas, and the *bashi-bazouks*), along with the local money lenders and tax collectors, kept the rural status quo, and the agrarian structure of the economy remained the same for a long period of time after liberation. By 1911 agricultural and livestock production still accounted for about 65 percent of national income. However, the tax on grain amounted to about 10 to 15 percent, and the revenues from tariffs were no longer being sent to Constantinople. Instead, they were used by the government for the development of the economy. Thus, the transportation network and the educational level of the country were improved. Foreign competition increased, however, and overwhelmed domestic producers of industrial and handicraft products, particularly after tariffs were reduced to less than 8 percent by the Berlin Treaty. Because of the heavy indebtedness of the country at that time, controls were imposed by foreign creditors over the revenue derived from tobacco taxes. Moreover, the division and subdivision of land into tiny plots and the low productivity of wheat forced changes in agriculture oriented toward the production of poultry, eggs, attar of roses, and tobacco, large quantities of which were exported.

During the interwar period Bulgaria went through stormy and violent years. The Internal Macedonian Revolutionary Organization (IMRO), which became an instrument of the Bulgarian government, continued its raids and assassinations, not only within Serbian and Greek Macedonia but also inside Bulgaria, where it liquidated leaders and people opposed to or not supportive of its cause. Alexander Stambuliski, the Agrarian Party leader, managed to implement extensive social reforms and to pursue a policy of cooperation with neighboring Balkan countries. He distributed large estates to the peasantry, and introduced compulsory labor service in place of military training, which proved to be beneficial for the infrastructural development of the country.

As premier, Stambuliski signed the Treaty of Neuilly in 1919, revised the tax system to benefit the peasants, and conducted elections (1920) in which the Agrarians received 39.1 percent, the Communists 20.5 percent, and the Democrats 11.0 percent; the rest of the votes were distributed among six other parties. His main goals were to mobilize support from other countries, to unite the peasants, and to establish a Green International in contrast with the White International of the royalists and landlords and the Red International of the Bolsheviks. In 1923, however, the military seized control in a coup that was recognized later by King Boris.[7] Thereafter, the country experienced disorders arising mainly from the activities of the IMRO, a group split between the Federalists, who supported an autonomous Macedonia, and the Centralists, who wanted its annexation by Bulgaria. From 1934 until 1943, when Boris died, the country was under military and royal dictatorship.

Before World War II scarcity of natural resources, lack of capital, and unskilled labor and management were the causes of the backwardness in industry and low productivity in other sectors. About half of the total capital in industry and transportation had been invested by foreigners. Agricultural exports, mainly fruits, tobacco, and animal products, accounted for more than 90 percent of total exports, two-thirds of which went to Germany to pay for imported machinery, chemical products, textiles, and other industrial commodities. However, the peasant families remained mostly self-sufficient, the educational level remained low, and even the limited number of university graduates had a difficult time in finding jobs, except in crowded government offices where corruption and open nepotism prevailed.

As mentioned earlier, during World War II Bulgaria became an ally of the Axis Powers, as did Romania, while Greece and Yugoslavia joined the Allies. Turkey remained neutral. When Germany occupied Greece and Yugoslavia, the Bulgarian army was permitted to enter Yugoslav Macedonia as well as Greek western Thrace and eastern Macedonia. With respect to troop allocation to other fronts, Bulgaria, under King Boris, managed to stay aloof, mainly because of the traditionally large Russophile sentiment in the country.

In the occupied lands of Yugoslavia, the Bulgarian forces tried to win over the inhabitants with the opening of schools, libraries, and theaters, especially in Skopje. But in Greece their policy was more ruthless, for they sought either to convert or to eliminate the Greeks, and replace them with Bulgarian colonists.

During mid-1942 the Fatherland Front was organized by Georgi Dimitrov, a Communist leader well known for his defiance of the Nazis during the Reichstag fire trial. The Front included Social Democrats, the left-wing Agrarian Party, and the Zveno group, which had connections in the army. The resistance against the Axis, however, was not as significant as in other occupied Balkan countries because the partisans had to concentrate against the Bulgarian army and the gendarmerie, rather than the Germans. Further aiding this decision was the fact that the peasants became more prosperous during the war, because of high prices received for agricultural products. As the Red Army approached Balkania, partisan bands, aided by Allied air raids and the delivery of British arms (dropped by parachute in Serbia), became more effective and finally took power.

As a result of the continuous advance of the Red Army, especially after the declaration of war against Bulgaria by the Soviets on September 5, 1944, the Bulgarian army turned against the Nazis and fought alongside the Yugoslavs and Russians in Yugoslavia and Hungary, where some 30,000 Bulgarian soldiers were killed. At the end of the war, Bulgaria evacuated the occupied Greek and Yugoslav territories.

During the postwar years Bulgaria has closely followed the Soviet economic model of central planning and strict government controls. However, in order to obtain a better performance from the economy, the government introduced some market-oriented reforms in the early 1960s. According to directives emanating from the country's leaders, technical rationalization and computerization were to be used in order to attain more efficient performance.[8] But these reforms did not accomplish much, mostly because of inflexibility in the centralized economy. It is difficult for the Communist Party to permit any loss of its authority because of an abstract and mechanical process that requires the use of precise information in order to obtain reliable results.

Capital formation, as a percentage of national product, was higher in Bulgaria than in other Comecon countries, but there was less independence in production enterprises (subsidiaries and subdivisions).[9] The gap between the growth rate of net national product and net economic welfare was greater than in Western market economies. Todor Zhivkov, the president of the country, and the planners responsible for policy making, tried to eliminate consumer frustration by keeping prices low, but inflation would have to rise if consumer lines were to be eliminated.

In the postwar years Bulgaria has experienced an unprecedented period of peace and progress, mainly because it has not had to confront any external threat and, unlike Romania, did not lose territory to its neighbors. Moreover, it does not suffer from internal disunity, as does Yugoslavia, or the political instability of Greece and the internal turmoil of Turkey.

Because of the common culture and linguistic and ethnic background with the Soviets, a high degree of cooperation has been developed between Bulgaria and Russia. The glorification of the Russian army, which liberated the country from Turkey in 1878 and helped it establish the present Communist regime, cannot escape the visitor to present-day Bulgaria. On the other hand, because of Bulgaria's strategic location (close to the Dardanelles and the Aegean coast), the Soviet Union has always kept a watchful eye upon the country, especially since 1979, when the Chinese attempted to sow the seeds of anti-Sovietism in the Balkan Peninsula.

It has been said that Russia can use its most faithful ally to stir up conflicts in the murky and sometimes conspiratorial world of Balkan affairs. This is especially so with Macedonia, where Yugoslavia fuels the issue, from time to time, to create an external threat and unify its diverse republics. However, the Bulgarians have declared publicly that they consider the present borders with Yugoslavia and Greece as permanent. On the other hand, although they decry U.S. military assistance to Turkey as meddling in the Balkans to exploit political instability in the region, they wait for more concrete results, an attitude that reflects the old Bulgarian saying "We count the chickens in the autumn."

GREECE

After the long struggle for liberation (1821–28), Greece began its independent status with borders extending to Thessaly (including the Cyclades Islands). Then, gradually, through wars and diplomatic pressures, Greece acquired the Ionian islands from Britain in 1864. Thessaly and part of Epirus, ceded by Turkey, were acquired in 1881.

By the eve of World War I, Greece had achieved a satisfactory degree of economic development. Paved roads, railways, and the construction of the Corinth Canal in 1893 improved the transportation network and stimulated agricultural productivity, especially after the abolition of the tithe in 1880. Exports of currants and tobacco were used to pay for imported grain. Fruits, olives, and wine were also some of the main agricultural commodities produced at that time.

In the meantime, Macedonia, Crete, and a few other Aegean islands (mainly Samos, Chios, and Lesbos), ceded by Turkey in 1913, and western Thrace, ceded by Bulgaria in 1918, joined the nation.

In 1920, as a consequence of the Allied victory, the Treaty of Sèvres allotted to Greece eastern Thrace, many islands in the Aegean (including Imbros and Tenedos), and the administration of Smyrna and its environs (with over 375,000 inhabitants, most of them Greek). However, the Allies deserted Greece. Then Turkish nationalists, headed by Mustafa Kemal (Atatürk), objected to this treaty. Moreover, the Greek army, which had landed at Smyrna in May 1919, advanced rapidly after March 1921 to the Sakarya River, within striking distance of Ankara, the capital of the new Turkish government; it met with strong resistance by August of the same year. In the meantime, Italy and France withdrew from Anatolia and, with Russia, started to support Turkey, formerly their enemy.

The eruption of a severe domestic feud between Venizelists and Royalists divided the country, particularly the army.[10] All these factors worked to demoralize the Greek soldiers, who retreated toward the Aegean coast with large numbers of refugees in September 1922. The Mudanya Armistice of October 1922 was followed by the Lausanne Treaty (July 1923), which established the present borders between Greece and Turkey. A compulsory exchange of Greek and Turkish minorities was concluded, involving some 1,300,000 Greeks and 400,000 Turks. These catastrophic events initiated a revolt by Greek officers, headed by Nicholas Plastiras, on the island of Chios. Six government officials, regarded as having been responsible for this situation, were executed.

The cheap skilled labor of the refugees was beneficial to Greek manufacturing, particularly the rug industry that had been transplanted from Asia Minor, where it had flourished. Also, there was a great amount of stimulation to other industries, including pottery, copper ware, textiles, shipping, and land reclamation and development, mainly in the Maritsa and Vardar River valleys.

The policy of friendship and conciliation, which was pursued later by Eleutherios Venizelos and Kemal, as well as other leaders in the Balkan Peninsula, was instrumental in stimulating trade and development in the area. Genuine efforts for closer economic and cultural cooperation among the Balkan countries occurred in the early 1930s. However, the feud between the Venizelist liberals and the conservative Royalists led in 1936 to the dictatorship of General John Metaxas, who supported King George II.[11]

On October 28, 1940, Italy attacked Greece from Albania. The Greeks managed to push the Italians back into Albania. This Greek victory bought time for the British to strengthen their position and to land forces in Crete, Lemnos, and other parts of Greece. In addition, the British sent five squadrons of planes to help the embattled Greeks, despite their doubts about Prime Minister Metaxas, who had been educated in Nazi Germany.

Implementing the directive of Operation Marita, Hitler invaded Yugoslavia and Greece on April 6, 1941, and Crete on May 20. The invasion of Russia and the implementation of Operation Barbarossa took place on June 22, 1941. Then Greece came under a tripartite occupation by Germany, Italy, and Bulgaria. During the occupation years Greece, Yugoslavia, and to some extent Albania suffered great human and material losses, while Bulgaria and Romania continued to serve as Axis satellites.

From the first months of the Greek occupation, the Germans printed inflationary money, buying everything they could, and drained the country of products needed for the survival of the people. This practice, together with the drop in imports because of the Allied blockade, led to the country's bankruptcy and starvation. More than 500,000 people perished in battle or through starvation. Civilian massacres, such as that at Kalavrita, where some 1,300 unarmed persons were gunned down, were carried out by the Nazis.

The Greeks formed the resistance movement EAM (National Liberation Front) in September 1941. EAM served as the resistance's political organization and included people from all walks of life: priests, teachers, army officers, labor leaders, workers, and mainly peasants. However, it gradually came under the domination of the well-organized and disciplined Greek Communist Party. Members of the party, known as Ipefthinoi (the responsible ones), who were planted in each village and town, and the Kapetaneoi (guerrilla leaders such as Ares Velouhiotes), who commanded the partisan bands of ELAS (the National Popular Liberation Army), took over EAM-ELAS. Although only about a tenth of the EAM-ELAS members officially belonged to the Communist Party, they managed to control almost the entire resistance movement in Greece.

EAM attracted and organized other functional bodies, such as EPON (the United All-Greece Youth Organization), which was set up to provide training and recreation of young boys and girls; EEAM (Workers' National Liberation Front), for the cities; EA (National Mutual Aid); and ETA (Caretaking Committee for the Partisans). ETA was responsible for the collection of food and other supplies from the villagers, in a form of progressive taxation, to help feed and equip the partisans. All these organizations stimulated the peasants to help themselves and keep the fighting spirit alive. Communications, theaters, crafts, and a new cultural life spread rapidly through the countryside. Alarmed at the growth of resistance groups and their infiltration by Communists, the German puppet governments of Greece, especially that of the Royalist politician John Rhallis, used propaganda appeals to resistance fighters to "join together like good brothers, helping Greater Germany to crush . . . those two great enemies of the world, the Anglo-American-Jewish coalition and the Bolsheviks, the two evil demons of humanity, who tyrannize the world."[12]

Among other resistance groups that developed in Greece, EDES (the Greek National Democratic League), under Colonel Napoleon Zervas, was the most important one, operating mainly in Epirus. Zervas, like Draja Mikhailovich in Yugoslavia, wavered between a superficial democratism and a superficial nationalism, caring more for promoting his own interest than for arousing popular enthusiasm for resistance. EDES and other minor "nationalist" bands became increasingly dependent upon British help and, since they grew increasingly weaker compared with EAM, they became secretly collaborators with the Axis. On the other hand, during the turbulent years of occupation, certain heads of resistance groups committed many crimes for personal or ideological reasons. However, as noted by Colonel Chris Woodhouse (the chief of the British Military Mission to Greece, who regarded EAM as tyrannical and a threat to British imperial interests), the initiative of EAM-ELAS in fighting the Germans and reforming the countryside justified its predominance.[13]

Administratively, EAM formed district committees, which elected regional committees. These committees helped to set up the five-man Political Committee of National Liberation (PEEA) in March 1944. This body was responsible for the administration of liberated areas and for securing EAM's representation in the government-in-exile in Cairo.

As a result of the Moscow Conference (1944), at which it was stipulated that Britain would have a 90 percent influence in Greek affairs, Churchill decided to crush EAM-ELAS, and ordered General Scobie to use British troops to support the royal government under George Papandreou in order to restore the king. British troops reached Patras on October 4, 1944, and ten days later were in Athens, where ELAS had a dominant position. On December 3 a mass demonstration sponsored by EAM turned into a battle as the police, composed mostly of German collaborators, opened fire on the first lines of the demonstrators, who were carrying Greek, American, British, and Russian flags. The fighting escalated, and extended to clashes between ELAS and the British until the Yalta Conference took place in February 1945. There, Stalin stated that he had no objections to British intervention, adding that "Since the Greeks had not yet become accustomed to discussion, they were following the practice of cutting each other's throats."[14]

Although fighting stopped after the surrender of EAM-ELAS forces, and the king was restored in 1946, the mutual hatred between left-wing and right-wing Greeks continued to flare up into a severe civil war that lasted until 1949. With the enunciation of the Truman Doctrine in March 1947, economic and military aid with army advisers (under General James Van Fleet) was made available to suppress the leftists, who by then had managed to dominate large parts of Greece, especially in the north. In 1949, when Tito also stopped his support and refused sanctuary to Greek Communist forces, the civil war was won by the royal government. In the meantime, Greece acquired the Dodecanese Islands (in which Rhodes was included) through cession by Italy (1947).

From then on, Greece engaged in a difficult struggle for rehabilitation and economic development. The country first had to cope with the ravages of occupation and of civil war, and then to turn to urgent problems of increasing overall and sectoral productivity of the economy. Improvements in social and educational conditions and a better organization of public administration, by reducing bureaucracy and changing an inequitable tax structure, were imperative. By 1958 the country had become self-sufficient in production of wheat. Electric power was doubled, and rice output increased by seven times over the prewar level. However, the problems of surplus rural labor and inequalities in the distribution of income and wealth remained unsolved for several years more. Only through massive emigration of some 800,000 workers (about one-third of the labor force), mainly to West Germany during the 1960s and the early 1970s was the labor surplus alleviated.

Large numbers of rural people migrated to large cities, particularly to Athens, where the urban sprawl and the lack of urban planning created problems of housing, sewage, and pollution. The lack of confidence, the limited use of checking accounts (only 28 percent of the money supply), and the economic and political instability in the country were responsible for the extensive channeling of savings into residential construction and short-term investment in services. Commercial banks, primarily the National Bank of Greece (absorbing more than half of savings deposits), the Commercial Bank of Greece (absorbing about 20 percent of savings deposits), and the Greek Industrial Bank, lent their support to the mainly oligopolistic industrial sector (mining, textile, cement, and other industries). On the other hand, the Agricultural Bank of Greece, which was (and still is) controlled by the Currency Committee, as the other banks are, provided the farmers with government-subsidized credit. Investment was directed primarily to real estate in large cities. This led to a dramatic increase in the value of urban land (25 times from 1958 to 1978, while the consumer price index increased by 2.2 times). (Economic growth and foreign trade problems of Greece, as well as of the other Balkan countries, are dealt with in later sections.)

ROMANIA

Throughout history, Romania has perhaps been the nation in Balkania most affected by foreign cultures. During the Byzantine era the Slavonic language and tradition were prevalent, while during the Ottoman period Greek culture was spread by the Phanariots and the monastic schools. Toward the end of the Ottoman occupation, revolutionaries and writers from Bucharest and Jassy spread the ideals of the French Revolution and introduced the French language into the schools of Walachia and Moldavia. However, in reaction to the Greek revolution of 1821, the Turkish authorities replaced the Phanariot *hospodars* with Romanian boyars. On the other hand, a number of Romanian students, educated in Jesuit schools at Rome, started a systematic movement to replace the mainly Slavonic language with Latin, which was the tongue of their Dacian and Roman ancestors. During the post-liberation years the influence of France and the rest of western Europe was predominant.

As mentioned earlier, the long tenure in office of Carol I (1866-1914) helped the economic development of the country. Some 2,000 miles of railroads were constructed. A large bridge at Cernavoda on the Danube connected Dobruja with the rest of Romania, and the Iron Gate was blasted to open the Danube to large ships. Moreover, the ever-increasing oil production around Ploesti (from 50,000 tons in 1890 to 1,885,000 in 1913) helped improve the financial and borrowing position of the country until 1917, when British engineers blew up the wells to avoid their falling into the hands of the Central Powers. By 1921 oil production was restored to prewar levels and, together with grain and lumber exports, provided enough foreign currency to pay for industrial imports.[15]

During the interwar years Romania, like the other Balkan countries, went through a turbulent period. Under pressure from the poor peasant masses and in order to stop the Bolshevik revolutionary spirit from crossing the Dniester River, King Ferdinand enacted a drastic land reform program between 1918 and 1921. Of 6 million hectares of land expropriated from absentee proprietors, foreigners, the crown, and large landowners, about two-thirds were distributed to some 1.4 million peasants; the rest was held for public use (forests, grazing, model farms, and roads). Although these reforms had political importance, mainly for the Liberal and the National Peasant parties, economically they were insufficient to increase farm productivity. Moreover, under the pressure of the depression of the 1930s, many poor peasants sold their plots and became part of the growing rural proletariat class.

The death of King Ferdinand in 1927 and the succession of his son Carol II, a shrewd maneuverer, led Romania to further turbulence and instability. Although he had as a tutor Professor Nicholae Iorga, an internationally known historian, his unwise policies and his favoritism stimulated the fascist movement of the Iron Guards, and led to the dictatorship of 1938–40. Old nationalist feelings of the Romanians, surrounded by a sea of Slavs, and endemic anti-Semitism were growing. Apathy and lack of cohesiveness, similar to that prevailing in Yugoslavia, brought on a national crisis in 1940 that resulted in the cession of Bessarabia and northern Bukovina to Russia, of northern Transylvania to Hungary, and of southern Dobruja to Bulgaria. Carol and his mistress, Magda Lupescu, fled the country to avoid prosecution by avenging nationalists.

Despite the efforts of the government and the political parties to carry out rapid industrialization, the Romanian economy remained largely agrarian. Close to 80 percent of the population lived in the rural sector by 1941, while only about 40 percent of the existing labor in this sector was needed. Ownership of small plots was prevalent. About 58 percent of the plots were less than 3 hectares. Increase in land productivity and employment of surplus rural labor, rather than land distribution, seemed to be the most pressing problems. Land productivity (9.5 quintals per acre) was very low, less than one-third that of Denmark (29.4 quintals per acre). This average output was the lowest in Balkania, except for Greece. Lack of equipment, limited use of fertilizers, the practice of strip farming, and primitive methods of cultivation vere the main reasons. In addition, the decline in agricultural prices by half, during the depression of the 1930s, intensified the dismal economic conditions of the population.[16]

Heavy indirect taxes on consumption and high tariffs on agricultural exports (up to 50 percent of their value) made things worse for the starving peasantry. On the other hand, high import duties and quotas to protect domestic industry did not greatly help to stimulate industrial growth. Other restrictive measures on foreign investment (not permitting more than 40 percent foreign ownership and less than three-fourths native personnel) proved to hamper technological development. However, the rich mining and lumber resources of the country helped to establish a few raw material-processing and metallurgical industries. Shortly before World War II petroleum was providing 46 percent, and lumber 12 percent, of the export total. By that time Germany had imposed a semicolonial treaty on the country that called for specialization in the production of minerals and agricultural raw materials.

Great inequality in incomes, class stratification, a low level of education (nearly half of the population was illiterate), and poor health conditions (the highest infant mortality rate in Europe next to Yugoslavia) also intensified misery and poverty in Romania. Average per capita income remained very low ($60 to $70 in 1937). As in all Balkan countries, education was limited and misdirected. Classical education was preferred to technical or agricultural training. Students prepared themselves for white-collar bureaucratic positions and gathered in the towns to swell the mass of applicants for the already overcrowded government offices. Nepotism, favoritism, and corruption were widespread.

Toward the end of the 1930s, the pressures from Italy and Germany were mounting. Italy tried to organize Yugoslavia, Romania, and Hungary in order to avoid Russian penetration across the Danube. At the same time Turkey, Greece, Bulgaria, and Romania tried to form an alliance supported mainly by Britain. Both efforts were unsuccessful, and by 1940 the Balkan Entente had become ineffective.

Romania then faced serious problems of dismemberment. (It has already been noted that Russia demanded and got Bessarabia and northern Bukovina, Hungary partitioned Transylvania, and Bulgaria took over southern Dobruja.) To avoid further partitions, and pressured by its people, Romania joined the Axis. In the meantime Hitler had decided to invade Russia, and he needed a secure Balkan Peninsula. German troops were sent to Romania in October 1940 while Mussolini launched his invasion of Greece.

Under the dictatorship of General Ion Antonescu, Romania provided Germany with oil, munitions, and grain, as well as some 30 army divisions for the Russian front. During the war the country suffered severe losses in Russia, especially during the winter of 1942–43 and the battle for Stalingrad. When the Soviet army crossed the Prut River and entered Romania in April 1944, the Russian dominance in the area became obvious. Moreover, after the Teheran Conference, Romania was assigned to the Soviet Union and Anglo-American nonintervention was assured. On August 25, 1944, King Michael, who was sympathetic to the Allies during the war, broke away from the Axis and declared war. The Romanian army then turned against Germany, fighting alongside the Russians in Transylvania, Hungary, Czechoslovakia, and even Germany. Casualties suffered in this fighting totaled some 170,000.

In contrast with the primarily Communist-led resistance movements against the Nazis in Yugoslavia, Greece, and Albania, no significant resistance movement developed in Romania, mainly because of the territorial disputes with Russia over Bessarabia and Bukovina. At the end of World War II, Romania gave up Bessarabia and northern Bukovina, which had been ceded to Russia in 1940, and regained Transylvania from Hungary.

After 1945 and under the Petru Groza regime, Romania was bound to the Soviet bloc and its interests were interwoven with those of Comecon. However, after the death of Stalin in 1953 and under Gheorghe Gheorghiu-Dej, initiatives were taken toward some degree of independence and restoration of cultural relations with the West.[17] Despite the Soviet interventions in Hungary (1956), Czechoslovakia (1965), and Afghanistan (1980), Romanian leadership (under President Nicolai Ceausescu since 1965) managed to maintain a precarious position while attempting to develop its own identity. Still classifying itself as a Communist country, it pronounces, from time to time, its opposition to both NATO and the Warsaw Pact, and wishes to retain its national independence.[18] Although an ally of the Soviet Union, Romania is not as close an ally as Bulgaria, first because its population is primarily non-Slav and second because of the existing problem of Bessarabia. Moreover, Romanians feel that the Soviet Union and Comecon exploited their country's natural resources during the postwar years.

TURKEY

The defeat of Turkey during World War I led not only to its loss of vast occupied areas in Arabia, Syria, Mesopotamia, and Balkania, but also to the determination of its present boundaries. The Treaty of Lausanne (1923) restored the boundaries of 1914 and changed the Treaty of Sèvres (1920), which provided, among other things, for the expulsion of Turkey from Europe (eastern Thrace) and the creation of an independent Armenian state. After the extermination or dispersion of the Armenians and the elimination of the Greeks from Anatolia (Asia Minor), Turkey achieved a national homogeneity with the exception of the non-Turk Kurd minority in eastern Anatolia, which from time to time rebels, seeking independence. From time to time, dispersed Armenian avengers renew the decades-old feud, assassinating and launching bomb attacks against Turkish diplomats and tourist offices in retaliation for the massacre of over a million Armenians in 1915.

Mustapha Kemal, born at Salonika in 1881, proved to be a good military commander, an effective diplomat, and a great reformer of modern Turkey. He joined the Young Turks and later organized his own nationalist movement, which finally led him to the presidency of the newly created republic of Turkey. He rapidly abolished the autocratic sultanate and caliphate, which had prevailed for centuries in the Ottoman Empire. Kemal introduced a policy of secularization and westernization. He appropriated all religious endowments and foundations, abolished the institution of polygamy, replaced the Arabic with the Latin alphabet, and introduced a number of economic reforms aimed at securing higher agricultural productivity and self-sufficiency.[19] Along with the emancipation of women and the abolition of the veil came the replacement of the Oriental fez with the Occidental hat. Protective tariffs were raised, domestic savings were encouraged, and the building of highways, railroads, and other public works was expanded. Intellectual and social progress proceeded vigorously, parallel with industrial progress.

After the death of Kemal in 1938, the government of Ismet Inonu (1938-50) emphasized higher agricultural growth instead of rapid industrialization. However, this policy failed to increase productivity substantially.

The weakness of the private sector and the lack of entrepreneurial know-how during the years of "emergence" of the Turkish economy (1923-50), under the governments of the Republican People's Party, may be considered the main reasons of growth of state enterprises. The state economic enterprises (SEEs) started with the creation of the State Railroad Company, and were expanded in the 1930s and later.[20]

Turkey did not suffer great destruction as a result of World War II, and was not compelled to rebuild and modernize its industry, as Greece and Yugoslavia were. Moreover, special-interest organizations, which remained and increased over time, inhibited the effective competititve functioning of the economy and led to inflation and balance-of-payments deficits.

In 1950-60 the government of Adnan Menderes pursued a policy of expansion. The growth of the economy may be attributed to the rapid growth of agricultural exports, especially during the Korean War, which resulted in the inflow of foreign investment and the establishment of needed infrastructure. However, the more liberal economic policies of the government aimed at achieving great leaps forward that were unrealistic for the culturally and religiously conservative Turkish society.[21] Furthermore, the opening to the West increased the propensity to import, with no equal rise in exports, and led to trade deficits and the gradual depletion of foreign currency reserves.

On the other hand, the implementation of some form of indicative planning after 1963 was not integrated into the "financial programming" suggested by the International Monetary Fund (IMF), and it proved to be ineffective in solving the problems of inflation and the balance of payments. Such macroeconomic planning, which also was used in Greece after 1958, usually includes optimistic projections for the overall and sectoral growth of the economy with little, if any, practical effect. Only for the projection of public investment may they have some importance. The continuation of the ineptly administered development policies and the overexpansion of the money supply led to even higher inflation.

The inflationary policy of money and credit expansion, which continued during the 1970s, was due primarily to the significant increase in remittances from Turkish workers in Europe. In order to avoid social unrest due to high inflation, the government froze the prices of products of state enterprises. However, because of the lag in tax collection, large deficits appeared in the public sector and were financed by further increases in the money supply, thereby fueling more inflation. Moreover, interest rates were fixed, and as a result the quantity and quality of investments were lowered. These unwise domestic policies, as well as the use of fixed exchange rates in foreign transactions, led to extensive balance-of-payments deficits and further weakening of the Turkish lira. It would seem that in recent years the political structure of the country has become more sophisticated and its social awareness more acute; people now demand higher standards of living that the economy is unable to provide.

The Turkish government has begun unpopular reforms, scrapping subsidies and eliminating protectionism that has kept inefficient enterprises in operation. These austerity measures are used to reduce oil consumption, reduce inflation (which runs at rates more than 100 percent annually), and stimulate the economic growth of the country. Also, some $450 million of economic and military aid provided by the United States and its Western allies during 1980, and additional sums to be provided until 1985, are expected to help stabilize the ailing Turkish economy, which has an unemployment rate of over 20 percent. The geographical location of Turkey, between the Soviet Union and the Middle East, is a major factor influencing Western policies on foreign aid to the country.

Turkey is very much a country with a split personality. One segment of the population, living mainly in the cities, is in many ways modern and Western; the people in the rural regions form a traditional Middle East society where Islam holds sway. The process of economic development leads to the migration of poor, uneducated peasants into the slums of the cities, which in recent years have been the main areas of extremism.

A member of the North Atlantic Treaty Organization (NATO) since 1952, Turkey has received large amounts of military and economic aid from the United States under the Truman Doctrine (1947). The 1960s and 1970s have been marked by outbursts of public disorder and frequent changes in government. On September 12, 1980, the country came under a military dictatorship (the third in the postwar years) headed by General Kenan Evren.[22] This dictatorship seems to be milder than those in 1960 and 1971, and is expected by some experts to improve relations with neighboring countries, particularly Greece (over Cyprus), and reduce both the leftist and the rightist killings and the skirmishes between the Sunni majority and the Shiite minority of the Moslem population.

As mentioned earlier, the majority of the Kurdish population, estimated at 10 million, lives in Turkey. While the Kurdish nationalists are not as well organized as they are in neighboring Iraq and Iran, a number of attempts have been made to awaken nationalism and achieve independence. Another priority of the military rulers in Ankara is to discourage such movements and to calm the unrest that has been growing in the underdeveloped, predominantly Kurdish areas of eastern Turkey.

YUGOSLAVIA

The Yugoslav (South Slav) state was created in 1917 when representatives of the Serbs, Croats, and Slovenes gathered on the island of Corfu and decided to create their union under the Serbian Karageorgevich dynasty, with the aim of reviving the dynasty of the Hapsburg Slavs. By 1919 other nations, including the United States, recognized its existence as an independent nation. In addition to the external problems with its neighbors, the newly created federation faced internal troubles, mainly from Roman Catholic Croats and Slovenes, the Greek Orthodox Serbs, and the sizable Moslem communities of Bosnia-Herzegovina and Macedonia. Geographically the country is midway between the East and West, as is the whole Balkan Peninsula, and is affected by many cultures.

Two parties have been dominant in the political life of Yugoslavia: the Radical Party, under Nikola Pashitch (1881-1926), and the Croatian Peasant Party under Stefan Radich (1905-1928). Both parties remained active until the German invasion of 1941. In 1919 land reforms were enacted. Feudal and quasi-feudal institutions were abolished, and land was distributed among some 500,000 peasant families, despite strong opposition from (mainly Moslem) landlords. The constitution of 1921, influenced by the unionists of Pashitch, created a centralized monarchy that led to the dictatorship of King Alexander in 1929. The name of the country was then changed from the Kingdom of the Serbs, Croats, and Slovenes to Yugoslavia. Alexander was assassinated in 1934, and the regency continued until 1941.

Like the rest of the Balkan countries, Yugoslavia was devastated during World War I. The loss of livestock was extensive, especially of pigs and sheep (47 and 55 percent, respectively). Credit was limited, interest charged by individual lenders reached 200 percent or more, and taxation was heavy (40 to 50 percent of the peasants' cash income). Agricultural productivity was low, which discouraged new capital investment. A labor surplus of more than 60 percent was estimated in the rural sector (disguised unemployment), and illiteracy was more than 50 percent in the interwar period.[23]

It was realized that to carry out a rapid economic development, industry had to be stimulated through protective tariffs and other subsidies. As a result of the industrialization policy, foreign investment increased, transportation and communications were improved, and large lumber and steel mills and many manufacturing and mining units were established. However, domestic and intra-Balkan markets were poor, and Yugoslavia became largely dependent on German markets for economic survival.

After being conquered by the Nazis in World War II, Yugoslavia was divided among Germany and Hungary (in the north), Italy (in the south and west), and Bulgaria (Macedonia). Only Serbia and Croatia remained as German puppet states. Croatians, under Ante Pavelich and his terrorist group (Ustachi), opposed the Serbians and Catholics and, in an alliance formed with the Moslems, turned against Orthodox Christians and Jews. Out of the wave of murders and assassinations that swept the country, there emerged the unifying force of resistance. Josip Broz, known as Tito, a Croatian by birth and secretary-general of the Communist party since 1937, became the recognized leader of resistance in Yugoslavia. He had served in the Austro-Hungarian army during World War I and, after being captured by the Russians, had fought in the Red Army during the Russian civil war. Using guerrilla tactics, he managed to organize the partisans and exploit the enthusiasm of the people through such slogans as "Death to Fascism, Freedom to the People," and proclaimed the goal of self-determination and federation for all Yugoslav ethnic groups. Another resistance group, the Chetniks, under Colonel Draja Mikhailovich (a Serbian nationalist and an anti-Communist), became inactive, and finally collaborated with the occupation forces against Tito's partisans.

The partisan bands, using hit-and-run tactics, achieved many victories. The savage reprisals of the Germans, such as the massacre of 7,300 people (including schoolchildren) in the industrial town of Kragujevac, helped further the recruiting and resistance of the partisans. Moreover, Tito's strategy in organizing a national rather than a Communist resistance, coupled with the austere discipline of the partisans—no drinking, no looting, no sex—increased fighting spirit and aided in unifying the resistance movement. The local, popularly elected National Liberation Committees, like the Russian soviets in 1905, provided the resistance with needed supplies and new members. Using the slogan of self-determination and federalism, Svetozar Vukmanovich, a Montenegrin and trusted lieutenant of Tito, organized effective resistance in Macedonia and established liaison with the partisans in Albania, Greece, and Bulgaria. On November 29, 1943, the Anti-Fascist Council for the National Liberation of Yugoslavia, known as AVNOY, established a presidium with Dr. Ivan Ribar as president and Tito as the head of the 13 acting ministers, and forbade the return of the king and his government-in-exile.

The main problems Yugoslavia faced immediately after the war were the rehabilitation of the economy, which was devastated as a result of fighting with the Nazis; the pressure from the Soviet Union for the extension of the Russian perimeter of defense, particularly after the growing U.S. influence over Greece and Turkey that resulted from the Truman Doctrine and the Marshall Plan; and the need for national and ideological consolidation.

The Soviets were interested mainly in exploiting agricultural and mineral resources in the Balkan and other eastern European countries in order to repair their own war-torn economy. After the war they bought raw materials at low prices in exchange for expensive industrial goods and equipment of poor quality, a policy similar to that practiced by the Western powers with their colonies. However, Yugoslavia was in no better position than Russia after the war. One-quarter of the population remained homeless, more than half of the industrial capacity was destroyed, and about 10 percent of the population (1.7 million people) had died in the fighting.[24] Furthermore, investment in joint ventures with Russia did not prove to be very effective, except in air and shipping transportation.

In order to keep up production incentives and avoid apathy on the part of the peasants, the First Five-Year Plan of 1947–51 did not abolish private owner-ship. However, investment emphasis on industry, to the neglect of agriculture, led to low wages, high prices, and shortages in the consumer sector. Many of the goals of the plan did not materialize because they were based on unrealistic premises and overenthusiasm. This first plan, as well as the 1946 Constitution, provided for a closer connection between the various ethnic territories and the establishment of a federal state with six constituent republics—Bosnia-Herze-govina, Croatia, Macedonia, Montenegro, Serbia, and Slovenia—and two provinces (Kosovo and Voivodina).

Tito tried to establish closer relations with neighboring Albania and Bulgaria. The Bulgarians, subject to more control by Russia, proposed instead a looser and broader association among the Balkan countries. Stalin was suspicious of Tito's movement, which could establish a new Balkan power deviating from the direc-tives of Moscow. He summoned the Yugoslavs and Bulgarians to Moscow in Feb-ruary 1948, but Tito did not go. Charges of Trotskyism, Menshivism, and revi-sionism were directed against him. Russian advisers were withdrawn from Yugo-slavia, and economic sanctions were imposed. Tito was recognized as a national leader, and started following a policy independent of Moscow. He also stopped his support of the Communist side in the Greek civil war, in order to avoid involving his country in a conflict in which the Americans were involved with war materials and military advisers. Yugoslavia then accepted some $98 million worth of aid from the Export-Import Bank, the Economic Cooperation Admin-istration, and other Western relief organizations, and even aid from military programs. Tito, the first Communist to break away from Soviet ideology and control, developed a personality cult. He also proved that there are different socialist paths, a concept that was later accepted by Soviet Premier Nikita Khrushchev in his reconciliation agreement with Yugoslavia.[25]

TRENDS FOR BALKAN COOPERATION

The geographical position of the Balkan countries at the hub of three continents—Europe, Asia, Africa—attracts the competition of the big powers for politcal and economic influence and domination. As was indicated in the histor-ical review, there have been many antagonistic efforts made by the big powers, especially the neighboring ones, to impose their policies and even to annex parts of the Balkan Peninsula. Such influence has been responsible for divisions among the Balkan peoples that have led to open conflicts and even to civil wars.

The common historical experience of the Balkan peoples, under long foreign occupations and periods of influence, has tended to create social and cultural similarities among them, such as a common religion (mainly Christian Orthodox) and certain common social customs (such as the drinking of raki). Because of these and other characteristics, some writers, mainly the Romanian historian Nicholae Iorga, have proposed a common Balkan type and a common culture, "Balkanology."[26]

As the Ottoman Empire declined because of external wars and internal revolutions, the big powers of that time—Russia, Austria, France, and England—prepared schemes either for dividing the Balkan countries or unifying them under their individual control or influence. These schemes, which at times were abandoned and at times modified, aimed primarily at promoting the political and economic interests of the big powers. For example, the increase of trade between England and Turkey, mainly through the Anglo-Levantine Company, forced England to support the status quo and to discourage any effort toward Balkan liberation from the Ottoman rule. What prevailed for centuries in the area can be described by the Balkan saying "A few donkeys quarreled in someone else's barn" or, as they say in Africa, "When elephants quarrel, the grass is destroyed." In other words, big powers quarreled over the Balkan Peninsula, and the result was its socioeconomic backwardness.

Efforts to achieve cooperation and eventual unification were made from time to time, but with limited results. During the struggle against the Ottoman yoke, a number of Greek revolutionaries urged the Balkan Peoples to unite against their common enemy. Rhigas Pheraios (Valestinlis), Alexander Ypsilanti, the Poulios brothers (in Vienna), and Joannes Capodistrias (Russia's foreign minister of Greek descent) were the main supporters of closer cooperation. The "Thourios" (war song) of Rhigas, which called for unification and revolution against the common enemy, was for years the "national anthem" of the oppressed Balkans, mainly the Greeks, Bulgarians, and Romanians. Influenced by the French Revolution, Rhigas not only agitated with such revolutionary slogans as "One hour of free life is better than forty years under slavery" but also suggested the economic and political unification of all the peoples of the Balkan Peninsula on an equal basis.

Other groups or individuals, such as Georgi Rakovski and Lyuben Karavelov (Bulgarian revolutionaries), Illya Garashanin (a Serbian), Charilaos Tricoupis (a Greek premier), and Francesco Crispi (an Italian premier of Albanian descent), worked for a closer cooperation of the Balkan peoples and even proposed the creation of a United States of the Danube, a federation of the Danubian countries. In the 1860s a number of alliances were formed, usually between Serbia and one of its neighbors (Montenegro, Greece, Bulgaria, Romania), with provisions that other neighbors would join later. Under the influence of the big powers and the regional disputes over annexation of certain territories, primarily in Macedonia, Epirus, and Transylvania, these efforts for closer cooperation, especially the federative ideas of the Christian Balkan states of 1912, were abandoned. Moreover, the constant suspicions and disputes led to the Balkan wars of 1912–13.

More intensive efforts to achieve closer economic and sociopolitical cooperation began after the Balkan wars, and were particularly strong in 1924–31. Such efforts were supported by the agrarian parties of Croatia and Bulgaria, led by

Stefan Radich and Alexander Stambuliski, respectively. Also, a number of writers (mainly socialists) advocated the creation of a Balkan Federation, and for this purpose published the journal *La fédération balkanique*, which had a great influence in Balkania as well as abroad. During 1930-34 more concrete results were achieved through four Balkan conferences (Athens, October 1930; Istanbul, October 1931; Bucharest, October 1932; and Salonika, November 1933). The main supporters of these conferences were Alexander Papanastassiou (a former premier of Greece) and Nicolai Titulescu (foreign minister of Romania). At these conferences, resolutions calling for the improvement of communications and the construction of roads and railways from the Adriatic to the Black Sea and from the Danube to the Aegean were adopted. Moreover, for the development of intra-Balkan and foreign trade, the conferences urged economic collaboration in tourism, credit, tariffs, and protection of Balkan agricultural products.[27] Resolutions also were adopted for the establishment of the Balkan Chambers of Commerce and Industry, Agriculture, and International Commerce, as well as a Central Tobacco Office, a Central Cereal Office, an Inter-Balkan Grain Exchange, and a Central Union of Cooperative Societies.

In February 1934, Greece, Romania, Turkey, and Yugoslavia initiated a Balkan Pact that was signed at Athens. It was hoped that Bulgaria would join them later. In October of that year those four states created the Balkan Entente, which replaced the Fifth Balkan Conference, scheduled to take place at Istanbul. The Entente, which was designed to make decisions and take actions on both economic and legislative matters, met at Belgrade in May 1936, and signed a treaty of friendship with Bulgaria at Salonika in July 1938. However, its importance was overshadowed by the expansionary policies of Italy and Germany.

The dependence of all Balkan countries on German markets for their exports was another factor in contributing to a strong German influence in the area. This economic dependence increased during the international economic depression, when the prices of Balkan agricultural products decreased by about 50 percent and exports to Germany increased from 16 percent in 1933 to 27 percent in 1937 for Bulgaria, Greece, Romania, and Yugoslavia, and from 19 to 51 percent for Turkey. In addition to engaging in economic competition over exports, the Balkan countries considered proposals for bilateral agreements, such as the federation of Greece and Turkey (by Venizelos and Atatürk) and the closer ties of the Slavs of Bulgaria and Yugoslavia, promoted by France against Italy. England tried to exert influence over Greece and Turkey in order to steer them away from the Soviet sphere of influence. All these factors had a repressive effect on the efforts to set up a pan-Balkan federation.

Interventions or influences of foreign powers frequently resulted in divisions and conflicts among the Balkan peoples. Big powers frequently used the principle of "divide and rule" to enhance their own interests. Thus, efforts by the Balkan countries to establish closer cooperation among themselves, independent of the desires of their "patrons," were frustrated.

There seems to be a desire for closer cooperation, and even federation, among the Balkan nations. In addition to the efforts to achieve unity of the people in the Balkan Peninsula for political reasons, moves toward a Balkan federation took place in the postwar years. Yugoslavia, under Tito, was always desirous of such a federation or wider union.[28] Bulgaria, under Dimitrov, proposed a Balkan Customs Union in 1948. In 1954, Greece, Turkey, and Yugoslavia signed an alliance agreement. Although this alliance faded into obscurity, good relations among these countries continued for years thereafter. In 1957, Romania's Prime Minister Chivu Stoica proposed a Balkan conference that would include Albania, Bulgaria, Greece, Romania, Turkey, and Yugoslavia. This proposal, which was renewed in 1959 and was accepted by all the others except Greece and Turkey, was aimed at gathering the Balkan leaders to consider economic and security problems of the region.

Regardless of which big power is behind some of these proposals (presumably Russia for those of Bulgaria and Romania), the idea of an association of Balkan nations seems to acquire a life of its own. On its own initiative, Bulgaria has assumed a more active role in settling regional disputes with Greece and Yugoslavia, in order to prepare the ground for further economic and cultural cooperation. A new Balkan conference, broader than that of Athens in 1976, is contemplated by the policy makers of the various countries. Statements and appeals for further cooperation have been made by almost all the leaders of the region.[29] Activities including scholarly conferences, music festivals, athletic games, and tourist and trade agreements have taken place frequently. These efforts, which have been intensified in recent times, are expected to continue.

National individualism and great-power imperialism have always been the main obstacles to closer cooperation among the Balkan countries. A working association of the previously hostile Balkan peoples requires the downgrading of the hatred and emotionalism that have promoted ethnic and territorial disputes. The recent worldwide trends of cooling fiery nationalism and of instituting closer communications may provide new impetus for the improvement of the economic and social relations of the Balkan peoples. In such a peaceful and progressive environment, agitation by minorities in these countries may cease and more energy may be devoted to the common goal of improving the economic conditions of all the peoples in the area. Although nationalism should be treated with respect, partisan indoctrination should be avoided if some form of federation or closer economic cooperation is to be realized. In order for a new federative venture to succeed, a nobler human purpose with an international outlook should replace the hates and rivalries that have devastated the Balkan peoples for centuries.

On many occasions the agreements or disagreements over closer cooperation among the Balkan countries have depended on the personalities or the ambitions of the leaders. Recent visits of these leaders to their neighbors have helped to iron out differences among them and to prepare the ground for closer economic and sociopolitical relations. Emphasis should be given to commercial and economic exchanges, and sooner or later improvements in the sociopolitical arena will follow. Then all the Balkan peoples will be able to visit and work in any of the areas of the peninsula in which, in addition to so many differences and conflicts, they share many common interests.

There is always the possibility of regional or political disputes and frictions. But these probably would not lead to greater isolation, restrictions on resource movements, loss of potential economies from large-scale production, and less economic and cultural development. Similar nationalistic differences existed among almost all the EEC countries, but the need for a common economic policy and development subordinated them to a considerable extent. On the other hand, contemporary technological advancements in transportation and communications have helped to liquidate national and territorial differences, and to support trends toward closer friendship and even regional unification. The improvement of economic and political relations among the Balkan countries would induce a reduction in military spending, not only among these countries but also among the big powers that have alliances with them.

NOTES

1. For more details see L. Stavrianos, *The Balkans Since 1453* (New York: Holt, Rinehart and Winston, 1958), pp. 709-31; W. Gewehr, *The Rise of Nationalism in the Balkans, 1800-1930* (Hamden, Conn.: Archon Books, 1967), pp. 116-17.

2. David Andelman, "Albania Dips a Wary Toe into the European Pond," *New York Times*, October 28, 1979; Faik Lama, "The Balance Sheet of the National Liberation War," *New Albania*, IV (Tirana: N. Librit, 1979), p. 16.

3. In 1978, China broke definitely with Albania, and Tirana was deprived of Chinese trade and aid (at least $5 billion over the previous 20 years).

4. More detailed figures on Albanian emigration are provided by Mahir Domi, "Albanian Settlements in the World," *New Albania*, V (Tirana: N. Librit, 1979), p. 20.

5. For details on reforms in Albania compared with other eastern European countries, see M. Kaser, "Albania," in H. Höhmann et al., eds., *The New Economic Systems of Eastern Europe* (Berkeley: University of California Press, 1975), ch. 9; Ramadan Marmullaku, *Albania and the Albanians* (London: C. Hurst, 1975), ch. 8.

6. Andelman, op. cit. A trade agreement with Greece in 1980 provided for $50 million, compared with only $4 million in 1975. In 1980, trade ministers from Greece, Turkey, and Romania scheduled visits to Albania.

7. Stambuliski was then captured and handed to IMRO terrorists, who tortured him and made him dig the grave in which he was buried. For the political success and the downfall of Stambuliski and the Agrarians, see Stavrianos, op. cit., pp. 646-50; F. Schevill, *The History of the Balkan Peninsula*, rev. ed. (New York: Harcourt, Brace, 1933), pp. 509-11.

8. For a survey of technical progress, planometrics, and incentives, see G. Feiwel, *Growth and Reforms in Centrally Planned Economies: The Lessons of the Bulgarian Experience* (New York: Praeger, 1977), chs. 4, 7, 9.

9. The reform "theses" of decentralization, suggested by Professors Angel Miloshevski and Petro Kunin, included the use of an incentive portion of wages in addition to the guaranteed portion. J. Brown, "Economic Reforms in Bulgaria," *Problems of Communism*, May-June 1966, pp. 17-21.

10. Venizelists were the followers of Eleutherios Venizelos, a Cretan revolutionary who became an outstanding statesman of Greece during the turbulent years of 1910-33.

11. The royal family continued to rule Greece until 1967, when the military junta, headed by Colonel George Papadopoulos, abolished the Glücksberg dynasty. With the fall of the junta in July 1974, democracy was restored in the country. For the causes of the coup on April 21, 1967, see S. Rousseas, *The Death of a Democracy: Greece and the American Conscience* (New York: Grove Press, 1967), chs. 2, 4.

12. Stavrianos, op. cit., p. 786 (from a leaflet distributed widely in Greece in 1944).

13. C. Woodhouse, *Apple of Discord: A Survey of Recent Greek Politics in Their International Setting* (London: Hutchinson, 1948), pp. 146–47. For further comments see C. Myers, *Greek Entanglement* (London: Rupert Hart-Davis, 1955), chs. 10, 18; W. McNeill, *The Greek Dilemma: The War and Aftermath* (New York: Lippincott, 1947). Heinz Richter, a German historian, presents a detailed and well-documented survey of the occupation years in Greece in *1936-1946: Dio Epanastasis kai Antepanastasis stin Ellada* (Two Revolutions and Counterrevolutions in Greece), 2 vols. (Athens: Exantas, 1975), translated from German.

14. Edward R. Stettinius, Jr., *Roosevelt and the Russians: The Yalta Conference* (Garden City, N.Y.: Doubleday, 1949), p. 218, reprinted in Stavrianos, op. cit., p. 829. A more detailed account is in G. Giannaris, *Mikis Theodorakis: Music and Social Change* (New York: Praeger, 1972), ch. 2.

15. For oil statistics see C. Jordan, *The Romanian Oil Industry* (New York: New York University Press, 1955). In 1975 crude oil production reached 14,590,000 tons. *Romania: Yesterday, Today and Tomorrow* (Bucharest: Romanian Institute for Cultural Relations with Foreign Countries, 1976), p. 53.

16. For more statistical data see H. Roberts, *Romania: Political Problems of an Agrarian State* (New Haven: Yale University Press, 1951), p. 177.

17. For Romania's decentralization reforms and trade increase with the West, see chs. 4 and 7; also John Montias, *Development in Communist Rumania* (Cambridge, Mass.: M.I.T. Press, 1967).

18. For additional sociopolitical considerations, see A. Damianakos, "Romania: In Search of Identity," *The Balkan Observer* (New York) 1 (1980): 7–9.

19. The main Turkish crops were tobacco and grain. Mining, textiles, leather, and food processing were also important and, with tourism, provided badly needed foreign currency. For an extensive discussion on Atatürk's reforms, see M. Price, *A History of Turkey: From Empire to Republic* (London: Allen and Unwin, 1956).

20. The shift from private to public enterprises ("statism"), in which the government owned at least 50 percent, presented serious problems of efficiency, especially in mining, wood and paper, oil refining, basic metals, and chemical industries. OECD and IMF economists have been critical of such subsidized inefficient SEEs. Richard Nyrop, ed., *Turkey: A Country Study* (Washington, D.C.: American University Press, 1980), ch. 3.

21. Morris Singer sees a reverse trend of westernization promoted by Kemal Atatürk and the Islamic revival. See his *Economic Development in the Context of Short-Term Public Policies: The Economic Advance of Turkey, 1938-1960* (Ankara: Turkish Economic Society, 1978).

22. The two main parties before the dictatorship were the Justice Party under Suleiman Demirel, who was prime minister in 1965-71, 1975-78, and 1979-80; and the Republican People's Party under Bulent Ecevit, prime minister in 1974 and 1978-79. Nyrop, op. cit., ch. 4 and pp. 303–04.

23. More detailed statistics are in J. Tomasevich, *Peasants, Politics and Economic Change in Yugoslavia* (Stanford, Calif.: Stanford University Press, 1955); Stavrianos, op. cit., chs. 31, 32.

24. For further details see S. Pavlowitch, *Yugoslavia* (New York: Praeger, 1971), p. 187.

25. On the policies of decentralization and the constitutional reforms toward a laissez-faire socialism, see ch. 4 of this book. Also see F. Singleton, *Twentieth Century Yugoslavia* (New York: Columbia University Press, 1976), chs. 12, 16; D. Rusinow, *The Yugoslav Experiment, 1948-1974* (Berkeley: University of California Press, 1977), chs. 5, 8.

26. In the countryside there are many physical similarities and numerous common characteristics, especially in music and peasant dances such as the Slav *kolo*, the Romanian *hora*, and the Greek *choria*. L. Stavrianos, *Balkan Federation* (Hamden, Conn.: Archon Books, 1964), pp. 2–4.

27. For a thorough review see R. Kerner, *The Bankan Conferences and the Balkan Entente* (Berkeley: University of California Press, 1963), chs. 2–6; T. Geshkoff, *Balkan Union: A Road to Peace in Southeast Europe* (New York: Columbia University Press, 1940), chs. 5–8.

28. The present president, and the other members of the ruling Presidium, elected in rotation for one-year terms after Tito's death, expressed similar desires for closer Balkan ties.

29. Constantine Caramanlis, the present president of Greece, who was prime minister in 1955–63 and 1974–80, was (and still is) instrumental in promoting Balkan cooperation, as are Premier George Rhallis and the opposition leader, Andreas Papandreou.

PART II

Organizational and Developmental Aspects

INTRODUCTION TO PART II

The preceding chapters emphasized the importance of historical events in shaping developmental trends in the Balkan countries. The following chapters deal with such domestic issues as the main characteristics of the Balkan economies, growth of natural and human resources, inflation, taxation, and productivity on the national and sectoral levels.

To improve economic efficiency, almost all Balkan countries have introduced material and/or moral incentives, and in some cases labor comanagement. This principle of workers' sharing in enterprise decision making, which has been implemented in a number of market and planned economies, creates the feeling of involvement among employees and workers, and stimulates innovations and productivity.

The market economies of Greece and Turkey, as well as of Yugoslavia, face serious problems of inflation and unemployment; the planned economies of Albania, Bulgaria, and Romania face the equally serious problems of efficient allocation of resources and inadequate supply of consumer goods. Economic development in the planned Balkan economies has emphasized industrialization at the expense of agriculture and services. In Greece and Turkey, on the other hand, the services sector has been emphasized at the expense of other sectors, primarily manufacturing. Although there are great difficulties in measuring and comparing economic indicators in these countries, empirical research indicates that during the postwar years, more capital per unit of output was used in Yugoslavia and less in Turkey, while labor productivity was higher in Romania, Greece, and Turkey than in the other Balkan countries.

4

ECONOMIC ORGANIZATION

MARKET ECONOMIES: GREECE AND TURKEY

The economies of Greece and Turkey, like all market economies, are affected by business fluctuations. They face never-ending movement up and down, comparable to what Sisyphus, the mythological ruler of ancient Corinth, faced when he was condemned to push a boulder up a mountainside time after time, only to have it roll back down upon him. In the upswing of the economy, factor imbalances and sectoral bottlenecks lead to price increases, which in turn reduce the power of the monetary unit and create the economic and psychological environment for the downswing. To avoid sharp ups and downs of the economy or to smooth out the cycles, economists and governmental officials in these countries have suggested both temporary and permanent measures. They aim at reducing inflationary pressures during the upturn stage of the economy and at stimulating demand and employment during the downturn.

With resource shortages expected on a worldwide scale, primarily in petroleum, metals, and other raw materials, perpetual inflation and stagnation threaten the economies of Turkey and Greece as well as the other Balkan economies. This is so because rising demand outstrips the supply of existing resources. As a result, prices of energy and other basic commodities are rising while the terms of trade for the Balkan importers of such goods become unfavorable.

To maintain high levels of employment and low rates of inflation, large amounts of resource-related investments are required in Greece and Turkey. Moreover, new investment is needed to replace worn-out capital equipment, especially in transportation, communications, and mining; to improve the land in places with extensive soil erosion; and to restore deteriorating irrigation projects. To accomplish this, government expenditures should be directed toward the supply side, emphasizing productive investment more than meeting demand. It would seem then, that the Keynesian emphasis on effective demand has run its course, and is inappropriate to the present stage of development in these countries.

Because of the prevalence of bureaucracy and political favoritism in both Greece and Turkey, a great deal of criticism has been directed against their public enterprises. Strong arguments are presented for denationalization and dismantling, instead of erecting welfare-state structures, even though it may be at the expense of higher unemployment. At the same time, the reluctance of private investors to make long-term productive investments, and their preference for investment in real estate and ventures intended to provide quick profit, may require increased investment activities by the governments of these two countries.

The following questions, however, may be asked: Is the public sector able to direct private enterprises or undertake economic activities where the private sector fails? Or can better results be achieved by getting the government out of economic activities? It may be argued that civil servants are subject to the same, or even more serious, shortcomings as private entrepreneurs, particularly in Greece and Turkey, which have a long history of bureaucracy in the public sector.[1] From a managerial point of view, the government may be considered a good policeman, but a poor adviser. Government subsidization of new private ventures, through easy loans, matching grants, tax rebates, and the like, may have greater significance than direct public investment.

In these two market economies some degree of subordination of extreme individualism to collective or group decision making, a sort of discipline and togetherness, may be needed for long-term growth. Also, some training for consensus and cooperation in effective decision making on economic and social matters, rather than endless argumentative discussions and stubborn, strongly opinionated conclusions, may be required for higher economic efficiency.

All Balkan countries use some form of planning for their economic development. Greece and Turkey use five-year development plans that can be characterized as indicative (or perhaps decorative), compared with the imperative plans used by the planned economies of Albania, Bulgaria, and Romania, as well as the Yugoslav economic plans, which are in between. The Yugoslav, and to some extent the Greek, plans have some similarities to the indicative planning of France. Advocates of such national planning believe that the dilemma of inflation and unemployment, as well as of bottlenecks or shortages, can be avoided or limited. However, others think that in such planning, a self-appointed elite of bureaucrats will try to regulate the private sector.

Concerning economic efficiency the question remains: Is the market mechanism in Greece and Turkey making possible the best allocation of resources? John Kenneth Galbraith's arguments for allocative inefficiencies of the present market mechanism may very well be applied to these Balkan market economies. Big businesses in these economies have a pervasive power to whet appetites and set objectives. This power derives from the goods and services they produce, the jobs they create, and the income they provide with their investment. Large domestic and foreign corporations are given incentives and enjoy high profits, autonomy, and other advantages provided by the respective governments. They may compel governments to provide tax breaks, subsidies, and favorable legislation on corporate matters, and may even (explicitly or implicitly) impose their will on important national or international decisions, as has happened on a number of occasions.

It is widely believed in Greece and Turkey that monopolistic and oligopolistic firms are largely responsible for recent inflationary price increases and supply manipulations, especially in the distribution of meat, dairy products, vegetables, and a number of manufactured goods. Usually prices in the cities are unjustifiably higher than those in the countryside. Furthermore, corporate investment has been directed primarily to the more advanced urban areas of Athens and Salonika in Greece and of Istanbul, Ankara, and Izmir in Turkey—a trend that has increased inequality between rich and poor regions.

To a large extent, production and distribution in these two market economies are performed by individuals and private companies directed by the principle of profit maximization. However, as long as the distribution of income is highly unequal, there may be a preference and demand for luxurious goods. This would mean greater use of resources for the construction of villas or the importation of jewelry, cars, and the like, at the sacrifice of production of basic goods needed by the masses. Thus, this type of misdirected production may be considered a form of waste, and total social utility may not be maximized.

In countries like Turkey, Herculean efforts are needed in the economic and social fields to improve social mobility, reduce sex and class discrimination, and eliminate serious barriers imposed by the landed aristocracy and the status quo. The demand for land reform, industrialization, employment, freedom, better health, and better education continues to be strong in Turkey, and at times leads to violence. At the same time, low-income people must be educated to give up their propensity to proliferate, which, as Malthus argued, perpetuates poverty. Certain governmental measures, such as direct employment in rural public works, diversification of manufacturing, proper taxation to stimulate investment incentives, extension of credit to small entrepreneurs, and institutional reforms to reduce bureaucracy and red tape, can reduce income inequalities.

In terms of income distribution, empirical findings suggest that Turkey is among the low, Greece among the intermediate, and Yugoslavia among the good performers. The percentage income share of the bottom 60 percent of the population is around 25 percent for Turkey, 30 for Greece, and 35 for Yugoslavia, compared with about 45 percent for Bulgaria and Romania. For Greece and Yugoslavia this percentage share remained about the same during the 1960s and 1970s, while that of Turkey increase slightly (from 21 to 25 percent). The results are worse with respect to the distributive share of the lowest 40 percent of the population. It is around 10 percent for Turkey, 16 for Greece, 20 for Yugoslavia, and 25-30 percent for Bulgaria and Romania.[2] This means that although large numbers of low-income workers and peasants have emigrated from Turkey, Greece, and Yugoslavia to other countries, mainly to West Germany, inequalities remain relatively high, particularly in Turkey. The main reason is the difference in income between urban and rural populations.

Such inequality generates differences in education, consumption, health, shelter, and even in the length of life. A low level of education is associated with low productivity and a low level of income, which in turn are responsible for the low level of education and skills. This is one segment of the vicious circle of poverty in the developing countries, in which Turkey is included.

Economic development in the Balkan countries, especially in Greece and Turkey, is a cause of rural-urban inequality through the transfer of resources and talented and educated people from the backward agricultural to the modern industrial and service sectors. Improvements in income distribution may be achieved by a reverse development process that places more emphasis on the rural sector, where average per capita income is low. However, this may lead to lower rates of overall economic growth, especially if redistribution is associated with lower rates of saving and investment. The dilemma, therefore, for Greece and Turkey may be how to correct inequalities, particularly in poor regions, without reducing the growth rate of their economies.

In certain cases, development policies may not promote income equality— will hurt poor people—unless they include guarantees of social justice. The frightening implication of empirical findings is that economic growth, planned or unplanned, promotes social injustice and makes things worse in many cases.[3] It increases the wealth and power of existing and newly created elites or oligarchies at the expense of the poorest segments of the population.

Capital-Labor Comanagement

Workers' participation in the decisions of their enterprises is an emerging issue not only in the Balkans but also in a number of market economies, such as almost all the EEC countries. Any enterprise wishing to be incorporated as a European rather than a national organization is required by the EEC to place workers on its boards. Thus, Greek and Turkish enterprises are expected to adjust their managerial structure to the new EEC requirements. Such an implementation of industrial democracy may help stabilize political democracy in unstable regimes such as that of Turkey.

There may be complaints that a new labor elite will be created by the elected representatives, who enjoy high wages and other benefits because they share in the decisions of the enterprises (as has happened in West Germany). Also, labor unions may fear that worker comanagement will blur the distinction between labor and management, and eventually destroy unionization. Thus, comanagement may be anathema to labor unions.

On the other hand, the dwindling power of unions raises the need for some kind of worker participation in the decisions made by enterprises. Moreover, not all working people are organized or unionized, especially in Greece and Turkey. There may be individuals with equal or even better skills and productivity who are paid less because they are unorganized. Thus, some form of labor comanagement may be instrumental in reducing unjustified and extreme inequalities.

Such sharing of authority as well as responsibility by workers may increase incentives for production and reduce governmental intervention. It may be the mule that eventually hauls these countries out of their ditch of stagflation. However, it should not lead to another form of bureaucracy. Comanagement probably will be effective in overall strategies such as macro planning, human relations, investment projections, and market orientation, but not in tactical and day-to-day operational activities that require quick decisions.

Practicing industrial democracy at the microeconomic level may solve many problems of inflation and sociopolitical instability. It may aid in avoiding what frequently takes place in almost all Balkan countries: the preaching of democracy and the practicing of dictatorship. Comanagement may help to increase incentives and reduce suspicion on the part of employees and employers, and to create the feeling that employees work for their own enterprises.

On the economic front, it seems that all Balkan economies, whether market or planned, face similar problems. Policy makers in Greece and Turkey try to fight inflation by exhorting labor and industry to restrain wages and prices and to increase productivity. Likewise, planners in Albania, Bulgaria, Romania, and Yugoslavia plead with administrators and workers to increase production, cut idleness and waste, and improve quality in order to avoid shortages, particularly in consumer goods such as meat, vegetables, and fruits, and in housing. On many occasions both types of economies resort to moral suasion in order to raise the aspirations of the workers and make them put maximum effort into their work. In the planned economies, such moral suasion is, at times, directed toward ending mutual recrimination between managers at each level of the production hierarchy, who blame each other for their own failures. In the market economies it is directed mainly at producers (monopolists or oligopolists) and labor unions, in order to make them refrain from blaming each other for contributing to the development of inflation and unemployment. The introduction of some form of industrial democracy in these economies may prove to be less painful and more effective in solving a number of these difficult problems.

With the exception of Yugoslavia, which is using the principle of worker-managed enterprises, the other Balkan countries use the principle of workers' sharing in decision making to a limited extent, if at all. Thus, in Greece and Turkey labor's share in decisions made by the enterprises is almost nonexistent. Some semipublic or public enterprises have implemented this principle from time to time. In Greece, for example, during the prewar years, particularly between 1928 and 1936, the first management-labor factory councils were introduced, mainly in the tobacco and shoe industries. After the war the principle of labor sharing in decisions was introduced for short periods in the Greek National Railways, the Piraeus Port Authority, the Bank of Greece, and the National Bank of Greece. Also, as a result of a special law passed in 1911, Councils of Economic and Social Policy were established; they included representatives of the state, management, and labor. Their success was limited. Moreover, a number of enterprises, such as Paraiki-Patraiki, Petzetakis Company, Lavreotiki Company, and the Commercial Bank of Greece introduced some form of workers' profit sharing, primarily in order to stimulate cooperation and higher productivity. Also two shipping companies in Crete and one in Lesbos, as well as the Macedonian Bank, began their operations on the basis of relatively equal ownership, being considered public-owned firms. Because of the widespread application of labor comanagement in the EEC countries, Greece and Turkey are contemplating the introduction of this principle in conjunction with Article 35 of the International Labor Treaty (concerning job protection of labor representatives).

While bureaucracy in the Balkan planned economies destroys the possibility of workers' democracy, the expansion of multinational enterprises and the formation of modern industrial working classes in these economies may dig the grave of bureaucracy. However, political levers are stronger than economic ones, and the process of debureaucratization is slow.

The Growing Public Sector

In Greece and Turkey, as in many other market economies, the public sector is growing proportionally faster than the overall economy. Thus, government expenditures in both countries increased from 18 percent of gross domestic product (GDP) in 1960 to more than 25 percent in 1980. As expected, budget expenditures in Bulgaria and Romania were high—58 and 65 percent of net material product (NMP) and national income, respectively—while for Yugoslavia they were 18 percent of national income in 1977.[4]

The expansion of the public sector is the result of the ever-increasing demand for governmental services (including those by regional and local units of government), which leads to high elasticities of government expenditures with respect to GDP. Such elasticities were 1.37 for Greece in 1960–78 and 1.58 for Turkey, compared with 1.46 for the EEC.[5] This means that the public sector grows proportionally more rapidly than the private sector in Greece and Turkey (as it does in the rest of the EEC), and more taxes are needed to finance growing expenditures. In Yugoslavia government expenditures grow relatively less rapidly than the overall economy.

Although the private sector in Greece and Turkey is far larger than the public sector, rapidly growing semipublic or public institutions in these two market economies present new problems that are difficult to solve with old theories. Large-scale industries such as shipbuilding, refining, communications, banking, transportation, energy, and insurance are under total or partial government control. In such "state capitalism" the government, or another public institution, takes over ownership and related managerial or entrepreneurial activities.[6]

The merchant marine has escaped state ownership and controls, mainly in Greece, because of its flexibility and its opportunity to move to another country in case of a threat of nationalization or other form of state control. Also, retirement plans for doctors, lawyers, engineers, and other groups who have major roles in these economies have a semipublic character. Management of these plans and groups, which is appointed by members and regulated by the government, can influence investment, and even social policies, through the use of large portfolio holdings.

Greece and Turkey are slowly becoming dual economies, with some form of joint partnership between private enterprises and government. The private sector concentrates on the production of material goods, while the government provides a wide range of services, such as social security, health, education, and community projects.

In Greece, in addition to the direct "fiscal monopolies," such as those of salt, matches, and playing cards, there is a growing number of independent public or semipublic institutions. They include the Public Power Corporation, the Organization of Telecommunications of Greece, the Railways of the Greek State, and Olympic Airways, as well as the newly established Public Real Estate Company, which administers government property. In the financial sector almost all banks belong to this category. The Bank of Greece, the Greek Bank for Industrial Development, the National Bank of Greece, the Commercial Bank, and the Ionian Bank are all under total or partial governmental control. The Public Enterprise of Petroleum, established in 1975, explores and deals with petroleum resources in cooperation with foreign companies. Such companies include the Romanian enterprise Rompetrol, which performs drilling and other operations and promotes use of petroleum products, primarily in northern Greece. Parallel public or semipublic institutions also exist in Turkey.

The psychological and economic urgency for Greece, Turkey, and Yugoslavia to develop closer cooperation with the European Common Market forces their industries and enterprises to form cartels, trade cooperatives, and other business associations so that they can meet future competition from larger foreign companies. This need for cartelization and the inflated profits earned by middlemen have forced the formation of more consumer cooperatives and public supermarkets in Greece and Turkey. Also, agricultural cooperatives for the sale of fruits, vegetables, and other products, similar to those operating in western Europe (mainly Germany and Italy), are spreading in these countries. Their main effort is to eliminate the monopolies held by middlemen who buy at low prices and sell at high prices, or manipulate supply and demand in order to reap sizable profits. Agricultural cooperatives, looser than those in planned economies, that combine agricultural production and some form of processing also are contemplated as a means of improving productivity and marketing in these countries.

In centrally planned economies, on the other hand, there is a tendency toward the denationalization of retail stores and the redistribution of some state lands to the peasantry in order to provide strong incentives to increase productivity. This trend can be observed in the Balkan centrally planned economies as well as in other east European countries, especially in Poland and Hungary. For large enterprises socialization seems to be more attractive than nationalization, especially in Yugoslavia. It is also suggested that even nationalized industries in market economies be handed over to a mutual fund in which every citizen would have shares that could be introduced into a free market.[7]

PLANNED ECONOMIES: ALBANIA, BULGARIA, AND ROMANIA

In recent years reforms and innovations, which were central in Schumpeter's analysis of capitalist economies, have become the main concern of the centrally planned Balkan economies. These reforms focus on technological progress involving new methods of production, new products, and new managerial techniques for more efficient and less costly production. As a result, decision makers have more flexibility in choosing among alternatives, in promoting incentives, and in determining rewards.

The reforms implemented in the planned Balkan economies—with, in one way, the exception of Yugoslavia—are not sufficient in terms of welfare. There are still problems of economic and political resistance to fundamental innovations, the dehumanizing effects of the rush to industrialize, and the satisfaction of consumers' wants. But the obstacles to innovation do not come primarily from the managers and the people involved; they are structured within the system. State enterprises enjoy some form of monopolistic protection against other enterprises. Managers hesitate to introduce innovations and risk not fulfilling the plan's requirements because they may lose bonuses, be demoted, or, in extreme cases, end up in "correction camps." One of the main problems that planners have to face is how to achieve planned targets while allowing more autonomy to search for and apply new techniques and innovations. In an analogy to Adam Smith's "invisible hand" in capitalist markets, what may be required is an invisible foot to jolt managers into the introduction of new technology. However, bureaucracy continues to thwart efforts to promote innovation and increase efficiency. This is more so in the public sector, where work expands to fill the time available for its performance (Parkinson's Law).

To stimulate efficiency and increase production, Balkan planned economies have started to reorganize their economic mechanisms. This includes changes toward more autonomy and self-sufficiency for state enterprises, through adjustment of production to related market demand; reduction or elimination of subsidies; and increases in material reward to the workers with high productivity. This economic strategy has been introduced in Romania and to some extent in Bulgaria. Similar innovative measures have already been applied in Yugoslavia and Hungary. They aim at improving quality and increasing productivity, through more competitive cooperation and less inflexible planning, so that products can be made more competitive with those of the Western economies. Also, the institution of private property has gradually been enlarged to include retail trade and housing, as well as small agricultural plots. Private agricultural plots and the raising of small numbers of livestock, permitted in Romania, provide more reliable sources of food than state stores.

Like the market economies, the centrally planned economies of Albania, Bulgaria, and Romania are not free of economic fluctuations. Although inflation, in the form of frequent price increases, does not occur because of price controls, disequilibrium between supply and demand is common. Inflation, therefore, cannot be measured by price increases, but by the length of the lines outside retail stores.[8] Perhaps this is the main reason why the currencies of those countries are not convertible and are not accepted in international markets. One can conclude that these currencies are not "money," but ration coupons.

To avoid shortages and inconsistencies during the plans' implementation, rolling or sequential planning is more practical because it provides for adjustment to changing conditions. In such circumstances, planners in Balkan socialist economies would solve the problem of waste that arises from useless reserves, which long-term plans set aside to meet unpredicted shortages during plan execution. In addition, many problems of storage and transportation, especially of fertilizers, and delays in housing construction might be solved by sequential or rolling plans.

Bulgaria and Romania are under pressure to liberalize their economies by removing subsidies from a number of consumer products and allowing prices to adjust to the market forces of supply and demand. Such a removal of subsidies and of price controls has been implemented in Hungary as a result of the "new economic mechanism" introduced in 1968. The main goals of this new policy are to reduce bureaucracy; relieve the budgets of their heavy burden of subsidies, which are responsible for a drain of about one-third of total revenue; and make production enterprises stand on their own feet. Also, a gradual lessening of emphasis on investment in heavy industry and improvements in the consumer sector appear to be occurring in Balkan and east European planned economies. The slogan "invest now, consume later" seems to have less appeal, because it has been overused and consumers are tired of waiting indefinitely for the better life.

As an objective visitor can observe, the main problems of the planned Balkan economies are an insufficient distribution system, low incentives for sellers, interruption of sales of certain products, and excessive demand (compared with supply) for consumer goods, which is made so evident by the long lines of customers outside retail stores. Adjustment to changes in fashion is another serious problem; production cannot be quickly adjusted to new styles and materials (such as synthetics). Moreover, customers are more affluent, and therefore more selective. Previously, when a suit was needed, it was bought—whatever was available. Now, customers who are buying a second or third suit are more discriminating. Thus, lines form in front of clothing stores selling Western products, such as blue jeans or stockings, despite their high prices.

Rigidities in central planning cause stagnation in production, severe shortages of food and industrial products, shoddy quality, mismanagement, and sometimes corruption. Illegal barter deals and serious bottlenecks bedevil the distribution of goods. Agricultural products such as fruit, eggs, and meat may take a month to get from the cooperatives or the state farms to the cities because of delays instigated by governmental purchasing agencies that interfere with the processing chain. By the time products reach marketplaces in central cities, a significant portion may be unfit for use. Some food products, such as fish and fruits, may be in short supply because a portion has been reserved for party officials and other very important persons or dignitaries. Tractor plants may produce machines that do not meet standards; and new television sets may have faults such as wavy lines, blurred images, or dark screens to the point that they are unacceptable to consumers. Managers and workers in car industries and shipyards are interested primarily in meeting the official quantitative targets of the plans rather than turning out high-quality products. Lengthy delays occur in the construction of factories, schools, hospitals, and houses. Many buildings are three to five years behind schedule because of delays in the allocation system and the scarcity of materials. However, similarly or even more defective or low-quality products appear in Greece and Turkey; but they cannot last long under competitive conditions.

Consumers in these planned economies do not have a large and varied package of consumables, as do their counterparts in market economies. The heroic efforts to achieve big increases in output have taken their toll in the form of lower quality. There seems to be a sort of coexistence between archaic, low-productivity organizations, with inefficient processes, and advanced, modern techniques. In many cases incremental modifications and improvements in technology take place before basic transformations are undertaken.

Problems of Efficiency

One of the main headaches of the planners in the centrally planned economies of the northern Balkans is the adjustment of production to consumer needs and preferences. Such preferences change with fashion, as well as with the level of development of a country, and it is difficult to predict or to try to change the taste of consumers. As development progresses, it becomes more difficult for planners to foresee the reactions of consumers and to satisfy their demand effectively. That is why some degree of advertising, marketing, and sales promotion can be noted in these countries.

In order to stimulate incentives and increase productivity, the centrally planned and managed system of the northern Balkans has become flexible in wage differentials. The same flexibility can be observed in other east European countries, mainly Hungary, Poland, and Czechoslovakia. Thus, coal miners can earn as much as $1,000 per month, about five times the average salary of a factory worker and ten times the salary of a grade-school teacher or a priest. In addition to bonuses, huge pensions, insurance against accidents, and generous fringe benefits are used to attract workers to the coal and similar hard-labor industries where the labor shortage is serious. After strikes, demonstrations, and complaints from coal miners, as in Romania's Jiu valley, for example, the planners realized that it is easier to shift money than people. In other industries, piece rates and incentive pay for high productivity were introduced. Moreover, by implementing more intelligent policies for commercial farmers, these economies have managed to zigzag back to output-oriented incentives in order to increase agricultural productivity. Such incentive policies, through some form of rural Keynesianism, may be needed for higher agricultural production and overall employment.

The limited production incentives in state or even cooperative farming led the planners of the Balkan socialist economies to consider a policy of private uses of public lands, which Aristotle suggested in his criticism of Plato's ideal communist state more than 2,000 years ago. Probably, under such an arrangement, the rural people would use limited supplies of tractors, spare parts, fertilizer, and other equipment and materials more efficiently. Moreover, the recent introduction of agrarian-industrial complexes, with emphasis on quality products and a better coordination of the rural and urban sectors, would lead to lower costs. These new policies may help to reduce regional inequalities that prevail in these planned economies, though not as extensively as in Greece and Turkey, and to stop the trend of migration from villages to big cities and industrial centers.

To discourage hoarding of materials, practiced by some managers of the Balkan planned economies to meet future quotas, and to avoid false reporting, physical quotas have been gradually replaced by valuation and criteria of profitable performance that are similar to those of the market economies.

To implement such policies, turnover taxes are used by these planned economies to siphon off resources from consumption to capital formation. Also, discount rates are used in the planning process to decide on investment priorities, in a fashion similar to the one that prevails in market economies. The main goal for managers of state enterprises is finding methods and techniques that economize on input requirements. That is, they use pricing and profitability criteria in the production and distribution process, as their counterparts in market economies do, to reduce cost and increase profits. However, innovations and reforms can be implemented only slowly and painfully, and not with "great leaps forward," as the Chinese experience has indicated.

To motivate managers and workers to act efficiently in the economies of Albania, Bulgaria, and Romania, more material incentives and/or shorter hours of work per week are more effective than penalizing them by assigning still higher targets when they fulfill their previous plan goals. It would seem that workers and managers care more for their own interests than for social interests. Thus, bonuses, reduction of work hours, and other incentive norms are expected to stimulate the assimilation of new technology and to increase productivity for each enterprise and each manager.

The paradox of our time is that socialist nations are yearning for the benefits of the capitalist materialism they have condemned for decades, while capitalist nations are questioning the goals of materialism and the values of their cultures. Moreover, Communism is no longer a monolithic ideology. There are many centers of power with different degrees of influence instead of a unified Communist world. There seem to be more disagreements among Communist countries than between Communist and capitalist countries. There is a trend toward negotiated settlements and economic, rather than ideological, competition between countries with different economic systems, especially in the Balkan Peninsula. Even the distinction between "capitalist" and "Communist" has been replaced by the less ideological and more economic terms "market economy" and "planned economy."

Wages

Wages in the socialist Balkan economies are determined primarily according to the principle "From each according to his ability, to each according to his work." Socialism in these countries has not reached the stage in which the distribution would be "to each according to his needs."

Rent, transportation, and telephone prices are fixed and maintained artificially low. However, there are substantial differences in rewards and status that support the argument that there is a deviation from the classless society that remains constant, or even widens. Such economic and social inequalities were inherited from the previous capitalist system, and they are reproduced through the social division of labor required for continuing economic growth and high productivity.

Depending on the nature of work—"regular," "heavy," "extra heavy"—wages can differ in a ratio of 1 to 3 or more. Underground miners, for example, make far more than workers in local industries, and professional and technical workers may earn even more. In addition to regular wages, special payments in the form of bonuses, seniority supplements, and overtime pay can be given.

The Balkan planned economies have adopted widely divergent approaches to managerial decision making and labor remuneration. Romania has the most highly centralized system, followed by Albania and Bulgaria. Bonuses in Romanian enterprises are too low, relative to basic income, and plans are on many occasions overly optimistic. That is why the Romanian plans are frequently modified during the period of their implementation. Important decisions are made at the ministerial level, while managers of enterprises and *centralas* (trusts) are confined to activities similar to those of foremen and junior managers in market economies.

There are great differences in wages between unskilled and skilled workers. Managers of factories, for example, earn four to five times more than manual workers. The same is true of laborers working in hard and risky jobs, as in coal mines or in underdeveloped regions. In certain cases low-skilled jobs may involve extra material remuneration because, for instance, they are in stores selling scarce goods. For example, salesclerks in food stores can put aside food for themselves or their acquaintances. Although average wages are relatively low in the Balkan planned economies (around $200 per month, compared with $240 monthly minimum wage in Greece), medical services and education are free, and rents are very low (from $10 to $45 per month).

In certain cases party members or managers are incompetent to deal with problems of resource allocation, or they use resources for their own benefit. Technicians, for example, may be placed by managers in menial jobs unsuited for their training. Other managers may embezzle large amounts of money, while still others may promote their relatives or favor female personnel in exchange for sexual favors.[9]

In the past, planned economies, including the Balkan ones, referred to labor as the primary factor of production, in accordance with Marxian dogma. In recent years, though, an effort has been made to fuse scientific and technological achievements with the advantages of socialism. As a result, more and more emphasis is placed on management, specialization, improvement of productivity, and import of foreign technology. Recently introduced reforms aim at specialized education, professionalism, more research, and decentralization of decision making, moving gradually away from central controls and sterile dogma. These innovations lead to the advancement of knowledge and a gradual international integration. The policy makers in the planned economies expect that the fusion of science and technology with the socialist economic system will undermine capitalism, just as the industrial revolution undermined feudalism.

New chains of stores, named Intershops, have been established in the planned Balkan economies to import highly coveted Western goods for selected consumers. Such goods, which include blue jeans, panty hose and stockings, television sets, French brandy, coffee, and chocolate, are available to holders of Western hard currencies and to high-salaried or party elite. Thus, a bourgeoisie with a higher standard of living than others and a second capitalist economy coexist with the socialist economy. This privileged class is entitled to shop at special stores and to be given preference on the waiting list for an apartment or a car.

Young people have dreams like those of their Western counterparts. They want to advance in education, improve their living standards, acquire the symbols of status, live in a capital or large city, and succeed in careers that can provide a materially comfortable and culturally attractive life. They want to get into a prestigious institution of higher education or university, to be appointed manager of a state or cooperative enterprise, and to join the party elite. However, social mobility, which primarily means advancing from the rural to the urban life, or from manual labor to skilled work, or from secondary to higher education, is not easy for a large number of persons. Some will remain manual workers on the farms or in the factories, some will go to inferior vocational schools, and a small number will advance to a higher managerial and educational class. Connections and bribery, along with true merit, determine who "makes it." Such a stratification of society creates problems of favoritism, nepotism, political hypocrisy, and even outright corruption. Fictitious marriages take place so that people can get an apartment and stay in large cities.

In many cases young people serving in the army or in the party, or working on farms or in factories, may have priorities in housing, higher education or managerial jobs. Usually, after two to three years on a job, they are free to change jobs within their specialty. There is virtually no unemployment; rather, there is a shortage of workers in a number of labor-intensive industries. However, some young factory workers end up with nothing to do because the unwieldy and highly centralized bureaucracy sends them where they are not needed. Also, people with education are not willing to do manual work. As a result, labor productivity does not match wages paid, and full employment takes place at the sacrifice of efficiency. The stage of rapid industrialization, in which the whole society is upwardly mobile, seems to be tapering off, and advanced technology and high skills are required. Thus, social mobility in these planned economies is limited to highly educated and skilled persons.

In the socialist Balkan economies there may be more competition on lines of consumers waiting to buy goods than on production lines (to achieve high performance). It is difficult for planned economies to find a replacement for the stimulus of market competition as a guarantee of high productivity. To get workers to compete in the production of more and better goods and services, honors, titles, bonuses, trips, and other privileges are offered. However, such remunerations, especially "honor rolls," have lost a good deal of their importance. Even higher money wages do not have much meaning, as long as they cannot be used to buy goods. Moreover, when everybody in a factory, from the director to the cleaning lady, gets a bonus for overfulfilling the plan, there may be complaints that the outstanding workers receive less, and the lazy ones more, than they deserve.[10] Such practices, which also apply to the professions, may undermine competition and reduce productivity.

YUGOSLAVIA

After the break with the Soviet Union and the other Cominform countries in mid-1948, Yugoslavia began to develop a new economic system characterized by social ownership with workers' self-management and decentralized decision making. Such decentralization to the republics and local governments reflected recogniton of the nationalities and ethnic minorities. Gradually, and especially after 1953, the country's resistance against Soviet-style collectives increased. Since then, half of the state-owned acreage has been returned to the private sector, and most of the state farms have been transferred to collectives.

Since the reforms of 1965, the country has moved further toward the "self-management" principle.[11] Under this principle, seeds of which can be found in the Commune of Paris (1871) and which became a great "myth" of Yugoslav society, control should be exercised by representatives elected by the workers (Workers' Councils) of each enterprise; full-time managers or directors should follow the directions of these representatives. That is, labor does the managing instead of being managed. A serious question arises, however, as to the degree of influence exerted by the governmental representatives on the committees selecting the managers, and the effectiveness of such a principle in a country containing different nationalities (and thus possibly subject to conflicting group interests). Furthermore, one cannot ignore political and doctrinal constraints, as well as the problem of production efficiency, given that the system is based on a policy of full employment and almost perpetual job maintenance.

The constitutional amendments adopted in 1971 and the Social Development Plan of 1971-75 introduced further decentralization in decision making, lessened governmental and bureaucratic controls, and provided more autonomy for the six republics and two autonomous provinces. Only a limited number of activities, such as national defense and internal security, monetary and foreign-exchange policies, and development of poor regions, continued to be the responsibilities of the federal government. At the same time interrepublic committees were established to deal with the harmonization and coordination problems of the country.

In spite of all these experimental structural changes and unique institutional arrangements, which have been hammered out by trial and error over more than 30 years, Yugoslavia has achieved good results in terms of economic growth, foreign trade, investment rates, and industrialization. However, the tendency for self-managed enterprises to increase personal incomes and high rates of investment led to inflationary pressures and an increasing capital/output ratio, particularly in industry. Such an increasing capital/output ratio does not necessarily indicate a decline in the productivity of capital, but it implies the use of more capital per unit of output, probably at the sacrifice of labor, thereby bringing about unemployment or underemployment. Moreover, greater autonomy of enterprises on investment decisions caused "territorialization" of development, elimination of federal investment funds, and lack of growth in infrastructural facilities, mainly in transportation, communications, and electric power.

Since Tito's death in May 1980, Yugoslavia has faced the increasingly serious dual problem of retaining its socialist but nonaligned policy and the federated unity of the states and provinces. Already there has been some uneasiness among the inhabitants of Albanian descent in less-developed Kosovo[12] and Macedonia, as well as opposition in Croatia and Bosnia-Herzegovina. The main opposition comes from groups of émigrés in Australia, the United States, and (to a lesser extent) West Germany. However, locally these groups, which are either remnants of fascist groups (Ustachi) of Croatia or anti-Communist groups (Chetnik) of Serbia, do not have much support. They live mostly in nostalgia for the past.

There are also groups in a few east European cities, mainly Prague and Kiev, that would like to see the country return to the system of hard Communist rule that prevailed before 1948. Such groups tried to infiltrate and to influence the country's policy in 1954, 1971-72, 1974, and 1976 (on a relatively larger scale).

Planning and Decentralization

The First Five-Year Plan (1947-51) was a rigidly centralized Soviet-model plan for economic development. All accumulated capital was channeled into the federal budget, then reallocated to the various regions. Emphasis was placed on the movement of capital from the advanced regions of Slovenia and Croatia to finance projects in the poorer regions of Bosnia, Macedonia, and Montenegro. The plan determined the amount of production and trade for each state enterprise, and specified the places from which its raw materials should be supplied and where its products should be sent. An elaborate bureaucratic mechanism with some 217 federal or republic ministries was established to supervise its implementation. By 1951 the operation of the plan began to hinder rather than help economic development, primarily because there were no incentives for the people responsible for its implementation. This inefficient performance, coupled with a new ideological spirit that began after the decision of the Cominform to expel Yugoslavia from the Soviet socialist camp, brought about the replacement of the monocentric "state capitalist" planning by the polycentric "social" planning with its worker-managed enterprises and market-incentive socialism.

Detailed planning led to the development of such bottlenecks as bureaucracy, inefficiency, alienation of workers from decision making, and neglect of consumers. After 1950, when Yugoslavia started to veer away from the Soviet model of detailed planning, the country was gradually directed toward a market economy. Regarding the overall development strategy, however, Yugoslavia continued, as did the other planned economies, to invest large amounts in heavy industry at the expense of consumption.

As mentioned previously, after Tito broke with Stalin's Russia, he followed an independent policy, replacing the Soviet-style centralized planning with decentralized or "indicative" planning. The private sector, especially agriculture, was given more importance, and the workers of each enterprise became the decision makers on matters of production, capital expenditures, income distribution, and other vital functions of the firm.

Recently greater reliance has been placed on private activities, not only in farming but also in housing, retail trade, restaurants, and small-scale industries. Many people are making their living without drawing paychecks from the state, and a great number of others are augmenting their government wages by "moonlighting." The second job, however, tends to become more important than the government job. Workers often sleep in their government offices in order to be able to earn more on their outside jobs. New enterprises can be opened by any person or group of persons, the communes, or the public authorities.

There are nearly 6 million private farmers, owning more than 80 percent of the agricultural land. The country also has about 250,000 small private businesses. Half of the restaurants are privately run, and 60 percent of the houses built in recent years were erected by the private sector. The regime allows the import of goods by individuals, especially if they are shipped by the 1 million or more Yugoslavs working in West Germany and in other Western countries. Small private firms are predominantly run by the working people on an equal-shares basis, so that exploitation "of man by man" can be avoided, in conformity with the Marxian doctrine.

Communes, which are self-supporting economic and social units, have been established throughout the country. The Yugoslav commune (*obstina*) is an administrative arrangement similar to that of the local community in Western countries, but with wider socioeconomic functions. It has little in common with the Chinese commune. The main organ of the commune is the assembly, which has legislative and executive power similar to the residual power of the individual states of the United States. The commune is in charge of education, welfare, health services, and maintenance of public order. It supervises the legal and, to some extent, the economic activities of the enterprises. It supplies them with credit and provides guarantees for the capital they obtain from the state. Even though the official Titoist theory claims that, through this communalization and decentralization, the Yugoslav development would lead to the fulfillment of Marx's prophecy that the state would "wither away," there is still a one-party system with all the trappings of a modern bureaucracy.

All the subsequent plans, as well as the 1974 Constitution, have extended the principle of workers' self-management to macroeconomic decision making, primarily on problems of overall resource allocation. The same spirit predominates in the Five-Year Plan for 1976-80 and the Ten-Year Plan for 1976-85, which emphasize resource mobilization, economic stability, and reduction in income disparities between the less developed regions of Kosova, Bosnia-Herzegovina, Macedonia, and Montenegro and the more developed regions of Croatia, Voivodina, Slovenia, and Serbia.[13]

The Yugoslav Firm

As a result of the political and economic movement of Yugoslavia away from Soviet hegemony, a new form of socialism with decentralized enterprises and labor management emerged. The property of the firm is not owned by the state, but is held in trust for society (social ownership). However, small firms with fewer than five employees can be privately owned. Each firm is run by a general manager selected by the nominating committee chosen by the Workers' Council, which in turn is selected by the employees of the firm.[14] A representative of the local government sits in on committee meetings to select the general director or manager. A set of bylaws governs the details of managerial responsibilities. The annual net income is distributed among the workers of each enterprise. Workers are not hired at contractually fixed wages, but at a given share in the net income of the firm. Each is guaranteed a minimum income, and benefits above this minimum wage depend on the performance of the enterprise.

This device of income sharing stimulates the workers to perform as efficiently as possible, because they feel that the firm belongs to them; and the more they produce, the better their remuneration. There is a danger, though, that strong Workers' Councils may try to maximize individual profits while ignoring the needs of the enterprise for expansion and long-run improvement. Also, the directors of enterprises, who have little security of tenure, may, at the request of the workers, manage the firms in such a way as to achieve the largest short-run profits at the expense of long-run social interests.

The Yugoslav system of market socialism tries to reconcile the autonomy of the individual firms with the interests of society as a whole. To achieve these goals, the Yugoslav firms must conform to the provisions of national plans and try to achieve planned targets more through persuasion than the use of force by the authorities. Capital taxes, turnover taxes, credit, and other fiscal and monetary instruments are used by the federal government and the Investment Bank to allocate resources efficiently among the sectors and regions of the country. Antitrust laws and, to some extent, price and wage controls also are used to prevent major maladjustments, to minimize disequilibriums, and to encourage competition within the socialist framework. Thus, about a quarter of the output of intermediate goods, such as steel, is subject to price ceilings; and price increases of about one-third of consumer goods are subject to prior approval by the Federal Price Office. Furthermore, about 40 percent of total retail trade is subject to maximum markups. Besides the 6 percent capital or interest tax, there is a turnover tax averaging between 10 and 15 percent. About 60 percent of the tax revenue goes to the federal government, 20 percent to the communes, and the rest to the republics and districts.

Industrial enterprises are highly concentrated in Yugoslavia. The largest 200 enterprises account for about 60 percent of the total assets of industrial firms, excluding handicrafts. More than three-quarters of domestic production is sold by 20 or fewer producers, and about half of this production is sold by 5 producers. The same high concentration can be observed in retail firms.

In order to restrict monopoly and encourage competition, antitrust legislation has been introduced. Article 30 of the Constitution prohibits mergers or associations that promote inequality, prevent free trade, and practice discrimination. Recent legislation also prohibits price fixing, production limitations, deceptive advertising, and other practices that may damage other firms, the consumers, or the economy. However, price and other agreements between firms may be permitted if they are not contrary to law and contribute to improvement in organization or specialization, and higher productivity. Furthermore, in order to avoid duplication and to save costs, mergers may be permitted, especially in the exporting industries. Thus, more than 9,000 enterprises merged in the 1960s, reducing the total number of firms from 25,015 to 14,232.[15] The liberalization of foreign trade after 1965 further increased the number of mergers so that Yugoslav firms could survive foreign competition, but created some problems for firms producing commodities that could be imported at lower prices, such as automobiles, tires, steel, petroleum derivatives, cellophane products, and electrical appliances.

In this labor-managed system the firm does not own any productive resources, and serves merely as a vehicle for transactions initiated by its workers. However, the question remains of whether the labor-managed enterprise operates in a competitive environment (as Jaroslav Vanek assumes), being a price taker for both inputs and outputs, or whether it operates in a monopolistic or oligopolistic structure, being a price giver. Or, finally, is it a price taker that is instructed by the planning commission or any other governmental agency? To what extent are earnings distributed to workers or retained for investment in further expansion?

Although the economic system is based on self-managed enterprises that are independent of the central state apparatus, easy access by workers to managerial information frequently overturns designed policies, and may lead to the dismissal of top directors. This may be an additional reason why managerial decisions on wages, hours of work, holidays, vacations, dismissals, and the like are supposed to be attractive to workers and meet with their approval. This sharing by workers in enterprises also means participation in the obligations and losses, a fact that makes managerial efficiency difficult.

A peculiar method of workers' participation in decisions pertaining to internal organization, wage determination, bonus payments, and similar matters has been gradually introduced in the Soviet Union. This is known as the "method of Zlobin," named for Nicolai Zlobin, who first used it on the construction project in 1970. It permits a workers' team (brigade) to decide how to achieve the goal determined by the plan and how to distribute the assigned total income for the specific project or enterprise. The team, as an autonomous economic unit, tries to assign jobs and income to the most productive workers, and retrain or get rid of the lazy and unproductive ones.

In worker-managed firms there are problems of ownership rights to capital, the right to a market rate of economic rent, and the right of liquidation. An individual worker, for example, should be compensated for the capital contributed to a firm through underpaid labor, especially when he or she leaves the firm. Also, differences in income-leisure preferences of workers, as well as inflexibility in short-run adjustment of labor input, can pose problems in the process of decision making, since workers may be suspicious of changes affecting their share in income and decision making. When they deal with leased capital goods, they may show little interest in preserving the equipment. Workers may prefer short-run activities with quick payoff, neglecting long-run capital formation. These difficulties may lead the system away from optimality and toward something less than the best social utility, in which the winners gain more than the losers lose.

The incentives to worker-entrepreneurs for the formation of a new enterprise or the introduction of innovations into an established enterprise seem to be weak, because they do not have unique claims to the residuals generated by these enterprises, which they must share with the other workers. Although certain nonpecuniary rewards may be offered in place of income remuneration, there may be dissatisfaction with private benefits for entrepreneurial activities; this could result in fewer innovations, fewer new firms, and inefficient factor allocation. Moreover, in the voting procedures a well-organized and energetic minority may dominate an apathetic majority of workers who may be ignorant of policy making. This can take place through manipulating voters, using demagoguery, shifting positions, and forming coalitions. All these factors tend to decrease efficiency in factor allocation and welfare distribution.

To enhance motivation and increase productivity, opportunities for promotion and recognition of personal progress on the job should be instituted. Underappreciation on the job, limited opportunities to get ahead, short promotion ladders, and early dead ends undermine effectiveness and lower efficiency. To tap sources of productivity, everyone on the job should be given the chance to contribute and get recognition, instead of being "stuck" and underutilized. This can be achieved through developing a "progress ethic" and lessening the "pyramid squeeze."

NOTES

1. For such arguments see Xenophon Zolotas, *International Monetary Issues and Development Policies* (Athens: Bank of Greece, 1977), pp. 370-73.

2. M. Ahluwalia, N. Carter, and H. Chenery, "Growth and Poverty in Developing Countries," in Hollis Chenery, ed., *Structural Change and Development Policy* (Oxford: Oxford University Press, 1979), ch. 11; A. Tsantis and R. Pepper, *Romania: The Industrialization of an Agrarian Economy Under Socialist Planning* (Washington, D.C.: World Bank, 1979), pp. 496, 560. For more details, see Shail Jain, *Size Distribution of Income: A Compilation of Data* (Washington, D.C.: World Bank, 1975); S. Mourgos, "Economic Development and Distributional Trends in Post-War Greece," Ph.D. dissertation, New York University, 1980, p. 167. A comparative review is provided by N. Mouselis, *Modern Greece: Facets of Underdevelopment* (London: Macmillan, 1978), chs. 3, 5.

3. For such findings see M. Ahluwalia, "Income Distribution and Development: Some Stylized Facts," *American Economic Review*, May 1976, pp. 128-35. For good effects of the increase in schooling on the distribution of income, see A. Marvin and G. Psacharopoulous, "Schooling and Income Distribution," *Review of Economics and Statistics*, August 1976, pp. 332-38.

4. For the EEC countries in general, government revenues (average of Britain, France, Germany, Italy) increased from 35 percent of national income in 1960 to 45 in 1976, while for the United States they remained around 30 percent. See United Nations, *Statistical Yearbook*, and OECD, *National Accounts*, both various years.

5. Further statistical data are presented in N. Gianaris, "Indirect Taxes: A Comparative Study of Greece and the EEC," *European Economic Review* 15 (1981): 111-17; S. Kuznets, "The Share and Structure of Consumption," *Economic Development and Culture Change* 10, no. 2 (January 1962): 1-92; R. Bacon and H. Karayiannis-Bacon, "The Growth of the

Non-Market Sector in a Newly Industrialized Country: The Case of Greece," *Greek Economic Review*, April 1980, pp. 44-62.

6. On the gradual shift of investment emphasis from the private to the public sector, and the growth of state economic enterprises in Turkey, see Anne Krueger, *Turkey* (New York: National Bureau of Economic Research, 1974), ch. 1; Richard Nyrop, ed., *Turkey: A Country Study* (Washington, D.C.: American University Press, 1980), pp. 134-37.

7. M. Friedman, *From Galbraith to Economic Freedom* (London: Institute of Economic Affairs, 1977).

8. When government or party officials are expected to visit, there are plenty of goods on the shelves and lines are eliminated. However, when the officials leave, the lines reappear.

9. G. Feiwel, *Growth and Reforms in Centrally Planned Economies* (New York: Praeger, 1977), pp. 227-30.

10. About half of the working population in Bulgaria receives wages close to the minimum (80 leva in 1973). Farmers receive around the same minimum amount of nontaxable income. For some 60 percent of all workers in industry, wages are based on the piece-rate system. The five-day workweek has gradually been introduced, starting in the Kabrovo and Zagora districts. Pensions are modest, and a serious problem is the increasing share of pensioners in the population, not only in Bulgaria but in all Balkan countries. Feiwel, op. cit., pp. 222-27.

11. For reforms in the banking system and the autonomy of enterprises, see Vinod Dubey et al, *Yugoslavia: Development with Decentralization* (Baltimore: Johns Hopkins University Press, 1975), pp. 216-33; L. Sirc, *The Yugoslav Economy Under Self-Management* (London: Macmillan, 1979), chs. 6-8, 14.

12. Kosovo was the center of the Serbs during the Ottoman occupation, but most of the inhabitants migrated north, near the Austro-Hungarian borders, in 1690, under pressure from the Turks.

13. Martin Schrenic et al., *Yugoslavia: Self-Management Socialism and the Challenges of Development* (Baltimore: Johns Hopkins University Press, 1979), ch. 5.

14. For a stimulating discussion see F. Ian Hamilton, *Yugoslavia: Patterns of Economic Activity* (New York: Praeger, 1968), pp. 107-13; Jaroslav Vanek, "Economic Planning in Yugoslavia," in Max F. Millican, ed., *National Economic Planning* (New York: Columbia University Press, 1967). Also see Branko Horvat, "Yugoslav Economic Policy: Problems, Ideas, Institutional Development," *American Economic Review* (suppl.), June 1971, pp. 71-169.

15. Joel Dirlam, "Problems of Market Power and Public Policy in Yugoslavia," Testimony before the Subcommittee on Antitrust and Monopoly, Committee on the Judiciary, U.S. Senate, 90th Congress, 2nd Session, April 17, 1968.

5

RESOURCES AND PRODUCTIVITY

LAND AND NATURAL RESOURCES

The Balkan Peninsula is primarily a rugged, mountainous area jutting from central Europe into the Mediterranean Sea. To the east and southeast it is separated from Asia by the Black Sea, the Bosporus, and the Aegean Sea. In the west the Adriatic Sea separates it from Italy. The easy accessibility from Europe and Asia, and the geographical complexity of the peninsula, have been two powerful factors affecting the economic and cultural statuses of the Balkan peoples.

The major seaports of the peninsula are Rijeka, Sibenik, Split, and Dubrovnik in Yugoslavia; Vlorë in Albania; Constanta in Romania; Varna and Burgas in Bulgaria; Istanbul and Izmir (Smyrna) in Turkey; and Kavalla, Salonika, Piraeus, and Patras in Greece.

The main mountain ranges that crisscross the area are the Carpathian Mountains in the north and the Transylvanian Alps in the center of Romania, the Dinaric Alps in western Yugoslavia, the Balkan Mountains in central Bulgaria, the Rhodope Mountains on the border of Greece and Bulgaria, and the Pindus Mountains in central Greece.

The principal river in the area is the Danube, which runs from central Europe down to Yugoslavia (via Belgrade) and, passing the narrow Iron Gate, flows quietly along the border of Bulgaria and Romania, then of Romania and Russia, finally reaching the Black Sea. In Yugoslavia there are the Sava River in central Yugoslavia, the Tisza and Drava rivers in the north, the Morava in the east and south, and the Neretva in the west. The Prut River is located on Romania's border with Russia, the Siret in the north, the Olt in central Romania, and the Ialomita in the south; the Iskur, Yantra, and Maritsa rivers are in Bulgaria. All these rivers, except the Neretva and the Maritsa, are tributaries of the Danube. Other rivers in Balkania are the Drin, the Shkumbi, and the Vijosë in Albania; the Evros (Maritsa) and the Greek-Turkish border; and the Nestos, the Struma

79

(Strimon), the Vardar (Axios), and the Akheloos in Greece. All these rivers flow south and east, except the Morava, which flows north to the Danube. A number of fertile valleys are located in northern Yugoslavia, eastern Romania, northern Bulgaria, and central Greece (Thessaly), primarily along these rivers. A number of small lakes are scattered throughout northern Greece, and two larger ones (Ohrid and Prespa) are located near the borders of Albania, Greece, and Yugoslavia.

Greece has been known since ancient times for its merchant fleets and fisheries. Recently, however, Bulgaria and Romania, along with other east European countries, have rapidly developed their ocean fisheries with ships built mainly in East Germany and Poland. These four countries, together with the USSR and Cuba, own 60 percent of the total world fishing fleet tonnage, according to Lloyd's Registry of Shipping Statistical Tables.[1] Unfortunately, the recent expansion into distant fisheries has not resulted in a proportional increase in catch. As a result, intersectoral disequilibriums have been created in the planning process and the respective governments have tried to meet production deficits in one group of commodities (such as fish, meat, bread) by taxing others (cars, clothes, television sets).

All the Balkan countries have good subsoil resources. The main mineral products are bauxite, nickel, lignite, chromite, copper, aluminum, and iron. Greece is the leading country in the production of bauxite in western Europe, with 2.7 million tons produced in 1976, followed by Yugoslavia with 2 million tons and Romania with close to 1 million tons in the same year. Production of iron ore is about 100 kilograms per person for almost all these countries. Crude oil is produced primarily in Romania—98 million barrels in 1976—but there is fear of rapid depletion, and imports from Libya, Iran, and Iraq are growing. Limited amounts of oil are also produced in Albania, near Vlorë; in Greece, on the island of Thasos; and in Bulgaria, in the Black Sea. Nuclear energy is produced in Bulgaria, and is expected to appear in almost all the other Balkan countries during the 1980s. Mineral resources are primarily used by domestic enterprises rather than being shipped abroad or exploited by foreigners.

Except for the valleys mentioned previously, the Balkan countries consist mainly of nonfertile lands. In Greece and Turkey, where private ownership prevails, land is largely divided into small lots (stamps) that are widely scattered. Although incentives for production are high on such privately owned lots, especially for labor-intensive crops such as vegetables and fruits, the extensive subdivision of land into noncontiguous plots is not conducive to the application of mass-production technology in agriculture, and thereby reduces the productivity of land and labor.

However, on the large plains of the Balkan planned economies, where there are no fences and cultivation of crops can be diversified, uniformity and mass-production technology help to increase land productivity, although incentives are low. Vast areas planted to corn, wheat, sunflowers, cotton, and other plantation crops are interspersed with huge herds of cows grazing on large cooperatives or state farms. On such cooperatives the peasants have given their farms voluntarily or involuntarily, and they share the labor and the distribution of the final product. However, there are many acres of land that do not belong to cooperatives or state farms, but remain under private ownership. Each member of the cooperative may sell his or her private land to the cooperative, to another member who possesses little or no land, or to the state.

Most of the Balkan soil is poor, and in many areas resources are meager. Extensive mountains of barren limestone are covered with bare rocks, and occasionally there are some inaccessible forests. There are also many low hills where running water is usually absent. The peninsula is situated in the temperate zone, with the warm Mediterranean climate prevailing in the south along the shore, and the cooler continental climate prevailing in the interior. The long, dry summers of the south, where high temperatures force people to take a siesta, stimulate tourism. Prolonged periods of hot, dry weather promote the production of such products as olives, grapes, figs, and other fruits. Goats and sheep prevail in the south, where there are limited grassy pastures, while cows and pigs are raised in the northern and central Balkans.

The Valley of Roses, which runs through central Bulgaria, provides a unique combination of soil and climate for the cultivation of exotic roses with pungent, long-lasting aroma. This Valley of Kazanluk, named for a Turkish governor of the area who was the first to produce and market this exceptionally aromatic rose oil in 1580, is protected from the north winds by the Balkan Mountains, and from the summer heat by the Sredna Gora Range. Its sweet-smelling, pink and white roses make it a spectacular tourist lure. At present some 17,000 acres are cultivated, a considerable decline from the peak at the end of the nineteenth century, when 24,000 acres were ablaze with blossoms. During World War II, Germany, Bulgaria's ally, encouraged the farmers to uproot rose bushes in order to plant potatoes. Since 1842, when the attar was brought to Paris, it has provided the country with valuable foreign exchange, despite the fact that a few other countries, notably Russia and Turkey, also produce rose oil. The present price of this rose oil, which is the best in the world, is about $2,300 per pound.

The geographical location of the peninsula has often been called a curse by its inhabitants. Being at the crossroads of three continents (Europe, Asia, Africa), it beckons to invaders and superpowers. Its position halfway between the tropics and the cold North attracts northerners, who come to enjoy the warmth and natural beauty. There are thousands of miles of wildly beautiful and strategic coasts. Only about a third of the peninsula is flat land or low, tillable hills. The rest is mountainous. Less than a third of the land is covered by forest.

HUMAN RESOURCES

There is a great variety of ethnic groups in the Balkans. There are five main races and several scattered minorities within the area. The most numerous race is the South Slavs, who live primarily in the center of the peninsula, from close to the Adriatic Sea (Slovenes and Coatians) to the center (Serbians), to the east, near the Black Sea (Bulgarians). In the northeast are Romanians; in the southeast, Turks; in the southwest, Albanians; and in the south, Greeks. The Bulgarians, an Asiatic people related to the Huns, were conquered and mostly assimilated by the Slavs. Minorities include the Vlachs (some 140,000), the dispersed ancient Thracians, now largely nomadic shepherds scattered throughout the mountains of Balkania; the Germans in northern Romania (about 750,000) and Yugoslavia (around 500,000), who first came during the Hapsburg rule; the Hungarians (more than 1 million in Romania and about 500,000 in Yugoslavia); and the Gypsies (about 500,000), who live mainly on the edges of towns, plying their trades as musicians, peddlers, and fortune-tellers.

Before World War II the Jews were a sizable minority in Romania (about 1 million) and in Greece (Salonika). However, during the war large numbers were shipped to extermination camps in Germany, and many others migrated to Israel. The German minorities were greatly reduced after the war. Greek minorities exist in Turkey, Albania, and Yugoslavia; Slavs are near the northern borders, and Moslems are located on the eastern borders, of Greece; groups of Albanians, Romanians, and Italians are in Yugoslavia; Armenians (some 60,000 out of more than 2 million during the Ottoman period) and Kurds are in Turkey. Large minorities of Moslems arrived when the Ottomans ruled, and remain all over Balkania. Yugoslavia and Bulgaria have about 10 percent Moslem population (as the Soviet Union does); Albania, 50 percent; and Turkey, 98 percent.

Before World War II the majority of the Balkan peoples belonged to the Greek Orthodox Church, especially in Greece, Bulgaria, Romania, and most of Yugoslavia; Roman Catholics were found mostly in eastern and northern Yugoslavia and northern Romania; Protestants inhabited a small part of central Romania; and Moslems lived mainly in Albania, eastern Thrace, and some smaller areas. After the war such distinctions became less important, since religious practices were either prohibited or suppressed in the Communist Balkan countries.

Table 5.1 shows the total population of each country, the density, and the population growth for 1937-78. Population growth in Bulgaria, Greece, Romania, and Yugoslavia was relatively small during the postwar years, as was true in almost all European countries. In Albania and Turkey, however, the population was more than doubled in 28 years, which is in accordance with the Malthusian theory of geometrical growth of population. The birth rate in both these countries continues to be high (30-32 per 1,000), compared with other Balkan countries (15-19 per 1,000), while the death rate is about the same (10 per 1,000) for all of them.

The death rate of children aged one to four was 10 per 1,000 for Turkey, 2 per 1,000 for Yugoslavia, and 1 per 1,000 for the other countries. Overall population growth would have been more had emigration been included for Greece, Yugoslavia, and Turkey.[2] Population density does not differ much

TABLE 5.1

Population Statistics of the Balkan Countries, 1937–78

	Population (millions)			Population Growth		Area	Density
				Percent	Annual	(1,000 sq. km.)	1978
	1937	1950	1978	1950–78	1970–78		
Albania	1.0	1.2	2.6	117.0	2.5	29	90
Bulgaria	6.2	7.7	8.8	14.3	0.5	111	79
Greece	7.0	8.0	9.4	17.5	0.7	132	71
Romania	15.5	16.2	21.9	35.2	0.9	238	92
Turkey	16.8	20.9	43.1	106.2	2.5	781	55
Yugoslavia	15.2	16.1	22.0	36.6	0.9	256	86

Note: For Albania and Bulgaria the second and third years are 1951 and 1977; for Romania the second year is 1951.

Source: United Nations, *Statistical Yearbook*, various issues; World Bank, *World Development Report, 1980* (New York: Oxford University Press, 1980).

among these countries, except for Turkey, which is the least densely populated country in the Balkans.

Education, which helps to bring out latent abilities and talents, plays a pervasive role in the development of all countries, including those of the Balkan Peninsula, not only because of its direct economic effects but also because of its side effects on society as a whole. As Alfred Marshall has pointed out, the economic value of one industrial genius may be sufficient to cover the expenses of education for a whole town. That is why free and universal primary school education, as well as extensive secondary and higher education, have been accepted and implemented in all the Balkan countries as a basic requirement for socio-economic development. However, there is still a bloc of 2–15 percent illiterates in Bulgaria, Greece, Romania, and Yugoslavia, and as high as 28 percent in Albania and 40 percent in Turkey. There is a noticeable difference in the average number of students per teacher in primary school. Greece and Turkey have around 30 students per teacher, while the northern Balkan countries have around 20. In educational expenditures Greece has the lowest percentage of GNP spent on education (1.8),[3] while all the others spend more than 4 percent of their GNP for education. In 1977 the enrollment in secondary schools, by percentage of age group, was 43 in Turkey, 79 in Yugoslavia, 77 in Romania, 82 in Greece, and 88 in Bulgaria. In 1976, in higher education the percentage (of those age 20–24) was 8 in Turkey, 10 in Romania, 18 in Greece, and 21 in Bulgaria and Yugoslavia.[4]

Education frees the student from a life of drudgery on the farm or the stultification of the assembly line, and provides the opportunity for a good career and social advancement. However, it is hard to get into universities, which have strict examination requirements in all the Balkan countries.

Although throughout Balkania there is an official policy to reduce inequality in education, opportunities for postsecondary education are greater for the urban intelligentsia than for workers and peasants. Professions with high social prestige enjoy higher incomes, even in the planned Balkan economies. Women enjoy less power within the family and in the entire society, despite the doctrine of equality proclaimed by the socialist economies.

There is not much difference in availability of medical care in Balkania, except for Turkey. The average number of patients per bed varies from 108 in Romania to 115 in Bulgaria, 156 in Greece, 167 in Yugoslavia, and as·high as 476 in Turkey. On the other hand, population per physician is 440 in Bulgaria, 450 in Greece, 730 in Romania, 760 in Yugoslavia, and as high as 1,100 in Albania and 1,770 in Turkey. Life expectancy at birth varies from 61 years in Turkey to 69 in Albania, 70 in Romania and Yugoslavia, 72 in Bulgaria, and 73 in Greece.

In the planned economies open unemployment is replaced by concealed underemployment, which is expressed in the form of padded employment rosters and swollen payrolls. The result is pervasive economic inefficiency, especially in sectors that accommodate such low-efficiency labor. The increase in efficiency and the fixed structure of working hours may cause loss of jobs, unless there is sufficient demand to absorb additional output. Otherwise, a transfer of workers to other industries or a reduction in work hours may be expected. If these alternatives are not possible, the result may be higher unemployment or low average and marginal productivities of labor.

Although the sociopolitical system plays a significant role in the pace of development of certain sectors, the overall advancement of a country also depends on its work ethic and the discipline of its people, as well as on the training and technical skills of its human infrastructure. Differences in these areas can be seen among the Balkan peoples despite the fact that for centuries they were under common (Roman, Byzantine, and Ottoman) rulers.

Greece and Turkey are among the countries that lose large numbers of scientists and professionals. The United States, the United Kingdom, Canada, Germany, and France are the main recipient countries. The scientists move to places that respect and value their accomplishments, and offer favorable conditions for their ambitious programs. They prefer to work in countries that supply research facilities and appreciate their work, where meritocracy and achievements, rather than political affiliations and nepotism, determine advancement. Greece and Turkey are trying to adopt measures to reverse the "brain drain." Such measures include reorganization of domestic education and research, more academic freedom, and introduction of seminars and exchange programs for students and professors to facilitate "brain gaining" or "brain exchanging."

Comparatively speaking, Turkey has low percentages of women participating in the overall labor force and especially in industry, where the active female population is only about 5 percent, compared with 20-30 percent for the other Balkan countries. Historically, the status of women has been an inferior one, particularly in Turkey. Fewer opportunities, limited education, and social discrimination characterize their overall position. Reasons other than economic—primarily traditional conditions and religious beliefs[5]—seem to have been predominant in the determination of the participation of females in the labor force. Although the institution of polygamy was abolished by the reforms of Atatürk, the economic and social role of women is still limited. The answer to the argument that the utilization of more female labor may intensify the problem of high unemployment in Turkey may lie in training women for the improvement of home and child services, family budgeting, sanitary conditions, and (primarily) family planning, so that unnecessary spending and overpopulation can be avoided.

ECONOMIC GROWTH

Economic development—improvement of the material and nonmaterial conditions of the population—can be achieved through technological advancement, dissemination of knowledge, and structural transformation from a predominantly subsistence agricultural economy to a more productive industrial economy.[6] In all the Balkan countries such a transformation from the agricultural sector, where productivity is low, to the industrial sector, where productivity is high, has not materialized to a satisfactory degree. Hence, a large proportion of the labor force is usually engaged in agriculture, where extensive disguised unemployment and low income prevail.

Although there are certain common characteristics shared by the Balkan economies, a homogeneous analysis is difficult because of variations in economic conditions and institutions. Thus, the study of the economic framework of this group of countries with divergent institutions and policies is relatively new, and cannot yet lay claim to any high degree of coherence.

Almost all the Balkan countries are at a stage of intermediate development, perhaps somewhere between the takeoff stage and the drive-to-maturity plateau.[7] It can be said that they are comparable neither to infants nor to adults, but to teen-agers. Through the transfer of technology and capital from advanced countries, these economies can continue to achieve high rates of growth. The northern Balkan countries, with their command economies, can continue to emphasize high percentages of investment by withdrawing resources from consumers and placing these resources in the capital-producing sectors. Assuming a relatively constant capital/output ratio, their rates of economic growth can be expected to be high. But their economies may end up producing fewer consumer goods, a frequent problem in the past. As Table 5.2 indicates, the Balkan nations have

TABLE 5.2

Average Annual Rates of Growth of GDP, Constant Prices: 1950–78
(percent)

	Total				Per Capita			
	1950–60	1960–70	1970–78	Average 1950–78	1950–60	1960–70	1970–77	Average 1950–77
Albania	6.9	7.3	6.7	7.0	3.6	6.2	4.3	4.7
Bulgaria	8.9	8.2	6.3	7.8	7.9	7.4	7.0	7.4
Greece	6.0	7.5	5.0	6.2	5.0	6.8	3.9	5.2
Romania	9.0	8.6	10.6	9.4	7.6	7.6	9.8	8.3
Turkey	5.8	6.0	7.1	6.3	2.9	3.5	4.3	3.6
Yugoslavia	9.2	6.6	5.6	7.1	8.0	5.5	4.8	6.1

Note: In some cases fewer years' data were available.
Sources: United Nations, *Statistical Yearbook* and *Yearbook of National Accounts Statistics*, various issues; World Bank, *World Development Report, 1979* (New York: Oxford University Press, 1979), p. 129; and *1980*, pp. 111, 113.

had high rates of economic growth during postwar years. On a per capita basis all of them, except Turkey and perhaps Albania, are expected to continue to perform well because of high overall national growth rates and a low rate of growth in population.

Greece has the highest per capita GNP ($3,250 in 1978, about half that of the EEC), followed by Bulgaria ($3,230), Yugoslavia ($2,380), Romania ($1,750), Turkey ($1,200), and Albania ($740). Comparatively speaking, per capita income conceals greater inequalities in Greece and in Turkey, where 10 percent of households share 41 percent of national income, than in the other Balkan countries. However, there is a growing trend toward the development of wage and price determination (income policies), with the aim of achieving a better income distribution. Moreover, the gradual acquisition of corporate shares or company partnerships, and the spread of insurance, retirement, and similar mutual funds to large segments of the population, although not extensive in these two countries, alleviate the problem of inequality and tend to support the spread of what Joseph Shumpeter called people's capitalism.

Capital formation or investment, as a percentage of gross domestic product (GDP), was relatively high for almost all Balkan countries, generating high rates of economic growth.[8] As Table 5.3 shows, average rates of gross fixed capital formation (GFCF) were higher than 13 percent for all six countries considered, during the period 1951–78. For Albania, Greece, and Yugoslavia they were more than 20 percent during that period.

In the empirical parts of this study, gross (undepreciated) investment figures are generally used because new capital has superior efficiency and is associated with improved technology. The fact that gross investment is a major vehicle of technological progress makes gross figures more meaningful than net figures. Although estimates of capital goods in constant prices give more reliable figures, current prices seem to be preferable for projections because the machines and other capital goods have to be paid for at current prices.

Investment in the centrally planned Balkan economies is financed primarily through government taxes, while in the market economies of Greece and Turkey it is financed mainly by private savings, both domestic and foreign. In Greece and Turkey, where there is skewed distribution, high-income groups are expected to save more, although they have a high propensity to spend on luxury and imported goods. (For the relationships of investment, GDP, and exports for all Balkan countries, see regressions in Tables 2, 5, and 6 of the Appendix.) Also, net capital funds from foreign sources flow into these countries from time to time, and thus help to narrow the savings/investment gap.

Long-term economic development leads to the agglomeration of cities. The example of urban concentration in other countries is followed by all Balkan countries, although with less intensity in Albania, Bulgaria, and Romania. As per capita income increases, more people tend to move into urban areas in order to enjoy higher pecuniary and nonpecuniary benefits, the "bright lights" and other amenities of cities that act as magnets for peasants from rural areas. Such urban

TABLE 5.3

Investment (GFCF) as Percentage of GDP, 1951–78 (current prices)

	1951–60	1961–70	1971–78	Average 1950–77
Albania	21.0	23.6	23.8	22.8
Bulgaria	12.0	17.8	14.5	14.8
Greece	16.0	21.3	24.0	20.4
Romania	10.0	13.8	15.5	13.1
Turkey	13.0	16.0	17.3	15.4
Yugoslavia	33.0	31.5	31.7	32.1

Note: For Albania, GFCF/NMP; for Bulgaria, NFCF/NMP; for Romania, GFCF/social product.

Sources: United Nations, *Statistical Yearbook* and *Yearbook of National Accounts Statistics*, various issues; World Bank, *World Development Report, 1979* (New York: Oxford University Press, 1979), p. 129; and *1980*, pp. 111, 113; OECD, *National Accounts*, various issues; for Bulgaria, Greece, Turkey and Yugoslavia 1950-59, N. Gianaris, *Economic Development: Thought and Problems* (North Quincy, Mass.: Christopher Publishing House, 1978), pp. 180–81.

"demand pull" and rural "supply push" trends create problems of housing, sewage, and employment for overcrowded urban centers, especially in Athens, where more than one-third of the population of Greece is concentrated. Even in the Balkan command economies, where this type of transformation is planned and directed, there are problems of effective absorption and sectoral balancing within the economy. To keep rural people in their villages and to stimulate agricultural production, policy makers in these socialist economies permit ownership of larger plots of land and a greater degree of market freedom for the peasantry. However, despite all these capitalistic incentives, an increasing number of peasants prefer to migrate to the big cities.

The movement of the rural population to urban centers in all Balkan countries may be considered an advantage for carrying out industrialization that allows people to try to escape the lower standard of living in the countryside and to enjoy the amenities of the cities. Of course, there are disamenities and disadvantages of living in urban centers, but the fact that people continue to flow into the cities means that there are more advantages for them in the cities than in the villages. As a result, urbanization continues in all Balkan countries, although with more intensity in Greece and Bulgaria, where urban population is close to 60 percent, compared with 45 percent in Romania and Turkey, 38 percent in Yugoslavia, and 35 percent in Albania. However, there are indications that people, both young and old, are taking a new look at village life as the crowded urban areas have fallen victims to air pollution, traffic jams, and inadequate sewage disposal, mass transit, and educational facilities. It would seem that for people with a fierce love for the place of their birth, a day in the village is worth a month or more in the urban centers.

THE RELATIONSHIP OF CAPITAL TO OUTPUT AND THE CAPITAL/LABOR RATIO

In projecting capital requirements for target growth rates of output, all Balkan countries, explicitly or implicitly, use primarily the incremental capital/ output ratio (ICOR), which is the ratio of investment divided by the change in output. The capital/output ratio shows the amount of capital necessary to produce a unit of output per time period. The planners or policy makers in these countries project the growth rates of output or income and the investment required to achieve these growth rates, usually for five or more years. Such growth rates can deal not only with increases in the national income but also with increases in per capita income. If the rate of population growth in Yugoslavia, for example, is 1 percent per year and ICOR is 5, then the required investment to achieve a 4 percent increase in per capita income would be 25 percent of the national income or output.[9]

Table 5.4 shows the variations in ICORs of the Balkan economies over ten-year periods. These intervals were used to narrow the extreme variability of the year-to-year or short-run ratios.[10] Such variations are primarily due to changes in GDP that can be caused by variations in employment or productivity, over time, within each country and across the sample of countries. In almost all countries considered, the ICOR gradually increased during the postwar years, as it did in the developed Western nations. This means that more and more capital was used per unit of output. As the Balkan countries move to higher levels of development, they may expect higher ICORs and, probably, diminishing returns on capital.

Turkey and Albania had comparatively lower ICORs, as did all developing countries.[11] As we will see later, this does not mean that capital is more productive in these two countries than in the other Balkan countries; rather, less capital and relatively more labor are used per unit of output.

In order to determine in which country the productivity of capital (its rate of return) is higher, the relative contribution of the other factors, primarily labor, must be considered along with the capital/output ratio. To increase output by a given amount in Turkey and Albania might require comparatively less capital than in Bulgaria, Greece, Romania, and Yugoslavia, but it would require more labor.

Multiplying the relatively constant ICOR slope by the most recent GDP or NMP of a country, we can estimate the total capital stock in that year. Thus, for

TABLE 5.4

National ICORs for the Balkan Countries, 1951–60 to 1971–77 (constant 1975 prices)

	1951–60	1961–70	1971–77	Average 1951–77
Albania	3.4	3.1	4.0	3.5
Bulgaria	2.3	3.9	5.6	3.9
Greece	3.2	3.4	5.2	3.9
Romania	3.3	4.3	3.9	3.8
Turkey	2.2	2.8	2.9	2.6
Yugoslavia	3.8	5.2	5.7	4.9
Developing economies	3.5	3.3	3.5	3.4
Developed economies	4.4	4.7	5.9	4.9
Planned economies	3.0	3.9	3.8	3.5

Notes: For Albania, net material product (NMP) at 1966 prices and gross fixed capital formation (GFCF) at current prices. For Bulgaria, NMP at current prices, and for Romania, NMP at constant prices. In some cases fewer years' figures were available.

Sources: Calculations based on OECD, *National Accounts*, various issues; United Nations, *Yearbook of National Accounts Statistics*, various issues.

Albania the capital stock in 1975 was estimated to be 46.9 billion leks (13.4 X 3.5), in constant prices; for Bulgaria, 62.8 billion leva in 1977 (current prices); for Greece, 2,881 billion drachmas; for Romania, 1,643 billion lei; for Turkey, 1,528 billion liras; and for Yugoslavia, 2,700 billion dinars, all in constant 1975 prices.

To make comparisons easy, the per capita income or output in each country (in U.S. dollars) was multiplied by the population of that country. The alternative method of using official exchange rates for the expression of national output in dollars may not give more realistic figures because of the controls on the currencies of these countries and the parallel higher rates prevailing for tourism and some other activities, especially in Albania, Bulgaria, and Romania (see United Nations, *Monthly Bulletin of Statistics*).[12] For the determination of the capital stock in Table 5.5, the long-term and relatively stable ICOR (assumed to be equal to the average capital/output ratio) of each country was multiplied by its output.

The capital/labor ratio was higher in Greece and Yugoslavia, and far lower in Turkey and Albania. Investment efficiency, therefore, in the latter capital-thirsty countries is expected to be relatively high.

In Greece, Turkey, and Yugoslavia the capital/labor ratio would have been less if it were not for the emigration of large numbers of workers, mainly to West Germany. They not only reduced the labor force of each country, leaving more capital equipment per remaining worker, but also helped increase investment with their sizable remittances of close to U.S. $1 billion to Greece and Turkey and U.S. $2 billion to Yugoslavia per year. These remittances are equal to 35 percent of the export revenues of Greece and Yugoslavia and 50 percent of those of Turkey. Such remittances in Yugoslavia (some $3,400 per worker in 1977), which is the only socialist country permitting its nationals to work abroad, are directed primarily to investment in housing, taxis, tourist hotels, and small-scale farming. However, because of the official policy, there seems to be a saturation of investment outlets, especially in the excessively mechanized small farms, the ownership of which is subject to a ceiling of ten hectares. Turkish migrant workers have invested about half of their remittances in housing, one-fourth in small shops and factories, and only about 10 percent in land and farm machinery, despite the official attempts to channel their savings into agricultural investment through the Turkish Village Cooperatives Scheme established in 1963.

TABLE 5.5

Output, Capital Stock, Labor Force, and Capital/Labor Ratio in the Balkan Countries, 1977
(U.S. dollars)

	Output (billion dollars)	Estimated Capital Stock (billion dollars)	Labor Force (millions)	Estimated Capital/Labor Ratio (thousand dollars)
Albania	1.6	5.6	1.1	5.1
Bulgaria	22.7	88.5	3.9	22.7
Greece	25.6	99.8	3.4	29.4
Romania	34.1	129.6	10.3	12.6
Turkey	46.5	120.9	16.4	7.4
Yugoslavia	42.5	208.2	9.0	23.1

Notes: For Albania and Yugoslavia, total labor force (including the socialized sector) was estimated as 41.7 percent of the population. See V. Dubey, *Yugoslavia: Development with Decentralization* (Baltimore: Johns Hopkins University Press, 1975), p. 63. For Turkey, labor force is that of 1976.

Sources: Calculations based on OECD, *National Accounts*; United Nations, *Yearbook of National Accounts Statistics*; International Labor Organization, *Yearbook of Labor Statistics*, all various issues.

INFLATION AND PRODUCTIVITY

Inflation—a decline in the value of the currency or an increase in prices without a proportionate increase in real value—is a serious problem for the market economies, including those of Greece, Turkey, and (to some extent) Yugoslavia. Lenin said, "The best way to destroy the capitalist system is to debauch the currency." This argument was supported by J. M. Keynes, who said ". . . Lenin was certainly right" and "There is no subtler, no surer means of overturning the existing basis of society than to debauch the currency." A rate of increase in the money supply and credit that exceeds the rate of increase in production, which can be observed in the aforementioned countries, leads to demand outpacing supply and causes inflation—which, in turn, blunts initiative and weakens the link between effort and reward. Prolonged inflation may invite economic controls.[13] However, widespread price and wage controls are bureaucratic, and may feed inefficiency. Such controls, though, when imposed on large corporations and unions, and used as a protective ceiling above the market mechanism, may be preferable to runaway inflation.

It is argued that protection of wages from continuing inflation requires indexing (adding a cost-of-living escalator to wages). However, the indexing shelter could prove to be a leaky roof that makes inflation worse, particularly in countries with high rates of inflation, such as Greece, Yugoslavia, and especially Turkey. An increase in earnings now, because of past increases in the price index, may perpetuate inflation through the consequent increase in cost per unit of labor used in production (cost-push inflation), unless higher labor productivity takes care of the difference.[14] Thus, the cost-of-living indexing or wage/price guidelines implemented occasionally by the above countries seems to constitute a weak reed to lean on. Stagflation, the mixture of sluggish economic growth and inflation, saps the confidence needed for investment and plagues the economies of these countries.

There seems to be a trade-off between productivity and employment. Policies designed to sustain employment or avoid unemployment tend to reduce labor productivity. Unemployment can be solved at the expense of productivity or, as Keynes suggested, at the expense of efficiency and freedom. The full-employment policy implemented by the planned economies of Albania, Bulgaria, and Romania has the advantage of full utilization of labor, but at the expense of efficiency and the freedom of workers to change jobs.

Although there is an inverse relationship between productivity and inflation, the influence of productivity growth rates on inflationary rates seems to be less significant in Greece, Turkey, and Yugoslavia because other, more powerful factors are at work, such as a policy that promotes the expansion of the money supply and credit, and the increase in oil prices.

The curbing of protective attitudes toward backward "sunset" industries and the encouragement given to efficient "sunrise" ones is another proper policy to help attain higher productivity. In order to be able to compete in the modern growth race, Balkan enterprises and governments should allow resources to move from sluggish industries to more productive ones. This would mean the removal of subsidies and protective tariffs that perpetuate inefficiency, as well as the dismantling of the plethora of detailed regulations that discourage competitive incentives. Thus, the management of the regulatory process will be a serious problem for the Balkan governments in the foreseeable future. It would seem that long-term structural changes, rather than short-term policies, are needed to take these economies out of the present dilemma of inflation or commodity shortages.

The use of fiscal or monetary policy to stimulate productivity and curb inflation may not make people want to invest more and work harder. Increases in the money supply may simply produce more inflation without any expansion in output. For example, in Greece the money supply increased by 22 percent per year recently, in Turkey by 38 percent, and in Yugoslavia even more. Large amounts of money are spent to finance governmental expenditures, which absorb more than one-fourth of the GDP in all Balkan countries.

The socialist Balkan economies use extensive budget outlays to subsidize consumer products, thereby keeping pace with growing consumer demand and avoiding demonstrations and worker unrest arising from allowing prices to reach the market clearing levels. However, this policy leads to rising consumer demand for subsidized products and perpetuates concealed inflation.[15] Perhaps the introduction of gradual reforms with greater price liberalization may diminish the problem of shortages in the centrally planned economies of Albania, Bulgaria, and Romania, which have already begun to allow some degree of inflation (3–9 percent annually). The maintenance of balance in the consumer market in these countries necessitated price increases that were substantial, but significantly below those in Greece, Turkey, and Yugoslavia.

The rapid development of transportation and communications makes national economic policies on inflation and productivity less effective. The strength of the currency and the increase in real wages in each Balkan country depend not only on how fast productivity and inflation grow domestically, but also on how fast they grow in countries with which they trade. If other countries have less inflation and greater productivity, then foreign goods will be cheaper than similar domestic goods. Then imports will increase more than exports. To pay for the imported goods, the country in deficit has to buy foreign currencies, or its deficit will increase. That obviously drives down the value of its currency. To reverse this trend, comprehensive policies to reduce inflation and raise productivity to the level of other countries must be implemented. Balkan governments should stop stuffing people's pockets with inflationary "funny money," and try to increase both the supply and the competitiveness of their countries' products. This seems to be the way to avoid long lines in the stores of the Balkan planned economies, on which a shopper can spend the equivalent of one working day a week, with all the accompanying physical and psychological costs. This is also the way to avoid high rates of inflation, which prevail in Turkey (over 100 percent), Yugoslavia (about 30 percent), and Greece (more than 10 percent).[16]

There is a trend in the Balkan planned economies to adjust prices to realistic internal and actual world conditions, in order to encourage productivity. Such reforms in Bulgaria and Romania are not as liberal as those in neighboring Hungary. However, the recent trend in reductions of subsidies, which are as high as 20 percent or more of the GNP, allows prices to be determined by the forces of supply and demand.

TAX INCENTIVES AND PRODUCTIVITY

Economic behavior in Greece and Turkey focuses too much attention on consumption, and not enough on investment to increase productive capacity. To induce the private sector to consume less and save more, tax reforms, a decrease of regulations, and the introduction of policies intended to increase investment are needed to spur production incentives and expand supply. With such policies, total demand in the economy would not be diminished, but the mix would be different; spending for investment would replace spending for consumption. To reverse the slump in savings, which starves investment and feeds consumption, stimulation of long-term tax incentives for individuals and enterprises is required in these market economies.

Encouragement of savings and investment, by taxing wasteful spending rather than interest or dividends, and even replacement of personal income taxes with expenditures taxes, would stimulate work incentives and boost productivity.[17] The value-added tax (VAT), which has been used for some time in the EEC countries, and whose introduction has been contemplated by Greece and Turkey, may be able to boost investment and growth. The VAT is a tax collected, at each stage of production, on the addition that each firm makes to the value of its products or services. As such, it is a tax on consumption that encourages savings and investment—and, therefore, long-term productivity. The implementation of the VAT by Turkey and Greece may help reduce bureaucracy and stimulate employment through capital formation. Although it may increase inflation when first introduced, in the long run it will replace many other tax regulations that are complicated and confusing.

High tax rates on earned income destroy personal incentives to work, reduce productivity, and may have regressive effects. Although personal tax rates in Greece and Turkey are not as high as in Western developed countries, tax reductions to stimulate production in these countries may pay for themselves by creating a surge in investment and new work effort, thereby increasing tax revenue. However, if tax cuts are not matched with selective tax increases that minimally affect production incentives, budget deficits may be pushed upward. Therefore, tax increases may be directed to the portion of income that is actually spent. Thus, a cut of personal income tax and/or a reduction in social security payroll tax may be matched with a sales or value-added tax, which discourages consumption and encourages savings and investment, especially in Greece where the propensity to consume seems to be high.[18] Exceptions are needed for food and housing, so as to soften the tax impact on poor families. Also, a system of gradually decreasing income tax credits can make the VAT fair and progressive.

Although such a "right kind" of tax structure, emphasizing reduction on overspending, would not be an economic panacea, it might be expected that it would help stimulate investment, revive productivity, combat inflation, and encourage exports. It would, most probably, have an anti-inflation and anti-recession function, helping to solve the dilemma of simultaneous inflation and unemployment that plagues Turkey, Yugoslavia, and Greece.

Moreover, faster depreciation (higher deductions from taxable income for the cost of a productive asset) and low capital-gains taxes create an incentive to invest in more efficient equipment, which leads to higher enterprise productivity, more jobs, and (eventually) less inflation.[19] Such tax devices allow old enterprises to renew aging facilities, and young enterprises to satisfy their appetites for modern capital equipment. For companies with losses, and therefore paying no taxes, there might be provisions for refunds of the investment tax. Or there might be provisions for carrying a tax loss backward or forward, to apply it against taxes paid on an earlier or a later profitable year.

To stimulate competition and encourage investment in productive businesses, favorable loan terms and a tax structure favoring small firms and those that create new employment should be considered by the monetary or fiscal authorities of Greece and Turkey. Perhaps the widespread practice of borrowing investment funds from the private sector, by government or other public enterprises in these countries, should continue, because private businesses are unable or hesitant to invest in long-term infrastructural projects. However, if such borrowing takes place to finance further consumption, then the government competes with productive enterprises for a finite supply of lendable money, and the rate of investment will decrease while the rate of inflation increases from this type of deficit spending.

All the centrally planned Balkan economies maintain balanced budgets and price stability mainly through heavy hidden turnover or sales taxes (the equivalent of value-added taxes in market economies) and controls. Such taxes siphon off large amounts of income and purchasing power to finance government outlays. Despite these policies, chronic inflation is a serious drag on these economies, and frequently takes the form of shortages, long consumer lines, and even black markets or corruption. The policy makers in these economies try to deal with this problem by raising procurement prices above what consumers pay, covering the difference with subsidies. Therefore, large amounts of collected sales taxes are paid back through budget outlays to keep production of food and other necessities at proper levels. Policy makers in these countries seem to follow the well-accepted principle "If you tax something, you get less of it. If you subsidize something, you get more of it."

Additional tax revenues are provided by inflation, primarily in Greece and Turkey. This takes place through increases in income and spending, pari passu with inflation, and the automatic increases in rates under the progressive tax system. These additional revenues finance additional government expenditures, which stimulate inflation (as long as they are not directed toward productive investment), and the public sector keeps on expanding. For the government, then, inflation seems to be a wonderful tax. But for individuals it lessens incentives and melts away savings.

Therefore, inflation is a practicable way of transferring command over resources from consumers to the public sector, particularly in countries like Turkey, where the fiscal system is relatively inefficient and the number of taxpayers is not large. This can occur if the monetary authorities issue more money to satisfy the demand for higher nominal incomes that arises from inflation, which in this case can be thought of as an implicit tax that lowers the real value of unindexed incomes. It also can occur when tax rates are progressive.

FIGURE 5.1

Indirect Taxes as Percent of National Income: Greece, EEC, Yugoslavia, and Turkey, 1958–78

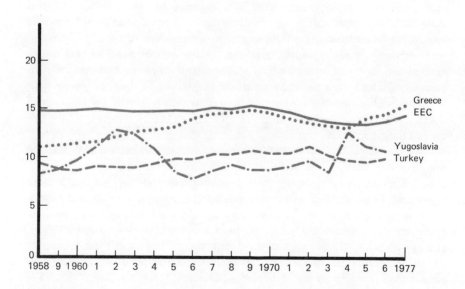

Notes: EEC is an average of France, Germany, Italy, and the United Kingdom. For Turkey, GNP is used, and for Yugoslavia, GMP, instead of national income.

Sources: OECD, *National Accounts*, various issues; United Nations, *Yearbook of National Accounts Statistics*, various issues.

TABLE 5.6

Central Government Revenues as Percentages of National Income, and Direct and Indirect Taxes as Percentages of Total Government Revenues, 1978
(current prices)

	Budget Revenues	Direct Taxes	Indirect Taxes	Ratio of Direct/Indirect Taxes
Bulgaria	58.5	28.0	72.0	38.9
Greece	22.8	24.3	67.8	35.8
Romania	65.3	18.6	72.1	25.8
Turkey	21.9	32.2	47.5	69.8
Yugoslavia	17.8	11.1	72.5	15.4

Note: In some cases the closest years' data available were used. For Romania, national income at 1963 prices; for Bulgaria, net material product.

Sources: Calculations were based on United Nations, *Statistical Yearbook* and *Yearbook of National Accounts Statistics* and OECD, *National Accounts*, all various issues.

For purposes of providing budgetary revenue and restricting personal consumption and wealth accumulation, progressive income taxes are used in all Balkan economies, including the socialist ones.[20] However, maximum tax limits are introduced to minimize disincentive effects on labor allocation, performance, and improvement of skills. Nevertheless, there are problems of tax evasion among scientists, artists, writers, and (primarily) middlemen in all the countries considered, particularly Greece and Turkey.

Indirect taxes (mainly turnover taxes, stamp duties, and tariffs) in Greece, Turkey, and Yugoslavia are around 10 to 15 percent of national income (not far from those of the EEC), as Figure 5.1 indicates. However, as percentages of total revenue, they are far higher in these Balkan countries (close to 50 percent for Greece and Turkey, and around 65 percent for Yugoslavia).

The gradation of turnover taxes is related to the classification of a product as a "nonnecessity," "luxury," or "socially harmful." Although recent reforms tend to reduce the fiscal role of turnover taxes in favor of new taxes on profits of enterprises, capital charges, and so forth, they still constitute about a third or more of the budget revenue in the planned Balkan economies. This is so because collection of turnover taxes is easier and manipulation by lower units is more difficult than in the collection of profit taxes.

Comparatively speaking, tax (budget) revenues in Romania and Bulgaria account for high percentages (more than half) of total national income or product; in Greece, Turkey, and Yugoslavia, for less than one-fourth of national income, as Table 5.6 shows. In developed countries such tax revenues vary from close to 30 percent of the national income for the United States to about 45 percent for the EEC countries and 60 percent for the Soviet Union. Higher indirect taxes (mainly turnover taxes, shares of profits of state enterprises, and tariffs) in the socialist Balkan economies are responsible for the differences. Recently there seems to have been a gradual shift from turnover taxes to shares of profits of state enterprises in Bulgaria and Romania and to value-added taxes in Greece.

During the 1970s the percentage increase in taxes divided by the percentage increase in national income (income elasticity of taxation) was positive and greater than 1 in all Balkan countries for which data were available: 1.2 in Bulgaria, Greece, and Yugoslavia; 1.1 in Romania; and 1.3 in Turkey. This indicates that government expenditures grew proportionally more than national income in all the countries considered.

The ratio of direct taxes (primarily income taxes and social security contributions) to indirect taxes levied by the central government varies from 15 percent in Yugoslavia to 26 in Romania, close to 40 percent in Bulgaria and Greece, and almost 70 percent in Turkey, compared with 90 percent or more in the four large EEC countries (France, Germany, Italy, United Kingdom) and far higher in the United States.[21] As per capita income increases, so does the ratio of direct to indirect taxes. In Yugoslavia and Greece, however, this ratio remains low, while customs duties remain relatively high (around 25 percent of total taxes). Greece and (perhaps) Turkey are in the process of adjusting their tax system to that of the EEC in order to achieve harmonization of tax rates, as Articles 95-99 of the initial Agreement of Rome provide.[22]

Indirect taxes, as percentages of national income, are about the same (around 15 percent) in Greece, Turkey, and Yugoslavia as in the EEC countries. However, as percentages of total government revenue, they are about double in these countries than in the EEC (around 30 percent).

LABOR PRODUCTIVITY

Average productivity of labor, which is measured by the ratio of output to labor input, varied from about $2,000 per worker in Turkey to around $7,000 in Greece, Romania, and Yugoslavia in 1977. The rate of productivity growth—the annual increase in output per worker—also varied among the different countries and among different periods, as Table 5.7 shows.[23] This annual increase in production per unit of labor is important because real income per worker is expected to increase in proportion to productivity.

According to statistical data reported to the United Nations and other institutions by the individual governments, the annual rate of growth of labor productivity was far higher in Romania (7.7) and Greece (6.8) than in the other Balkan countries, during the period 1961-77. These rates are among the highest in the world, with only Japan enjoying such high productivity rates in the postwar years.[24] Turkey and Yugoslavia have relatively good, but lower, productivity

TABLE 5.7

Annual Rates of Productivity of Labor: Balkan Countries, 1961-77

	1961-70	1971-77	1961-77
Albania	1.6	3.9	2.4
Bulgaria	3.1	2.2	2.7
Greece	8.8	3.5	6.8
Romania	6.3	9.5	7.7
Turkey	4.1	6.1	4.8
Yugoslavia	4.0	1.7	3.1

Notes: For Albania, NMP at 1966 prices, 1971-75; for Bulgaria, NMP at 1957 prices; for Greece, 1962-71 and 1972-77 (GDP at 1970 prices); for Romania, social product at 1965 prices; for Turkey, GDP at 1975 prices, 1971-76; for Yugoslavia, GNP at 1975 prices.
Sources: United Nations, *Yearbook of National Accounts Statistics*; OECD, *National Accounts*; International Labor Organization, *Yearbook of Labor Statistics*, all various issues.

rates. However, Greece, Turkey, and Yugoslavia would have had lower productivity rates if emigration had not taken place. Usually the unskilled, less productive, and underemployed rural workers emigrate. As a result, the number of workers in each of the above countries is reduced more than production, and productivity rates remain high.

The allocation of resources, including labor, to the most efficient sectors and industries of these countries and their combination in the right proportion increase overall productivity. Changes in the efficiency with which labor and other inputs are converted into output may result from managerial skills, work experience and education, economic organization, and changes in technology. Technological improvement—or advance in knowledge, as Alfred Marshall defined it—results in higher production, better quality of products, more leisure, and better working conditions.[25] New scientific inventions or discoveries—and mainly their commercialization or applications in the production process, by the innovating institutions and achieving adventurers—are responsible for increasing the wealth of nations, including that of the Balkan nations.

Technological improvements, in both the market and the planned Balkan economies, can be achieved by providing incentives for investors and managers through reducing the uncertainties and risks that inhibit innovations and slow growth. The key to improved technology is capital formation. Moreover, increased spending for research and development and investment-stimulating tax policies increase the capacity to innovate and encourage technical advances.[26]

Capital formation and work incentives play a vital role in the development of all the Balkan countries. Assuming the same amount of capital per worker (constant capital/labor ratio), productivity can rise through stimulation of work incentives and improvement of skills. More important, productivity can rise pari passu with the rise in capital investment per worker. (For the relationship of labor productivity, investment, inflation, and exports, see equations (1) and (2) of the Appendix.) Or it can rise—and this is more usual—through a combination of increased capital investment per worker and improved skills and incentives to production.

Part of the productivity growth in the Balkan countries during the postwar years, especially in Greece, Turkey, and Yugoslavia, has been due to the improvement of their international trade performance, which has given their economies the benefit of market growth abroad. For instance, Greek and Turkish shepherds were highly productive in the 1950s, mainly because of the economic boom in Europe at that time. Moreover, the transfer of people from agriculture to industry has been, and still is, a major reason for productivity gains in these countries. (As will be mentioned later, high agricultural productivity in Greece, and to some extent in Turkey and Yugoslavia, has been due to emigration of surplus rural labor to other countries.)

Inefficiency and low productivity are common in the public sector of Greece and Turkey, where civil servants cannot be dismissed or demoted without serious cause, and only after legal proceedings. Such employees are usually given other government jobs at the same level that may not fit their training and acquired skills. As governments change, new teams take over and pack the ministries, while the previous teams are moved in disadvantageous positions. Some highly capable employees may leave, but most of them remain in overcrowded government offices. Labor productivity declines, while payrolls remain swollen. The same thing can be observed in local government offices and in public enterprises where some degree of political patronage exists.

In the public sector of these countries, a new kind of entrepreneurship appears that affects the private sector. A number of risk takers can be found in town halls, provincial capitals, and parliamentary and public offices. They seem to be more aggressive than their counterparts in the private sector because they use taxpayers' money rather than their own. They influence the regional allocation of public as well as private investment through tax and financial incentives, fat depreciation allowances, free job-training programs, adjustment of pollution regulations, loan guarantees, and other devices to create infrastructural facilities that will attract corporations and private capital into their provinces. Such public entrepreneurship may not create jobs, but simply transfer them from one region to another. Moreover, tax revenues may be used for building highways, roads, sewers, hospitals, schools, and similar projects that may duplicate facilities and create excess capacity in certain locations. Such underutilized and overbuilt facilities tend to reduce regional and national productivity.

In the controlled economies of Albania, Bulgaria, and Romania, productivity suffers from the policy of accommodating large numbers of workers regardless of their efficiency. This effort to maintain full employment reduces the productivity of labor. Lack of proper skills, arriving late, extensive breaks, and leaving early are additional reasons for low productivity. Moreover, there is a parallel "invisible economy" in the socialist Balkan economies similar to the "underground economy" in the capitalist countries. Illegal construction of villas, cultivation of private plots, and other managerial and party favors are among the "underground" activites. These absorb valuable time, at the expense of official jobs.

To keep productivity from falling, some relaxation of controls and introduction of certain measures into the market mechanism are slowly occurring in the planned economies, including those of Bulgaria and Romania. Such measures may include reduction of wages and the eventual laying off of less productive workers. This seems imperative for enterprises in need of modern machinery, computers, and innovative technological equipment. Managers and skilled personnel with high productivity receive higher wages and more bonuses than the unskilled and less productive workers. The introduction of technical methods and computerization into decision making at the national, sectoral, and enterprise levels is expected to reduce bureaucracy and increase productivity in these countries.

For higher productivity it may be important not only that new investment incorporates technological innovations, but also that disinvestment takes place by closing obsolete facilities and industries that no longer enjoy comparative advantages. For example, steel industries using old-fashioned open-hearth furnaces should be closed or converted to modern basic oxygen furnaces. The same is true for old plants that fall behind technological innovations and make products for which there is stagnant or declining demand. Such structural changes are needed so that human and capital resources will be free to move from obsolete facilities to new and expanding industries with higher productivity. This process of modernization is required regardless of whether we deal with a market or a planned economy.

Increasing labor productivity does not always mean that we have to work harder. Better results may be achieved by thinking more and sweating less. Moreover, an increase in productivity, in the sense of raising output per labor unit, may not always be desirable. From a social point of view, better work conditions, a healthier and safer environment, and even more leisure time may be preferable to higher rates of productivity. Thus, long-term "social productivity" with quality output, better working conditions, and less or no unemployment may be a more beneficial and less costly social goal. Such a goal may approach Pareto's state of optimality, where no one could be better off without making somebody else worse off. In the Balkan countries, with their variety of economic ideologies and economic institutions, the criteria for social utility are different, and welfare comparisons are difficult to make.

To reduce differences in welfare benefits and improve resource allocation, reforms have been or are being introduced in the planned Balkan economies. They include the implementation of such models as "modifield centralism," "indirect centralization," and "market socialism." In the first case, mathematical techniques are used by large administrative units to remove accumulated inconsistencies, while the content of planning remains largely unchanged. In the second case, incentives and rules are determined by the central authorities and those responsible for the implementation of the plan. In the last case, major decentralization to independent units takes place while the party releases a large amount of its authority to enterprise managers.

CAPITAL PRODUCTIVITY

Given that population density has increased and land per laborer has declined in all Balkan countries, especially in Albania and Turkey, an increase in output per worker calls for an increase in capital. Capital, which Eugen von Böhm-Bawerk defined as the intermediate products that appear in several stages of the roundabout journey of production,[27] helps labor to increase the annual product of its country. As Adam Smith pointed out, this can be achieved through the improvement of machines and instruments that facilitate division of labor, and thereby increase productivity.[28]

As the quality of capital keeps improving, new capital to increase the capital stock or to replace that which is old and depreciated has a superior efficiency from a technological point of view. Because gross investment is primarily reported by the countries considered, and because it incorporates technological change, gross (undepreciated) figures are used in the subsequent empirical sections of this study.

TABLE 5.8

Investment/Efficiency Ratios, Balkans, 1951-60 to 1971-77 (ΔGDP/GFCF, constant prices)

	1951-60	1961-70	1971-77	Average 1951-77
Albania	27.2	32.6	24.7	28.2
Bulgaria	52.8	38.1	33.6	41.5
Greece	32.5	27.6	18.4	26.2
Romania	30.6	23.1	25.4	26.4
Turkey	31.5	35.5	34.7	33.9
Yugoslavia	22.5	19.4	16.2	19.4

Notes: For Albania, GFCF at current prices; for Bulgaria, NMP and NFCF at current prices; for Romania, national income instead of GDP. In certain cases fewer years' data were available.

Sources: Calculations based on OECD, *National Accounts*, various issues; United Nations, *Yearbook of National Accounts Statistics*, various issues.

TABLE 5.9

Labor Adjusted Investment/Efficiency Ratios:
Balkans, 1951–60 and 1971–77

	1951–60	1961–70	1971–77	Average 1951–77
Albania	5.4	8.5	15.8	9.9
Bulgaria	-1.6	19.0	8.4	8.6
Greece	28.2	31.4	14.3	24.6
Romania	n.a.	18.8	24.4	21.6
Turkey	n.a.	27.6	32.4	30.0
Yugoslavia	5.3	15.2	4.6	8.4

n.a. = not available.

Notes: For Albania and Yugoslavia, total labor force (including the socialized sector) was estimated as 41.7 percent of the population. See V. Dubey, *Yugoslavia: Development with Decentralization* (Baltimore: Johns Hopkins University Press, 1975), p. 63. For Turkey, labor force is that of 1976.

Sources: Calculations based on OECD, *National Accounts*, various issues; United Nations, *Yearbook of National Accounts Statistics*, various issues.

Some dissatisfaction has recently been expressed with the use of labor productivity as an indication of progress. More interest has been shown in the productivity of investment, measured with the efficiency-of-investment ratios, which can be adjusted for labor changes.

Table 5.8 shows the investment/efficiency ratios (IER = $\Delta Q/\Delta K$) for all Balkan countries; these figures are the inverse of the incremental capital/output ratio (ICOR). For a better measurement of the efficiency of investment, the growth of labor ($\Delta L/L$) was subtracted from the growth of output ($\Delta Q/Q$). Then, the "labor-adjusted" investment/efficiency ratio ($\Delta \dot{Q}/\Delta K$) can be determined as follows:

$$\frac{\Delta \dot{Q}}{\Delta K} = \frac{[(\Delta Q/Q) - (\Delta L/L)]Q}{\Delta K}$$

For example, the GDP (Q) of Greece in 1971 was 562.9, and in 1977, 738.6 billion drachmas (at 1975 constant prices), while the labor force was 3,140,000 and 3,359,000, respectively. Total investment (GFCF) in 1972-77 was 953.1 billion drachmas. Then,

$$\frac{\Delta \dot{Q}}{\Delta K} = \frac{[(175.9/562.9) - (219/3140)]562.9}{953.1} = \frac{(0.312 - 0.070)562.9}{953.1} = 0.143$$

That is, the labor-adjusted IER was 14.3 percent during the period 1971-77—every 100 drachmas invested brought about 14.3 drachmas increased production or output. This ratio, which measures the growth of return on investment, was 8.4 percent for Yugoslavia, 8.6 percent for Bulgaria, 9.9 percent for Albania, 21.6 percent for Romania, and as high as 24.6 percent for Greece and 30.0 percent for Turkey in 1951-77.[29] (See Table 5.9.)

Although investment helps improve labor productivity, it simultaneously increases the capital stock, which in turn may slow down innovations and make changes difficult. Enterprises with established bureaucracies and ways of doing things do not easily accept new methods with a high potential for productivity.

The full-employment policy of the planned Balkan economies may be a serious reason for their low or even negative labor-adjusted IERs in the early postwar years. The continuation of this policy keeps the growth of the rate of return on investment generally lower there, compared with the market economies of Greece and Turkey. Besides economic fluctuations, which affect output and, in turn, the IER, labor incentives play an important role in the variation and the level of the growth of the rate of return on investment.

Productivity usually increases through training of workers and use of more efficient machines. In both cases investment is needed either in intangible human capital or in tangible capital equipment. Consumption does little to provide a foundation for future production and jobs. The policy followed by the northern Balkan countries—emphasizing capital formation at the expense of the production of consumer goods—may be justified on these grounds. However, too much emphasis on the production of capital goods, through large investment in heavy industry, may mean severe sacrifices for consumers, a phenomenon common to all planned economies.[30]

NOTES

1. V. Kaczynski, "The Economics of the Eastern Bloc Ocean Policy," *American Economic Review*, Proceedings, May 1979, pp. 261-65.

2. World Bank estimates reveal that when the Balkan countries reach stationary population, there will be 100 million people in Turkey by 2075, 30 million in Romania by 2090, 29 million in Yugoslavia by 2095, 11 million in Greece by 2065, 10 million in Bulgaria by 2080, and 6 million in Albania by 2060. See its *World Development Report, 1980* (New York: Oxford University Press, 1980), p. 143.

3. There are cases where a university professor is responsible for grading 5,000 examinations. "A Survey of Greece," *The Economist*, September 20, 1975, p. 18.

4. For additional statistics on education and health see World Bank, op. cit., pp. 151-55.

5. Such beliefs prevail primarily among the Moslem population. For example, in southern Sudan, "a reasonably sound wife costs about 40 head of cattle, with perhaps a few goats and chickens thrown in." J. Goddard, "Kayaks Down the Nile," *National Geographic Magazine* 107, no. 5 (May 1955): 173. In Constantinople a seventeenth-century sultan (Ibrahim the Mad) ordered his 1,001 concubines trussed and tossed into the Bosporus, and filled the Great Harem of Topkapi with new ones. *Time*, September 13, 1971, p. 39.

6. For the difference between growth economics and development, see John Hicks, *Capital and Growth* (New York: Oxford University Press, 1969), pp. 3-4. For the structural transformation of the Balkan economies from the agricultural to industrial and services sectors, see ch. 6 of this volume.

7. W. W. Rostow thinks that for Turkey the takeoff started after 1933, when import substitution in light industry began. See his *The World Economy: History and Prospects* (Austin: University of Texas Press, 1978), ch. 39. Romania was considered to be at takeoff in 1966-75.

8. For comparisons with other countries of eastern Europe, see U.S. Congress, Joint Economic Committee, *Economic Development in Countries of Eastern Europe* (Washington, D.C.: U.S. Government Printing Office, 1970).

9. Using a simplified version of the Harrod-Domar-Tinbergen model, without gestation lag, we have

$$g = \frac{j}{v} - \pi$$

That is, $j/5 - 1\% = 4\%$, and $j = 5 \ (4+1) = 25\%$, where g is the per capita growth of income or output, j is investment as percentage of income, v is the ICOR, and π is the rate of population growth.

10. For the calculation of the ten-year ICORs, the total gross investment during the period was divided by the incremental GDP during the same period. That is:

$$\text{ICOR} = \sum_{t=1}^{t=10} I_t / Q_{t+10} - Q_t$$

Similar ICORs, obtained through the regression of GDP on cumulative investment, give more reliable results because the ICORs do not consider only the terminal-year outputs, as the ten-year ratios do.

11. Simon Kuznets also found low ICORs in low-income countries. See his "Quantitative Aspects of Economic Growth of Nations," *Economic Development and Cultural Change* 3, no. 4, pt. 2 (July 1960), pp. 1-96; N. Gianaris, "The Instability of the Incremental Capital-Output Ratio," *Socio-Economic Planning Sciences*, August 1969, pp. 119-25. For comparisons of these ICORs with those of other east European nations, see United Nations, *Economic Survey of Europe in 1976* (New York: United Nations, 1977), pt. II, p. 94.

12. In Romania, for example, there exist the official rate (4.47 lei per dollar), the tourist rate (12 lei per dollar), and the trading rate (18 lei per dollar).

13. Currency debasement and price increases are not new phenomena. In ancient Sparta (ninth century B.C.) and Athens (fifth century B.C.), in Rome (A.D. 301), England (twelfth century), India (1770), France (1789), and on many occasions in America, price controls have been imposed to curb inflation. For further discussion see N. Angell, *The Story of Money* (New York: F. Stokes, 1929); J. Backman, *Price Practices and Price Controls* (New York: Ronald Press, 1953).

14. For statistical information supporting the existence of "wage push" inflation in Yugoslavia, for the period 1952-70, see V. Dubey, *Yugoslavia: Levelopment with Decentralization* (Baltimore: Johns Hopkins University Press, 1975), pp. 320-21.

15. Inflationary pressures in controlled economies may surface under different guises, such as lower quality, discontinuing production of cheap commodities, narrowing available consumer options, increased shopping inconvenience, increased under-the-counter sales, black markets, and other forms of latent inflation.

16. The average annual rate of inflation in 1960-70 was 5.6 percent for Turkey, 12.6 percent for Yugoslavia, and 3.2 percent for Greece; for 1970-78 it was 21.5 for Turkey, 13.8 for Greece, and 17.3 for Yugoslavia. World Bank, op. cit., p. 111.

17. A bell-shaped tax rate structure that burdened upper-middle income brackets relatively more, existed in Greece during 1958–74. G. Provopoulos, "The Distribution of Fiscal Burdens and Benefits by Income Groups in Greece," *Greek Economic Review* 1, no. 1 (1979): 77–99. However, in a similar study, D. Karageorgas found a U-shaped tax rate pattern. See his "The Distribution of Tax Burden by Income Groups in Greece," *Economic Journal* 83 (1973): 436–48.

18. Athens, for example, has more clubs, cafés, taverns, bars, and cabarets, relative to the size of its population, than any other European city. It is in these places that many people are spending their incomes, and thereby fueling inflation.

19. However, tax incentives to corporations to increase productivity may not prove very effective if there is internal corporate bureaucracy and a tendency of corporations to increase their financial assets or withhold profits instead of investing in real assets.

20. Thus, for Bulgaria income taxes vary from 3.3 percent for 90 leva monthly income to 7 percent for 100, and 10.3 percent for 260 leva monthly income. P. Jonas, *Taxation of Multinationals in Communist Countries* (New York: Praeger, 1978), p. 66. For Greece they vary from 4.4 percent for income of 300,000 drachmas to 35 percent for income of 1,500,000 drachmas for a single taxpayer. *Oikonomicos Tahydromos* (Athens), October 23, 1980, p. 26.

21. N. Gianaris, "Indirect Taxes: A Comparative Study of Greece and the EEC," *European Economic Review* 15 (1981): 113. For tax reform arguments see A. Prest, "The Structure and Reforms of Direct Taxation," *Economic Journal*, June 1979, pp. 243–60; M. and R. Friedman, *Free to Choose* (New York: Harcourt, 1980), chs. 4, 5, 9, 10.

22. For comments on tax harmonization and problems of substitution, see the valuable articles in C. Shoup, ed., *Fiscal Harmonization in Common Markets* (New York: Columbia University Press, 1967); also N. Gianaris, "Fiscal Policy: Greece and the EEC," *Spoudai* (forthcoming).

23. For the calculation of labor productivity growth (q), the following equation in logarithmic form was used: $\log(Q/L)_n = \log(Q/L)_o + r \log(1 + q)$, where Q is output, L is labor, and n is time in years.

24. During the period 1960–78, Japan had an annual rate of labor productivity growth of 8.5; Italy, 6.2; France, 5.6; Germany, 5.5; United Kingdom, 3.2; and the United States, 2.6. B. Malkiel, "Productivity–the Problem Behind the Headlines," *Harvard Business Review*, May–June 1979, pp. 81–91. For comparisons of the OECD and the Comecon countries, see A. Bergson, *Productivity and the Social System* (Cambridge, Mass.: Harvard University Press, 1978), p. 199.

25. Empirical research in the United States and elsewhere revealed that about 85 to 90 percent of the long-term growth in per capita output was attributed to technological change and education. For an extensive review see D. Jorgenson and Z. Griliches, "The Explanation of Productivity Change," *Survey of Current Business*, May 1972, pp. 3–36; S. Fabricant, *A Primer on Productivity* (New York: Random House, 1969), ch. 5; R. Sutermeister, *People and Productivity*, 3rd ed. (New York: McGraw-Hill, 1976).

26. For related discussion see S. Kuznets, *Quantitative Economic Research: Trends and Problems* (New York: National Bureau of Economic Research, 1972); J. Schumpeter, *The Theory of Economic Development* (New York: Oxford University Press, 1961), ch. 6.

27. Eugen von Böhm-Bawerk, *The Positive Theory of Capital* (London: Macmillan, 1891), p. 22.

28. Adam Smith, *An Inquiry into the Nature and Causes of the Wealth of Nations*, E. Cannan, ed. (New York: Modern Library, 1937), p. 326.

29. For the United States the labor-adjusted IER was 12.8 percent in 1970–78; the "simple" IER was 27.9 percent for the same period. *Survey of Current Business*, various issues; and *Handbook of Labor Statistics*, 1978.

30. Also, extensive capital accumulation may lead to diminishing returns on capital. As tenuous as the estimates are, capital productivity, measured as average annual percentage change (growth rates of output per unit of fixed capital) in industry, was negative for Bulgaria (-2.0) in 1960-72 and -0.7 in 1970-75; for Romania it was -0.9 and -1.1, respectively. In agriculture and construction it was -5.6 and 6.2 in 1960-72 for Bulgaria and -4.3 and -2.3 for Romania. United Nations, *Economic Survey of Europe, 1976* (New York: United Nations, 1977), pp. 70-73; G. Feiwel, *Growth and Reforms in Centrally Planned Economies* (New York: Praeger, 1977), pp. 64-67, 317.

6

SECTORAL DEVELOPMENT

DUALISM AND MULTISECTORAL ANALYSIS

In the Balkan countries, as in other developing and somewhat developed countries, we can distinguish two broad sectors in the economy: the modern (or advanced) industrial sector and the traditional (or backward) agricultural sector. In all Balkan countries, primarily in Greece, Turkey, and Yugoslavia, the lagging rural sector is gradually losing the most trained and most progressive persons, while the modern sector is gaining their talents. Unfortunately, governmental policies in these countries have not done enough to discourage the trend toward regional concentration through public services, credit facilities, and technological transformation. In fact, they have neglected the development of backward regions.[1] Also, foreign investments, bringing in advanced technology, have concentrated on large-scale industries in limited areas that have advanced public, financial, and market facilities, thereby creating, in many cases, economic enclaves. The encouragement of this trend of "outward-looking" development policy has been detrimental to long-run regional industrialization.

It has been suggested that sectoral or regional dualism leads to a distortion in the allocation of resources, and impedes long-term economic and social development. An integrated domestic economy would provide more employment and higher standards of living. Dualistic rigidities and obstacles, on the other hand, are widening the gap between the advanced and the subsistence sectors, thus initiating political instability and social unrest.[2] The beneficial "spread effects" from the rich and dynamic regions to the poorer regions do not seem to be as powerful as the "backwash effects" in the Balkan countries. The idea of internal regional integration as a forerunner of external integration seems to be a better strategy of development, since a policy stressing external economic integration among the Balkan nations, as well as among other larger economic groups, may perpetuate and even aggravate the regional and sectoral gap in each country.

108

Balanced Growth

Concerning the problem of optimum allocation of investment and other resources among different sectors or regions in each Balkan country or in the Balkan Peninsula as a whole, a serious question may be asked: Should the allocation of resources be equiproportional, to produce balanced growth, or nonproportional, following an unbalanced growth policy in favor of a particular sector or region?

Some economists argue that development is best stimulated by a strategy of balanced growth, that is, a program of comprehensive simultaneous investment throughout the economy.[3] Diversified investment expansion in mutually supporting industries will provide the necessary additional purchasing power, thus creating a market for each firm's products and making the people working in these industries each other's customers. If economic development is concentrated on industrialization at the expense of agriculture—as, for example, happened in the northern Balkan and other planned economies—an acute shortage of agricultural products can be expected, and it may be difficult to dispose of manufactures. Moreover, progress at a snail's pace, through isolated advances, will only create bottlenecks in demand and sectoral deadlocks in the process of development.

The Savings Barrier and the Demonstration Effect

According to the supporters of balanced growth, an increase in savings to finance investments is needed. If the market mechanism is too weak to implement balanced growth and overcome the problem of absorbing income increases through consumption, which may be observed in the market economies of Greece and Turkey, then sectoral investment should be allocated and coordinated by national development plans. However, because of the highly unequal distribution of income in these two countries, particularly in Turkey, a great fraction of income may be saved by high-income people. But even families in middle-income brackets can save and invest if their income is higher than that of other families of the same group in the community.

In Greece and Turkey savings in the rural areas depend largely on the success or failure of crops, which in turn depends on weather conditions. The most prosperous peasants usually save and invest in the improvement of their land, in small-scale local projects, or, more frequently, in urban real estate, with the hope that they or their children will migrate there for a better life. People in the urban areas, whose income is two to three times greater than that in the rural areas, usually save more than the peasants. Their savings may be channeled into real estate, industrial projects, or stocks and bonds, depending on the expected rate of return, economic and political stability, and the efficiency of the capital market. However, in the socialist Balkan economies there are limited possibilities for private savings and investment. In these countries sectoral and regional allocation of investment is controlled by the government and takes place through the planning mechanism, and investment is financed through taxation.

An important obstacle to saving in Turkey, Greece, and, to a lesser extent, in Yugslavia, Romania, Bulgaria, and Albania is the demonstration effect. With an overexpansion of international trade, people are gradually shifting from domestic consumer goods to imported goods. The attractive lifestyles with so many desired objects of consumption, which become familiar through personal contact, motion pictures, the broadcast media, and the print media, tend to increase consumption and reduce saving. Also, domestically, low-income families tend to increase consumption because they want to "keep up with the Joneses." For the Balkan countries, however, the intraregional demonstration effect may not be as powerful and important as the international. As the Balkan economies (including the planned ones) are more and more exposed to international trade and tourism, the pressure for higher consumption levels, similar to those in advanced Western economies, is growing. In addition, the governments and public authorities of these countries tend to formulate development programs in which they seek to emulate advanced countries with high technical, social, and educational standards. The demonstration effect thus may be a major reason for deficits in the balance of payments and inflationary pressures in these countries.

Unbalanced Growth

Another group of economists argues that economic development at best can be achieved through a deliberate unbalancing of the economy, in accordance with a predesigned strategy.[4] This is the strategy that the socialist Balkan countries and all the other planned economies, including the Soviet Union, have followed in the past and continue to follow at present. In order to induce decision making through tensions and incentives for private entrepreneurs and state planners, a chain of unbalanced growth sequences should be generated. Thus, initiation of development in those sectors that present maximum backward and forward linkages with other sectors is advisable.[5] Such an unbalanced process of growth might be proper for overpopulated Turkey to achieve the gradual transfer of surplus population from the farming sector to a higher-productivity industrial sector. It is doubtful that a low-level balanced growth can eradicate poverty and backwardness from less developed countries such as Turkey and Albania.

Sectoral and Regional Pluralism

It can be argued that dualistic sectoral analysis should be replaced by multisectoral analysis. Emphasis has been placed recently not so much on two sectors, agriculture versus industry, as on a relatively large number of different sectors, such as agriculture, mining, manufacturing, transportation, electricity, housing, public administration, and trade/banking services. During the early stages of development, emphasis is placed on agriculture and mining. Then transportation, communications, electricity, and other public utilities, which are essential for the infrastructure of the country and for further development of all other sectors, are emphasized. In all the Balkan countries, perhaps with the exception of Turkey and Albania, such social overhead facilities are more or less established, and emphasis is placed on manufacturing, housing, and trade/banking services. Certain sectors, however, may have been overemphasized or priorities may have been misdirected in the past. In such cases, corrective actions may be necessary to avoid shortages and bottlenecks. For example, luxurious housing in Greece and Turkey should be discouraged, so that resources may be released for other productive activities. Also, the agricultural and consumer sectors in the socialist Balkan economies should be emphasized to avoid future shortages.

Similarly, regional dualism is losing ground in favor of regional pluralism or multiregional analysis. All Balkan countries contain a variety of geographical regions or areas with different degrees of development, instead of a clearly cut distinct backward section and modern section. There are a large number of big and small city centers, with different degrees of industrialization, spread throughout each country. Even in the regions of northwestern Greece (Epirus), southern Yugoslavia (Macedonia and Montenegro), and eastern Turkey, which are classic examples of dualism, there are locations with more economic development than others. As we move from villages to towns, to provincial centers or capital cities, and finally to the megalopolises or metropolitan areas, we can observe regional disparities, particularly in Greece, Turkey, and Yugoslavia. Underemployed resources, especially labor, move from poor rural areas to provincial cities and big centers in equal proportions or, as is more customary, in higher proportions to the large industrial citiies.

The resulting structural change, which takes place through the concentration of resources in industrial areas, is extensively criticized in economic literature as an undesired phenomenon.[6] One can argue, however, that if pollution and other urban disamenities are solved, there is nothing wrong with such concentration. As long as the productivity of resources—and, therefore, their reward—is higher, and as long as the beneficial side effects or amenities are stronger in the rich than in the poor regions, this structural change need not be inhibited. Thus, there is no need to fear such a transformation. Furthermore, certain regions may contribute more to economic development after a good part of the low-productivity labor force has moved to the cities, leaving the countryside for cattle raising or other more productive use. Recent development plans in all Balkan countries, which emphasize development of poor regions, might change the trend by providing the necessary infrastructural and technological improvements, thereby causing the comparative disadvantage of today to be the advantage of tomorrow, and increasing productivity in these regions. In such a case the "spread effects" (the diffusion of growth from the rich to the poor areas) may overwhelm the "backwash effects," and the development of the poor regions may start speeding up again. However, as long as the difference in productivity and remuneration persists, the trend of resource concentration will continue.

AGRICULTURE

Before World War II the Balkan economies were based on agriculture, which was organized and operated primarily under a feudalistic or manorial system. However, the gradual influence of Western capitalism and the movement away from subsistence agriculture to a market economy brought an increased dependency of the farmers on traders, middlemen, and loan sharks as well as bank credit and governmental bureaucracy. It became more obvious in Greece than in other Balkan countries. This may be considered the main reason for limited or no political movements among rural people in Greece (except for the creation of the weak Greek Rural Party in 1922), compared with other Balkan countries. Politically, economically, culturally, or otherwise, the Greek peasants followed largely the urban initiatives and changes. On the contrary, in other Balkan countries noticeable movements by the rural population took place, especially during the period between the two wars. In Bulgaria the Rural Union was in power from 1919 to 1923, when its leader Stambuliski was assassinated, and again from 1931 until the coup of 1934. Also, the formation and operation of farmers' cooperatives became more effective in that country during that period.

During the early years of the twentieth century, mainly the period between the world wars, agricultural reforms were initiated throughout the Balkan countries. The main result of these reforms was the reduction or the elimination of latifundia *(chifliks)*. As mentioned earlier, these large estates were unfairly acquired or inherited during the Turkish domination. Usually the regional Turkish rulers *(beys)* would grant ownership of large land areas as gifts to their collaborators. As a result, most the Balkan rural people were divided into the small class of landlords and the exploited peasant masses. For example, out of 658 villages in Thessaly, 466 were *chiflik* villages and 198 were free villages. Even today one can see remnants of these unfairly large holdings in the hands of heirs of the Turkish collaborators (for example, the Pahinas and the Caracosta properties in the Athens-Piraeus suburbs).

However, the rural reforms and the subdivision and distribution of many large *chifliks* to the tillers, combined with the more or less equal distribution of land through inheritance and dowry (equal sharing replacing primogeniture), led to the division of land into small strips (stamps) scattered in different places. (The average land holding in Greece, for example, is less than 9 acres, compared with 18 in western Europe.) Moreover, the gradual increase of agricultural exports to west European countries has led to specialization in the production of primary products (raw materials) that can be absorbed by the advanced Western markets in exchange for imports of more expensive machinery and industrial products.

This trend toward producing mainly primary products, so familiar in poor countries today, has kept Balkan nations at an underdeveloped stage until recent years.[7] At the same time, the rapid increase in population and the slow growth of industrialization have led to a surplus of labor in agriculture and, consequently, to extensive underemployment of rural workers in all Balkan countries. The move from rural areas to urban centers has been higher in Greece, where the agricultural sector used to be about 60 percent of the population in the 1930s (compared with about 80 percent in other Balkan countries during those years). The main urban center absorbing the Greek rural population has been Athens, which reached more than 3 million people in the 1970s, compared with 1 million before the war and only 200,000 in 1900. In the other Balkan countries, however, not only did the farmers remain in their villages, but some of the urban workers returned to agriculture during the prewar years, especially in Serbia.

Part of the surplus rural labor of Greece was absorbed by the rapidly growing shipping industry and emigration, mainly to the United States, to which about 445,000 Greeks had gone by 1932 (compared with fewer than 35,000 Bulgarians).[8] A golden stream of remittances from the thrifty emigrant sons (more than $120 million in 1921 alone) helped stabilize Greece's extremely unfavorable balance of trade. The other Balkan countries, however, did not have the same opportunities, and their population had to concentrate on the agricultural sector.

The limited movement of the population in the northern Balkan countries from the agricultural sector to the industrial and services sectors, as well as its limited opportunities for emigration, resulted in emphasis on the rural sector and the creation of farmers' organizations. In contrast, Greek farmers mostly looked outward, and their economic and political interests were linked to those of urban and foreign centers. Their political patrons, interested mainly in the cities and influenced on many occasions by foreign "protectors," left farmers unorganized and unprotected with respect to relative farm-product prices and rural development.

After World War II, when new reforms were introduced by Communist governments, the agricultural sector of the northern Balkan economies faced serious problems. The peasants were dissatisfied with the imposed collectivization of land (similar to the Soviet kolkhoz), and their incentives for production were reduced. This, together with the emphasis of the policy makers on heavy industries, led to shortages of consumer goods and forced the governments to impose compulsory deliveries of farm products in order to satisfy urban needs. Financing heavy capital investment required rigid curbs upon consumption and strict state controls on the economy through consecutive five-year plans.

It became obvious that it would be difficult to impose the Soviet model on the nationalistic and individualist-minded Balkan people. Therefore, land collectivization and forced industrialization had to be followed with severe state and local controls. However, in many instances where land had been subdivided into very small, widely scattered parcels, collectivization might have been the way to

TABLE 6.1

Agricultural and Mining Products of the Balkan Countries, 1978 (1,000 metric tons)

	Wheat	Corn	Potatoes	Sheep (1,000 head)	Fish Catch	Brown Coal and Lignite	Crude Petroleum	Crude Bauxite	Crude Iron
Albania	370	300	132	1,163	4	1,000	2,600	—	—
Bulgaria	3,450	2,300	390	10,145	138	24,868	129	—	707
Greece	2,660	537	944	8,004	106	23,572	—	2,874	881
Romania	6,235	10,179	4,450	14,463	151	19,416	14,652	900	633
Turkey	16,500	1,300	2,800	42,708	155	8,200	2,712	567	1,379
Yugoslavia	5,355	7,555	2,400	7,514	61	36,752	3,950	2,044	1,514

Note: In some cases, previous years' data were used.
Source: United Nations, *Statistical Yearbook*, various issues.

increase land productivity. The collectivization or communization process continued, and at present 68 percent of the land in Bulgaria belongs to the collectives, 21 percent is under state control, and 11 percent is within the private sector; in Romania the percentages are 60, 30, and 10, respectively.[9] In Yugoslavia, 30 percent of the land belongs to state enterprises (*kombinats*) and the rest to the private sector, with just a few cooperatives (*kolkhozy*) remaining.[10]

In all Balkan countries agricultural production increased satisfactorily during the 1970s, especially in Romania, Turkey, and Greece, through the use of growing numbers of tractors and other mechanical means of production. As Table 6.1 indicates, Turkey leads in production of wheat, followed by Romania and Yugoslavia; in the production of corn and potatoes, Romania is far ahead of all the other Balkan countries, followed by Yugoslavia in corn and Turkey in potatoes. Large amounts of corn are produced by Bulgaria, and relatively large amounts of potatoes by Yugoslavia. Greece is also known for the production of olives and olive oil, raisins, lemons, oranges, and other fruits; Bulgaria, for attar of roses; and Romania, for sunflower oil. Turkey is first in the production of cotton, followed by Greece. Romania, Yugoslavia, and Bulgaria are far ahead in the raising of pigs, while Turkey, with almost no pigs (because of the Moslem 'custom), is the leader in raising sheet. On a per capita basis, however, Bulgaria has been first in raising sheep and almost second in raising pigs for decades. In the production of eggs per capita, Romania is first, followed by Bulgaria, Greece, and Yugoslavia (where the use of brooding machines and the mass production of chickens are spreading rapidly). In per capita fish catch Bulgaria is first, followed by Greece and Romania.

The main mining products in the Balkan Peninsula are brown coal and lignite, produced primarily in Yugoslavia (36.8 million metric tons in 1977), Bulgaria (24.9 million metric tons), Greece (23.6 million metric tons), and Romania (19.4 million metric tons); crude petroleum in Romania (14.6 million metric tons in 1977), Yugoslavia (4 million metric tons), and Albania and Turkey (around 2.6 and 2.7 million metric tons, respectively); and natural gas in Romania, Yugoslavia, and Albania. Bauxite is produced mainly in Greece (2.9 million metric tons in 1977), holding first place in western Europe, and Yugoslavia (2.0 million metric tons); and iron, in all Balkan countries except Albania, primarily Yugoslavia, Turkey, and Greece. On a per capita basis, Greece produces large amounts of aluminum (15 kilos annually), followed by Romania and Yugoslavia (around 10 kilos annually). Moreover, gold is produced primarily in Yugoslavia (some 5,000 kilograms in 1977); copper, in Yugoslavia, Bulgaria, and Turkey; and nickel, in Greece and Albania.

To stimulate incentives and increase productivity, the planned economies of Bulgaria, Romania, and (to a lesser extent) Albania permit individual labor in handicrafts, farming, services for the public, and similar activities. Small private plots and the raising of a small number of privately owned cows, pigs, and other livestock are permitted in the countryside. The high productivity of the small private sector, yielding one-third or more of the country's vegetables, potatoes, meat, milk, and eggs, justifies the efforts to encourage collective and state farmers to raise vegetables and livestock privately. Furthermore, the manufacturing of good-quality hand tools and small-scale mechanized tools by the private sector supports efforts to encourage such self-sufficiency. However, the recent trend toward the creation of agro-industrial complexes has led some villagers to move into high-rise apartments, and has caused a reduction in the number of private plots.

INDUSTRY

The industrial development of the Balkan countries started primarily at the end of the nineteenth century, when capital from Western countries, mainly Britain, France, and Germany, moved into the area. The main reason for this capital flow was the military and political-economic interests of these Western countries rather than intra-Balkan development. The colonial powers of that time were engaged in fierce competition for new resources as well as market expansion, not only in remote colonies but also in the closer Balkan countries. Initially foreign capital flowed into the area in the form of governmental and private loans for the construction of railways, highways, and other infrastructural facilities. The first railroads connecting Varna with Ruse, Constanta with Cernavoda, and Belgrade with Salonika and Constantinople were constructed primarily at the beginning of the twentieth century; German enterprises extended the railways to Asia Minor and to Baghdad.

The unstable and frequently corrupt Balkan governments increased taxes to provide money to pay previous loans and to finance investment that would industrialize their countries. In the agricultural sector, emphasis was placed more on market or commercial farming than on self-sufficiency. This siphoned off farm products for the cities and for exports to help support industrialization and payment of foreign debts. However, industrialization did not advance much, mainly because Balkan markets were being flooded with industrial products from Western countries, a phenomenon similar to that in the less developed countries today. The few local family-owned monopolies that managed to survive substantially controlled the governments. Farmers had to pay relatively high prices for industrial products, resources were misallocated, and the development process was unable to utilize all the productive resources available. Flour milling, textiles, tanning, pottery, and the processing of olives, grapes, and other agricultural products were the main cottage industries in Balkania. Sailing vessels, and later steamships, were built and used mainly by wealthy overseas Greeks.

During the interwar years the pressure of surplus rural labor in the overpopulated Balkans indicated the need for emigration or industrialization. Moreover, low levels of land productivity and the consumption needs of the poor peasants left no surplus production for industrial investment. Foreign investment, on the other hand, was primarily directed to short-run ventures for quick, high profits, despite the tax incentives and other lucrative concessions given by the Balkan governments to job-creating industrial investment.

High import duties on such manufactured products as clothing, sugar, fertilizers, and agricultural machinery, designed to protect domestic industry, created inefficient quasi monopolies that aggravated the plight of the peasants instead of improving their economic conditions. However, investment in some agricultural industries, such as milling, manufacturing of sugar and alcohol, and vegetable oil refining, as well as in mineral production (copper, bauxite, iron, chrome) provided employment for a number of industrial workers, especially in Yugoslavia, where the number of workers in these industries increased by about 100 percent (from 200,000 to close to 400,000) from 1918 to 1938.[11]

During the postwar years the Balkan countries, which by then were on the road to industrial development, experienced great difficulties in meeting their industrial output targets, primarily because the resources for investment, including what was obtained from abroad, were not being made available as planned.[12] Also, the increase in petroleum and raw material prices in recent years has imposed a great burden on these countries. Albania, Bulgaria, Greece, and Romania experienced a slowdown in the industrial growth rate in the 1970s, and it is expected that it will become even lower.

Bulgaria, Romania, and Yugoslavia produce the largest amounts of meat, primarily pork, beef, and veal (about 50 kilos per capita annually), followed by Greece (close to 40 kilos), Albania (20), and Turkey (15), as Table 6.2 indicates. Greece, Turkey, and Albania produce mostly mutton and lamb. On the average, Greece and Bulgaria produce the largest amount of cheese per capita (close to 20 kilos annually), followed by Romania and Yugoslavia. Large amounts of meat and cheese are exported by the northern Balkan countries, primarily by Bulgaria, which exports close to 100,000 tons of meat per year.

Turkey, Bulgaria, and Greece are competitive in the production of tobacco. In absolute terms Turkey is the leader among the Balkan countries in the production of sugar and cement, as is Romania in wine and cotton yarn.

Bulgaria produces the largest amount of electricity per capita (close to 4,000 kilowatt-hours) per year, followed by Romania (3,000), Greece and Yugoslavia (about 2,200), Albania (1,000), and Turkey (about 500). About half of the total energy production in Albania, Turkey, and Yugoslavia, and around 10-15 percent in Greece and Romania, is derived from hydroelectric power.

In steel consumption per capita, Romania is first, followed by Bulgaria, Yugoslavia, and Greece. Comparatively speaking, Bulgaria, Romania, and Yugoslavia consume the largest amounts of energy per capita and Turkey the least. High consumption levels of energy and steel by the northern Balkan countries indicate their progress in industrialization, compared with Turkey and Greece. However, Greece, after Yugoslavia, has the largest number of tractors on a per capita basis.

TABLE 6.2

Selected Agricultural and Manufactured Products, Energy Production, and Steel Consumption in the Balkan Countries, 1978 (thousand metric tons)

	Meat	Cheese	Sugar	Tobacco	Cotton Yarn	Cement	Wine (1,000 hectoliters)	Tractors (units)	Energy Production (kwh)	Steel Consumption per Capita (kgs)
Albania	55	10	25	14	n.a.	800	203	9,400	2,150	57
Bulgaria	466	150	240	170	86	4,665	3,801	65,020	29,710	276
Greece	341	165	294	113	87	10,560	4,520	110,000	19,019	176
Romania	1,108	148	590	45	171	13,122	10,430	138,549	59,858	464
Turkey	624	120	1,158	290	167	13,390	662	324,669	20,565	112
Yugoslavia	1,057	132	647	60	121	8,233	5,200	296,825	48,580	239

n.a. = not available.

Note: In some cases, previous years' data were used.

Source: United Nations, *Statistical Yearbook,* various issues.

SERVICES

Tourism

Tourism continues to be a vital and growing sector for all Balkan countries, especially for Greece, Yugoslavia, and Turkey. For Greece alone the number of tourists increased from 2 million in 1974 to almost 6 million in 1979. Revenue from tourism in 1977 was $981 million for Greece, $841 million for Yugoslavia, $230 million (1975) for Bulgaria, $205 million for Turkey, and $112 million (1976) for Romania. Intra-Balkan tourism is not yet sizable, compared with overall tourism, as Table 6.3 shows. However, recent improvement in economic and cultural relations among these countries is expected to increase mutual tourism. At present the largest number of tourists in Bulgaria come from East Germany and Turkey; in Greece, from the United States, Yugoslavia, West Germany, the United Kingdom, and France; in Romania, from Poland, Czechoslovakia, and Bulgaria; in Turkey, from western Europe and the United States; and in Yugoslavia, from West Germany, Austria, Italy, and France.

To attract tourists, almost all Balkan countries continue to devalue (directly or indirectly) their currencies or offer certain other advantages. As the present writer observed on recent visits to Bulgaria and Romania, prices of hotels, restaurants, and related tourist services are comparatively cheap. Similarly, the gradual devaluation of the Greek drachma, the recent devaluation of the Yugoslav dinar by 35 percent, and the sizable devaluations of the Turkish lira aim at the improvement of the balance of payments through increasing exports and reducing imports, and attracting foreign exchange through tourism.

TABLE 6.3

Intra-Balkan and Total Tourism, 1977
(1,000 persons)

From/To	Bulgaria	Greece	Romania	Turkey	Yugoslavia
Bulgaria	—	10	539	4	30
Greece	86	—	26	2	114
Romania	186	6	—	4	15
Turkey	1,554	43	32	—	136
Yugoslavia	708	491	278	10	—
Total (intra-Balkan)	2,534	550	875	20	295
Total (world)	4,600	4,000	3,700	1,700	5,600

Source: United Nations, *Statistical Yearbook*, various issues.

The natural beauties, the variety of ethnic groups, and the pleasant climate of the Balkan Peninsula attract, and will continue to attract, foreign tourists. Greece, with so many picturesque islands and archaeological monuments, and appealing climate, is one of the most popular destinations for international tourists. Tourism would have particular importance for the Greek economy if the Olympic Games were held at their birthplace (Olympia) in Peloponnesus. The Yugoslav and Albanian Adriatic shores, the Bulgarian and Romanian beaches on the Black Sea, and the Turkish coasts also attract large numbers of tourists from all over the world. Recent efforts by the Greek and Turkish ministers of tourism and cultural affairs, aimed at reducing conflict over Cyprus, are expected to stimulate tourism and trade between these two countries as well as among the other Balkan countries.

Other Services

Annual international fairs, such as those at Salonika, Plovdiv, and other Balkan centers, have occurred more frequently in recent times, with ever increasing numbers of participants. Balkan film festivals (the fourth at Ljubljana, Yugoslavia, in April 1980 and the fifth at Athens in 1981), athletic meetings or Balkaniads (the thirty-ninth at Sofia in June 1980), and theatrical and other joint performances help to improve the economic and cultural relations between the Balkan peoples.

Comparatively speaking, the service sector is not contributing as much as the industrial sector to the development effort of the planned Balkan economies, but its importance is expected to increase with the gradual transformation from agriculture to industry to services. Such long-run sectoral priorities were followed by the developed countries, and it would be difficult for the Balkan countries to avoid such a developmental process.

It is argued that productivity grows less rapidly in services than in other sectors, particularly in manufacturing.[13] This means a reduction in the national productivity and growth, since the shift from agriculture and manufacturing to services continues in virtually every Balkan country. However, the introduction of computers in such services as transportation, communications, finance, office work, and the legal, medical, and other professions, as well as deregulation and encouragement of greater competition in the service sector, would help to increase output per unit of time. Moreover, low productivity in services may be due to the fact that its measurement is difficult, particularly in the diverse economies of the Balkans. With improvements in the methods and techniques of the computation of output per unit of time, productivity in this sector may prove to be equal to or higher than in other sectors.

To increase production incentives in services, Bulgaria, Romania, and to a lesser extent Albania permit private ownership of small-scale service industries and the increased use of private individual labor. For example, Romania recently permitted the establishment of small private restaurants, candy stores, laundries, repair services (for radios, bicycles, and similar items), tailoring, shoe stores, carpentry, garages, parking, barber shops, and the like. The entrepreneurs of these stores can employ up to three workers and share in the profits, paying income taxes on income above 18,000 lei. Also, the introduction of super-markets and self-service stores throughout the cities and towns of the centrally planned economies alleviates the problem of low performance of the employees in public stores, and improves overall efficiency in the service sector.

To facilitate tourism and communication services, attention is also given to the use of passenger cars and telecommunications. At present Yugoslavia has the largest number of passenger cars (about 2 million) in the area, followed by Greece (close to 1 million) and Turkey (about 500,000). There are about 25 telephones per 100 inhabitants in Greece, 11 in Bulgaria, 7 in Romania and Yugoslavia, and 3 in Turkey.

TRANSPORTATION

Sea Routes

The Balkan Peninsula is a natural gateway of eastern and central Europe to the countries of the eastern Mediterranean and the Middle East. Therefore, land, sea, and air transportation networks can be developed so that the area is trans-formed into a transit center, with all the beneficial economic effects that accom-pany such a status. The Danube and its tributaries can be improved to accommo-date the ever-growing transportation needs within the area. The same can be done for the Maritsa and Vardar rivers, which flow into the Aegean Sea. The all-waterway route from the Black Sea to the Aegean Sea, through the Bosporus and the Dardanelles, is another natural passage to help navigation and trade.

On both sides of the peninsula, seaports such as Constanta, Varna, Burgas, and Istanbul on the Black Sea and Trieste, Rijeka, Split, Dubrovnik, Vlorë, and Corfu on the Adriatic Sea play a vital role in facilitating sea transportation. Balkan ports in the south, particularly Salonika and Kavalla, are expected to be important junctions for the transportation of petroleum and other products from the Middle East to southeastern and central Europe and vice versa. Already some 35,000 Yugoslav trucks and a large number of freight trains transport petroleum from Salonika to Yugoslavia every year. However, instead of using trucks and trains, with their high cost and potential pollution, it would be pref-erable to construct an oil pipeline connecting the Aegean Sea with Yugoslavia via Salonika or, as Greece prefers, via Kavalla. Another proposition is to have Greece provide petroleum to Yugoslavia from the refineries located in Salonika.

A new gateway for the Balkan countries to the Middle East is through the port of Volos, Greece. This route is preferable to one through Turkey or Italy as the shortest direct connection between the Middle East and the Balkan interior. The improvement of this route and the creation of new ones are of vital importance to the area, in order that the system of issuing "transit cards" for trucks, practiced particularly by Yugoslavia, and the traffic congestion can be reduced or eliminated. In connection with that, it would be preferable to use the refrigerated freight trains instead of the refrigerated trucks currently being produced in Romania and France, especially for the transportation of fruits and vegetables.

The sea route from Volos to Tartus and Latakia, Syria, inaugurated in 1977, is about 760 miles and takes 42 hours to cover. Large trucks, mainly from Austria, West Germany, the United Kingdom, Sweden, and France, are gathered at Volos every day, to be loaded on large ships. The port accommodates more than 65 such trucks, which have as their destinations Syria, Saudi Arabia, Jordan, and other Middle East countries. More than 5,000 vehicles and some 6 million tons of cargo are loaded every year. It is expected that improvement in Syrian-Iraqian roads and the rapid modernization of the port would attract some of the traffic that now travels via Turkey, a more uncomfortable and expensive route. Already, the Volos-Tartus ferries handle some 2,700 trailer trucks a month, and work is proceeding so that fully loaded trains can be transported.

To decentralize operations and reduce bureaucracy, the Greek ports of Kavalla, Egoumenitsa, Patras, and Herakleion, in addition to Piraeus, Salonika, and Volos, are being developed. The improvement of these ports and their transformation into international transit centers would help relieve the heavy traffic through Salonika and Piraeus, and would facilitate the growing trade between Europe and the Middle East. The development of the port of Kavalla may be given high priority because of the need to relieve traffic through Turkey and because of the overall cheaper transportation through Bulgaria to the Middle East, where fees collected per truck are only $3,500, compared with $7,000 through Yugoslavia.

The ever-increasing traffic between Europe and the Middle East through Yugoslavia, Bulgaria, Greece, and Turkey indicates that closer cooperation, joint transportation ventures, and modernization of transport facilities are needed in the Balkan Peninsula. For these reasons Turkey is considering the construction of a new bridge over the Bosporus and the expansion of highways by some 3,600 kilometers. A more attractive proposal (by Professor Peter Bromhent of the United Kingdom) suggests the creation of a railway tunnel under the Bosporus and the expansion of rail transportation, which is cheaper (consuming less energy), safer, less affected by weather conditions, and less polluting than trucks.

An alternative means of transportation is ships that carry trucks loaded with commodities from Patras to Rijeka in northern Yugoslavia or from Patras to Brindisi or Ancona, Italy, and then to central and northern Europe. However, in addition to higher transport cost, there are problems with the issuance of a limited number of transit cards by Yugoslavia, Austria, and Italy.

In merchant shipping, Greece holds first place in Europe, with 34 million gross tons, followed by Yugoslavia (2.4 million), Romania and Turkey (1.4 million), and Bulgaria (1.1 million), compared with 31 million for the United Kingdom, 26 million for Norway, 22 million for the USSR, and 16 million for the United States. In oil tanker fleets, Greece also is far ahead of other countries (more than 10 million gross tons).[14] Thus, Greece can play a vital role in facilitating trade and tourism not only among the Balkan countries but between them and the rest of the world.

Further economic development in the Balkan countries is expected to take place through a new water transportation network. Greece and Yugoslavia are in the process of negotiations for connecting the Danube-Morava-Vardar (Axios) rivers to create a waterway from the Danube to the Aegean Sea. This would be accomplished through the construction of a navigable canal some 400 miles long between the Morava and the Vardar.[15] It is expected that the annual traffic of goods would increase from a present 3 million tons to more than 50 million tons after completion of the canal. Greece and Yugoslavia have already approached the United Nations Development Program for financing for part of the project. Such a project would facilitate transactions not only among the Balkan countries, but between them and other neighboring countries, such as Austria, Czechoslovakia, and Germany, as well as between Europe and the Middle East in general. Already, riverboats from Odessa and other Black Sea ports sail to Rotterdam by way of the Danube and the Rhine. Such a waterway would facilitate river traffic down to the Aegean Sea and reduce the cost of transportation between Belgrade and Salonika.

The economic advantages of such an important waterway are obvious. The present distance from Europe to Port Said by way of the Dardanelles or the Adriatic Sea would be reduced by one third, to 2,000 kilometers. As a result Salonika would become an important Europort, a natural gateway of the Balkans to the promising markets of the Middle East. Cities along the Morava River, such as Skopje, Kumanovo, Vranje, Lescovac, Nis, and Svetozareva, would receive developmental benefits from this waterway connecting Salonika with Belgrade.

Land Transportation

A highway from Belgrade, following the Morava and the Vardar rivers, leads to Salonika. Another route from the west, through the mountains to Sofia and the Maritsa River valley, leads to Adrianople (Edirne) and, via the Thracian plateau, to Istanbul. This route, which was an important road during the Roman period, plays a significant role in the transportation network of Balkania, connecting Europe with the Middle East.

Another transportation artery is the highway from Salonika to Bulgaria, Romania, Hungary, Austria (or Czechoslovakia), and Germany. The main problems with this road are that improvements are needed, especially in Romania, where border visas require much time, and that the distance is longer than the traditional route through Yugoslavia. For the development of this alternative route, Greece agreed to improve the route from Salonika to the borders of Bulgaria, and Bulgaria agreed to improve it from the Greek border to that with Romania.

Albania has announced the construction of a rail link between Titgrad, Bar, and the Albanian-Yugoslav border town of Shkodër, which will join the country to the European rail network. Another Albanian line to the Yugoslav border is being built near Lake Ohrid.

Trucking from Europe to the Mideast, via the Balkan countries, has become a profitable operation in recent years. About 180,000 tons of cargo, worth around $300 million, cross the Bosporus bridge every month. However, the frustrations of delays at border crossing points, the charges imposed by some countries on trucks in transit, and related restrictions are increasing rapidly. Turkey charges $800 for each loaded and $200 for each empty truck; Yugoslavia bans truck travel on Sundays; and Bulgarian policemen levy fines at will. In spite of these problems and the hazardous conditions of mountain roads, truckers continue to travel, occasionally bringing their wives and friends with them, making about $1,200 per trip.

SECTORAL INVESTMENT ALLOCATION

Productive resources, including investment, should be allocated among the various sectors or particular industries in such a way that the highest possible production is achieved. The allocation of resources to the most efficient industries improves factor productivity.

From an empirical point of view, the socialist economies of the Balkan countries seem to follow an unbalanced growth process in favor of industry, mainly the capital goods industry (maximum reinvestment criterion).[16] (See Table 6.4.) They also have lower percentages of investment in housing, transport, and services compared with Greece and Turkey. Like all centrally planned economies, they also have relatively high and stable percentages of agricultural investment, whereas developed Western economies have lower and declining farming investment.

High investment rates in housing and low investment rates in manufacturing present serious problems for Greece, and to some extent Turkey, in connection with industrialization, urban concentration, and environmental protection. In recent years development plans containing corrective measures have been introduced, but limited results have been obtained in their implementation. On the other hand, low investment rates in housing in Bulgaria and Romania present serious problems of apartment shortages. Young couples have to wait one or two years for new apartments. In Yugoslavia high rates of investment were channeled into the housing sector during the 1960s and 1970s. Nevertheless, one can

TABLE 6.4

Sectoral Allocation of Investment, Current Market Prices: 1950–59 to 1970–77 (percent of total gross fixed capital formation)

	Agriculture			Industry			Housing			Transport			Services		
	1950 –59	1960 –69	1970 –77	1950 –59	1060 –69	1970 –77	1950 –59	1960 –69	1970 –77	1950 –59	1960 –69	1970 –77	1950 –59	1960 –69	1970 –77
Albania	18	16	n.a.	45	48	n.a.	11	7	n.a.	11	10	n.a.	4	6	n.a.
Bulgaria	29	16	17	43	39	38	2	17	17	8	13	14	12	7	8
Greece	10	12	10	19	20	18	33	28	28	21	23	19	11	12	16
Romania	15	17	16	55	52	55	9	9	7	10	10	11	9	7	8
Turkey	n.a.	15	11	n.a.	32	38	n.a.	21	21	n.a.	16	16	n.a.	16	13
Yugoslavia	9	9	8	42	35	37	10	24	23	18	14	13	15	12	13
Developed economies	9	7	5	20	21	21	24	23	24	16	16	13	12	16	17
Developing economies	9	12	12	15	16	19	17	16	18	18	19	19	9	11	14
Centrally planned economies	15	14	14	43	40	38	14	17	17	11	12	12	10	11	11

n.a. = not available.

Notes: Industry includes mining, manufacturing, and electricity. For Turkey, industry includes construction, and services includes public administration. In some cases fewer years' data were available.

Sources: OECD, *National Accounts,* various issues; United Nations, *Yearbook of National Accounts Statistics,* various issues.

surmise higher percentage shares of investment in housing, primarily in Turkey, because of the underestimation that may occur in villages and remote rural areas where subsistence huts may not be counted.

Investment in mining and quarrying was negligible for all Balkan countries (around 1 percent). Because of oil and mineral shortages, investment shares, as well as costs of mining, are expected to rise in the future.

Sectoral priorities shown in Table 6.4 are visible in the long run. In the short run, however, political and social pressures, employment considerations, shortages of certain goods or services, environmental conditions, and biased developmental targets regarding rural development or urbanization may cause periodic fluctuations and deviations from the long-run trend. Admittedly, the number of sectors should be larger, but information on sectoral or subsectoral investment is limited or unreliable. Furthermore, differences in investment figures for certain years and sectors, especially in housing and services, may arise from statistical definitions rather than developmental considerations.

DIFFERENCES IN SECTORAL CAPITAL/OUTPUT RATIOS

In Chapter 5 national incremental capital/output ratios (ICORs) were considered. However, sectoral ICORs seem to be more useful than entire economy ICORs for projecting capital requirements of different industries. Our objective here is to see whether the sectoral ICORs are sufficiently stable to justify their use in projecting and allocating investment among the different sectors and industries of the Balkan economies.

All sectors of the countries considered have had wide annual variations. This is especially so for agriculture (which is subject to weather conditions), transportation, and housing. In planning, however, annual variations do not matter much because longer, mainly five-year, periods are used. Table 6.5 presents sectoral ICORS for the Balkan countries, compared with those of developed, developing, and centrally planned economies as groups.

For Bulgaria and Yugoslavia sectoral ICORs were relatively low. This indicates that prices of consumer goods increased relatively more than prices of capital goods and made for low ICORs at current prices compared to those at constant prices. As expected, all Balkan countries had high ICORs in transportation and housing. They are capital-intensive sectors, while manufacturing, trade, and other services use proportionally more labor than capital. But this does not mean that it is better to invest more in manufacturing and trade than in trains, buses, or houses. For in order to determine whether investment is more productive in one sector than in another, it is necessary to know the relative contribution of capital to output or income, as well as to know the ICORs. (See also the discussion in Chapter 5.)

The sectoral differences in the ICORs can be due primarily to the differences in the contributions of factors of production to output. Thus, the ICORs

TABLE 6.5

Sectoral ICORs for the Balkan Countries, 1955–77 (constant prices)

	Agriculture		Manufacturing		Transport		Housing		Services	
	1955–70	1971–77	1955–70	1971–77	1955–70	1971–77	1955–70	1971–77	1955–70	1971–77
Albania	2.0	n.a.	3.5	n.a.	n.a.	n.a.	n.a.	n.a.	n.a.	n.a.
Bulgaria	1.7	1.9	1.8	1.4	2.7	4.9	6.9	19.9	0.7	-1.3
Greece	1.9	4.1	2.0	3.0	9.2	9.9	14.9	14.8	1.9	3.1
Romania	8.8	4.3	3.2	3.1	5.9	7.5	8.2	6.3	3.0	5.2
Turkey	3.5	n.a.	2.1	2.9	6.5	n.a.	14.6	11.5	2.1	n.a.
Yugoslavia	1.0	1.0	2.4	1.6	4.3	2.3	4.0	4.4	1.6	1.4
Developed economies	6.5	5.9	2.3	2.8	6.6	6.1	28.3	28.5	2.0	2.6
Developing economies	1.8	1.4	3.4	3.2	8.6	9.1	14.7	16.5	2.0	1.7
Centrally planned economies	2.7	-2.0	2.0	2.3	4.9	5.8	5.8	9.5	4.7	-0.3

n.a. = not available.

Notes: For some sectors fewer years' data were available. For Albania, Bulgaria, Romania, and Yugoslavia, net material product (NMP) instead of GDP; manufacturing includes mining and electricity; housing includes construction. For Bulgaria and Yugoslavia, current prices.

Sources: OECD, *National Accounts,* various issues; United Nations, *Yearbook of National Accounts Statistics,* various issues; Y. Minxhozi, "Thirty Five Years," *New Albania 5* (1979), pp. 5–7.

in transportation and housing are higher than those in agriculture, manufacturing, and trade not because capital is less productive in the former, but because the relative share of capital in the latter is lower. In other words, labor participates more in agriculture, manufacturing, and trade than in transportation and housing. To increase output by a given amount would require less capital in the former industries than in the latter, but it would require more labor.

Thus, the ICOR is not a guide to the profitability or desirability of investment projects because it does not measure the marginal rate of return of capital. For example, if the manufacturing ICOR were stable and equal to 2 (as it was in most postwar five-year periods in the Balkan countries) and the relative contribution of capital to output in manufacturing were 10 percent, the marginal rate of return in this sector would be 5 percent (10/2 = 5). If the ICOR in transportation were also stable and equal to 5 and the relative contribution of capital to output in this sector were 60 percent, the marginal rate of return in transportation would be 12 percent (60/5 = 12), which is higher than that in manufacturing, even though the ICORs were stable in both sectors. Therefore, the constancy of the capital/output ratio might mislead policy makers to project investment uneconomically, in terms of marginal rate of return.

The practical planners, however, would be interested more in social or economy-wide productivity of capital rather than in encouraging development of one sector merely because its marginal rate of return of capital happened to be high. The consideration of the relative contribution of capital investment to output along with the ICOR is not necessarily a serious restriction on the usefulness of the ICOR when it is used simply to determine capital requirements. But it is a severe qualification if capital "requirements" so determined are taken to suggest investment that may be expected to be "profitable" or productive.

In sectors like manufacturing and transportation, where ICORs are relatively stable, extrapolated tends can be used for projections with some degree of caution.[17] Mutatis mutandis, these ICORs can also be extrapolated to other sectors and particular industries without historical data. Some flexibility and some alternative sets of estimates with different possible targets might be helpful in economic projections. Deviations are always possible, and projected ICORs must be subject to modifications during the implementation of economic plans.

SECTORAL LABOR AND PRODUCT TRANSFORMATION

The process of economic development is associated with a gradual transformation of labor and resources from agriculture to industry and services. It has also been proven statistically that there is an inverse correlation between the agricultural labor force and per capita income;[18] that is, as per capita income increases with economic development, the agricultural labor force declines, while that of industry and services increases. This is true for all the Balkan countries, as Table 6.6 shows.

TABLE 6.6

Sectoral Distribution of the Labor Force in the Balkans, 1960 and 1978
(percent)

	Agriculture		Industry		Services	
	1960	1978	1960	1978	1960	1978
Albania	71	62	18	24	11	14
Bulgaria	56	40	25	38	19	22
Greece	56	39	20	28	24	33
Romania	64	50	21	31	15	19
Turkey	78	60	11	14	11	26
Yugoslavia	63	33	18	32	19	35

Source: World Bank, *World Development Report, 1980* (New York: Oxford University Press, 1980), p. 147.

In all Balkan countries the percentages of the labor force in agriculture are far higher (varying from 33 to 40 percent in Bulgaria, Greece, and Yugoslavia, 50 percent in Romania, and 60-62 percent in Turkey and Albania in 1978) than in the industrialized countries (6 percent) and other centrally planned economies, mainly the Soviet Union (17 percent). In the services sector, however, the percentages of the labor force are lower (varying from 14 percent in Albania, 19 percent in Romania, 22 percent in Bulgaria, 26 percent in Turkey, 33 percent in Greece) compared with industrialized countries (55 percent) and other centrally planned economies. In the industrial sector the northern Balkan countries (Bulgaria, Romania, and Yugoslavia) have high percentages of labor, equal or close to those of the advanced countries (31 to 43 percent); Greece, Albania, and Turkey have lower percentages (28, 24, and 14, respectively).

The movement of labor from agriculture to services in Greece, Turkey, and Yugoslavia seems to be faster than from agriculture to industry because of the simpler requirements in the services sector. Such movement, therefore, seems not to be sequential from agriculture to industry and then to services, as was customary in developed countries, but simultaneous, or with higher percentages of labor going from agriculture to services than to industries. Similar movements probably would have taken place in Albania, Bulgaria, and Romania if labor mobility were not planned and controlled by the government.

It must be pointed out, however, that the figures in agriculture are overstated, while those in services are understated in all Balkan countries, particularly in Greece and Turkey. A large number of people reported as being in agriculture are engaged in operations, such as trading and other personal and community services, that are not agricultural. This is true especially during dormant seasons, when people work in spinning, clothmaking, entertainment, and other handicraft/tertiary labor. Such multioperational activities vary from country to country, and make regional and international comparisons difficult.

Greece and Turkey, with less industry than their northern neighbors, have relatively more middlemen and self-employed persons. In Greece, for example, some 60 percent of the active population is self-employed, primarily in trade and similar occupations. This is due mainly to limited opportunities for well-paid jobs in industry and other sectors offering steady work. Such a situation may present problems for effective cooperation with other countries or implementation of long-term social measures to increase productive employment. The existence of proportionally large numbers of short-run jobs in services creates uncertainty, and perpetuates an economy vulnerable to domestic and international disturbances of all kinds. Emigration from Greece, Turkey, and Yugoslavia, mainly to West Germany, helps diminish the severity of the problem of surplus labor and disrupts what John Kenneth Galbraith calls the poverty equilibrium in the poor sectors and regions. At the same time it helps to relieve the recipient country's labor shortage.

Additional support for a gradual transformation from the agricultural sector to the industrial and services sectors is offered by Table 6.7, which shows the

TABLE 6.7

Sectoral Production as Percentages of Total GDP, 1950–78

	Bulgaria	Greece	Romania	Turkey	Yugoslavia
Agriculture					
1950	30	34	34	49	32
1960	32	23	33	41	24
1978	18	17	16	27	16
Industry					
1950	34	20	44	12	42
1960	53	26	44	21	45
1978	64	31	61	28	45
Trade, other services					
1950	25	32	18	29	14
1960	15	51	11	38	31
1978	18	52	7	45	39

Note: In some cases data close to the above years were used.

Sources: United Nations, Statistical Yearbook, various issues; World Bank, World Development Report, 1979 (New York: Oxford University Press, 1979), p. 725, and 1980 (New York: Oxford University Press, 1980), p. 115.

TABLE 6.8

Average Annual Rates of GDP Growth, by Sector, in the Balkan Countries, 1950-78
(constant prices)

	Albania	Bulgaria	Greece	Romania	Turkey	Yugoslavia
Agriculture						
1950–60	4.9	5.4	4.4	3.5	4.1	5.6
1960–70	4.6	1.2	3.5	1.2	2.4	3.3
1970–78	6.4	1.3	1.9	5.5	3.9	3.3
Industry						
1950–60	20.4	11.5	7.8	12.7	5.9	10.7
1960–70	9.5	11.2	9.4	13.0	9.4	6.3
1970–78	7.7	8.4	5.3	12.6	8.8	8.0
Construction						
1950–60	14.5	11.1	10.2	13.4	8.1	6.5
1960–70	5.8	10.9	7.5	8.7	7.3	7.8
1970–78	n.a.	6.3	-0.4	9.5	6.1	5.6
Transportation						
1950–60	19.7	13.3	5.7	11.3	9.9	8.4
1960–70	5.2	11.6	8.6	10.5	8.7	6.4
1970–78	n.a.	12.7	7.1	12.8	9.3	4.7
Trade and other services						
1950–60	11.2	9.3	5.3	1.4	6.7	9.5
1960–70	4.7	6.2	7.1	-0.7	7.0	6.9
1970–78	n.a.	4.8	5.7	n.a.	7.9	4.0

n.a. = not available.

Notes: For Albania, Bulgaria, and Romania, NMP instead of GDP. In some cases fewer years' data were used.

Sources: OECD, *National Accounts*, various issues; United Nations, *Yearbook of National Accounts Statistics*, various issues; United Nations, *World Economic Survey, 1977 and 1978* (New York: United Nations, 1978 and 1979); World Bank, *World Development Report 1980* (New York: Oxford University Press, 1980), p. 113.

sectoral share of GDP between 1950 and 1978. The agricultural sector accounted for more than 30 percent of the GDP in all Balkan countries in 1950, but declined to 18 percent or less in 1978, except for Turkey (27 percent). The industrial sector kept growing in all these countries: 45 percent in Yugoslavia, 61 in Romania, and 64 percent in Bulgaria in 1978. However, in Greece (31 percent) and Turkey (28 percent) it was far less.

The relative shares of construction and of transportation in the GDP was around 10 percent or less for all countries considered. Some unevenness can be observed in the services sector, though. While the share of services in GDP was large and rapidly growing in the market economies of Greece, Turkey, and (to some extent) Yugoslavia, in the centrally planned economies of Romania, Bulgaria, and Albania it was small and almost constant or declining throughout the postwar years. These findings indicate that planned economies, in general, downgrade trade and other consumer services in favor of industry, especially heavy industry.

From these empirical findings it can be seen that agriculture is the weak sector of the developmental process. Even in the controlled or planned economies its share keeps declining. Expansion in industry and/or services seems to be important because both these sectors utilize labor, radiate stimuli throughout the economy, and improve living conditions. That is why the movement of labor and other resources from the laggard sectors and regions to the more productive ones is expected to continue in the foreseeable future. Care should be taken, however, to avoid extensive backwash effects upon traditional crafts and small-scale enterprises during the transformation period. Furthermore, such an expansion needs to be complemented by a simultaneous increase in agricultural productivity so that needed food and raw materials can be provided. Such trends of sectoral and regional transformation present common problems that require similar policies and closer cooperation among the countries considered.

The annual rates of growth of GDP in industry, during the postwar years, were far higher than those in agriculture for all Balkan countries, as Table 6.8 shows. The rates of growth of transportation and construction were also high, particularly in the 1950s, while the growth rates of services were comparatively higher in Greece, Turkey, and Yugoslavia than in Albania, Bulgaria, and Romania in the 1960s and 1970s.

NOTES

1. To reduce the gap between rich and poor regions, a number of policies have been used in different countries. The terms "pilot zones," "program regions," "pilot regions," "planning spaces," and "focal point of growth" have been used to indicate the implementation of regional development policies. See F. Perroux, "Economic Space: Theory and Applications," *Quarterly Journal of Economics*, February 1950; also a number of related articles in D. McKee, R. Dean, and W. Leahy, eds., *Regional Economics* (New York: Free Press, 1970); G. Myrdal, *Rich Lands and Poor* (New York: Harper and Row, 1957); D. Salvatore, "The Operation of the Market Mechanism and Regional Inequality," *Kyklos* 3 (1972): 518-36.

2. See, for example, H. Myint, *Economic Theory and the Underdeveloped Countries* (New York: Oxford University Press, 1971), pp. 315-18. C. Furtado, *Development and Underdevelopment* (Los Angeles: University of California Press, 1967), states that technological and wage-rate differences are preserving static dualism.

3. Even though such questions became important in the 1950s and later, earlier writers dealt, to some extent, with similar questions. The mercantilists stressed the foreign-trade sector; the Physiocrats and Adam Smith stressed the agricultural sector, for surplus food

production to support industrial workers; and Malthus placed emphasis on the industrial sector, which was characterized by increasing returns. Friedrich List, on the other hand, advocated a balanced growth among agriculture, manufacturing, and commerce, and wanted the state to bring this balance into existence. Recently, Rosenstein Rodan, R. Nurkse, W. Lewis, T. Skitovsky, V. Bhatt, and P. Yotopoulos and J. Nugent seem also to support the balanced-growth argument. N. Gianaris, *Economic Development: Thought and Problems* (North Quincy, Mass.: Christopher Publishing House, 1978), ch. 4.

4. A Hirschman, P. Streeten, H. Singer, N. Buchanan and H. Ellis, P. Alpert, P. Ohlin, and H. Chenery seem to support unbalanced growth. For a comparative analysis see H. Chenery and L. Taylor, "Development Patterns: Among Countries and over Time," *Review of Economics and Statistics*, November 1968, pp. 391-416.

5. Empirically, manufacturing was found to be a high-linkage sector, deserving priority over agriculture and services. P. Yotopoulos and J. Nugent, "A Balanced Growth Version of the Linkage Hypothesis: A Test," *Quarterly Journal of Economics*, May 1973, pp. 157-71.

6. See, for example, Myrdal, op. cit., ch. 3; A. Hirschman, *The Strategy of Economic Development* (New Haven: Yale University Press, 1958), p. 189.

7. For an extensive review see Gianaris, op. cit., chs. 10, 11.

8. For additional data on Bulgaria and Greece, see related statistics in N. Mouselis, *Modern Greece* (London: Macmillan, 1979), ch. 5; and his article "Ellada, Vulgaria, kai to Kinima tou Agrotismou" (Greece, Bulgaria, and the Agricultural Movement) in *To Vema* (Athens), May 14, 16, and 17, 1978.

9. A. Tsantis and R. Pepper, *Romania: The Industrialization of an Agrarian Economy Under Socialist Planning* (Washington, D.C.: World Bank, 1979), p. 229.

10. V. Dubey, *Yugoslavia: Development with Decentralization* (Baltimore: Johns Hopkins University Press, 1975), pp. 152-56.

11. J. Tomasevich, *Peasants, Politics and Economic Change in Yugoslavia* (Stanford, Calif.: Stanford University Press, 1955), p. 638.

12. Evidence that the existing medium-size manufacturing firms in Greece (employing up to 499 persons) are the most efficient units is offered by Kaliope Nikolaou, *Inter-Size Efficiency Differentials in Greek Manufacturing* (Athens: Center of Planning and Economic Research, 1978), pp. 168-69. For the high reliance of industry on imports of capital goods and raw materials, and the weak links between the different sectors of the Greek economy, see N. Vernadakis, *Econometric Models for the Developing Economies: A Case Study of Greece* (New York: Praeger, 1978), p. 130.

13. For example, the slowdown in productivity growth in the United States during the 1970s is attributed to relatively low output in services, low capital/labor ratio, and restrictive government regulations. *The Economist*, July 26, 1980, p. 14.

14. For further information see I. Tzoannou, *Elliniki Emporiki Naftilia kai EOK* (Greek Merchant Shipping and the EEC) (Athens: Institute of Economic and Industrial Studies, 1977), chs. 1, 3.

15. The distance from Salonika to the Danube is 648 kilometers, 575 in Yugoslavia and 73 in Greece.

16. The reinvestment criterion, emphasizing investment in industries producing equipment, machinery, and related capital goods (input for input), is also suggested for less developed countries confronted with the takeoff into the self-sustained growth stage of industrial development. W. Galenson and H. Leibenstein, "Investment Criteria, Productivity and Economic Development," *Quarterly Journal of Economics*, August 1955, pp. 363-70; M. Dobb, *Economic Growth and Planning* (London: Routledge and Kegan Paul, 1960), pp. 65, 73.

17. For the measurement of sectoral ICOR slopes, with regressions of GDP on cumulative investment for Greece and other countries, see N. Gianaris, "International Differences in Capital Output Ratios," *American Economic Review*, June 1970, pp. 465-77. For

comparisons of planned and actual ICORs in a number of sectors and countries, see Gianaris's "Projecting Capital Requirements in Development Planning," *Socio-Economic Planning Sciences* 8 (1974): 65–76.

18. S. Kuznets, "Toward a Theory of Economic Growth," in R. Lekachman, ed., *National Policy for Economic Welfare at Home and Abroad* (New York: Doubleday, 1955); N. Gianaris, *Economic Development: Thought and Problems*, pp. 202–06.

PART III
Foreign Trade and
Economic Cooperation

INTRODUCTION TO PART III

The following chapters deal with intra-Balkan and foreign trade and investment, as well as the advantages and difficulties of closer cooperation (and possibly regional integration) among the countries of the Balkan Peninsula. The facts that the Balkan Peninsula stands as a bridge between Europe and the Middle East, and that there is a growing need for mutual trade and intrabloc resource utilization, bring these countries closer together.

The questions posed are the following: Can Balkan countries with different economic systems and many ethnic groups achieve closer cooperation and eventual economic integration? Given that Bulgaria and Romania are members of Comecon, Greece a member of the EEC, and Turkey an associate member of the EEC, can initiatives for closer relations among them be successful?

Modern technology of mass production, better investment opportunities, and the expansion of multinational corporations require large markets and big enterprises. These factors point to the need for reduction of trade restrictions and improvement in economic relations among neighboring countries in the Balkans and, possibly, other eastern Mediterranean countries.

Despite periodic disagreements and skepticism, indications exist that the Balkan countries are moving from the stage of isolation to that of mutual cooperation and common developmental policies, which tend to submerge ideological and territorial differences among them and to prepare the ground for eventual "convergence."

7

INTRA-BALKAN AND
FOREIGN TRADE

FOREIGN TRADE

During the years immediately after the war, the socialist Balkan and east European countries had little choice but to trade with one another, mainly because of the prevailing cold war between East and West. However, the gradual warming of the cold war brought about a step-by-step increase in trade between East and West, and between the northern and southern Balkan countries. In recent years the increase in the intra-Balkan trade has been remarkable, some of it at the expense of trade within the socialist bloc. Joint ventures have already started or are being considered for implementation.

Intrabloc trade may impose costs upon the Balkan countries insofar as it means trade diversion. Moreover, the grouping of a number of countries in a protective arrangement may make the poor poorer and the rich richer, unless the more advanced countries are willing to run the risk of slowing their own trade and growth in favor of their poorer partners. However, the beneficial effects of intrabloc trade on the balance of payments, terms of trade, industrialization, and economic growth of the countries involved may be expected to be higher than the detrimental effects of trade diversion. That is, trade creation will most probably exceed trade destruction as a result of closer cooperation.

Regional trade among the EEC countries, for example, accounts for approximately 55 percent of their total exports, while trade among the Comecon countries accounts for about 60 percent of their total exports. The annual increase of trade in the EEC during the 1960s and early 1970s was about 8 percent, compared with 3 percent for the socialist countries. While international trade tripled in value, that between the EEC countries increased more than six times.

In any case, the creation and strengthening of regional markets among the Balkan countries does not imply renouncing the development of trade with non-Balkan countries. There seems to be no contradiction between the two. On

138

the contrary, the development of regional trade seems to be complementary to free trade in general.

In similar groupings of less developed countries, particularly in Latin America, the growth of mutual trade in manufactured goods has been slower than similar sales to the rest of the world. What we can expect in the Balkan countries, however, is a gradual increase of mutual trade in manufactured and other products, depending on the degree of specialization, economic cooperation, and customs accommodations. Historical, political, and nationalistic factors do not seem to favor rapid growth of trade in the area. What is definitely favorable to closer economic links is the geographical position of these countries, which facilitates land and sea transportation and joint investment ventures, as well as the differences in factor specialization.

A serious problem in the effort to achieve closer cooperation among these countries may be the degree of flexibility on industrial location, possibilities for subsidization, and a fair distribution of gains or losses from investment and trade transactions. There is a danger that the more industrialized northern Balkan countries would dominate Greece and Turkey in industrial production. The fact that half of the national product of Yugoslavia, Romania, and Bulgaria comes from industry, compared with only about one-fourth in the case of Greece and Turkey, means that the latter may face difficult problems in their efforts to speed up industrialization. The increase in imports of machinery and other industrial products by Greece and Turkey from their northern neighbors would prevent these countries from establishing their own industries in such products. This would mean less employment and income for them, as well as an increasingly unfavorable balance of trade. However, if the countries are complementary (in many aspects) in terms of production, close cooperation and the creation of customs unions would be beneficial for all of them, despite the differences in their degree of industrialization.

Another problem that may appear in the process of trying to obtain a closer economic cooperation among these countries with different systems, is the pricing of goods and services. Is the price system based on the average cost of production? Do prices include returns to nonlabor inputs, on the basis of "productivity" and costs of environmental protection? If they involve "full cost plus a markup," are they analogous to capitalist cost plus "surplus value"? In many cases even intra-Comecon trade is based on brute bargaining power or on political considerations, ignoring world market prices and relative production costs as bases for exchange ratios. Price and exchange controls, familiar in the Balkan planned economies, suppress inflation at the macro level (and more so at the micro level), and lead to the involuntary holding of excess amounts of money by the working people because there are limited amounts of goods, whether domestic or foreign, at official prices.

For the high rates of growth to continue and closer cooperation to be achieved, price disparities among the Balkan countries should be avoided and policies of regional balance adopted. However, one should not expect miracles, because it takes a considerable amount of time and effort for changes to be implemented, especially in the Balkan countries, with their great differences in political and economic philosophies.

Usually the planners in Bulgaria and Romania, as well as in other planned economies, overestimate the expected amounts of exports. They suffer from a salability or ex ante illusion, which leads to ex post deficits in the balance of trade, and consequently to a further reduction in the values of their currencies. As a result their currencies are not acceptable in other countries, and the official exchange rates serve only as units of account and not as real prices. Low quality, limited choice, poor marketing, and high cost are some of the characteristics of their commodities that make exports less demanded and imports more attractive. Their "fault" planning may result in a seller's market domestically, which cannot be extended abroad. Relaxation of controls and acceptance of free trade transactions by the policy makers probably would eliminate their "terms of trade" illusion and improve the foreign trade position of their countries, as has happened in the market economies with overvalued currencies. But all these measures require structural changes in the "systems of unequal exchanges" to adjust cost to international prices and to stimulate managerial and technological innovations. For these reasons and in order to raise productivity in general, the policy makers try to get associated technology rather than pure capital inflows from abroad—that is, they prefer "joint" capital-cum-technology.

Trade among the Balkan countries is based primarily on bilateral agreements. This is the system of clearings, according to which two countries agree on the amount of mutual transactions. In this case the value of exports would be equal to the value of imports between two countries for a specified number of years, and there would be no need for the use of hard currency by either country. Such equilibrating clearings offer many economic advantages for the less industrialized countries of Greece and Turkey in the sale of their agricultural products in exchange for machinery and other industrial products. At the same time the northern Balkan countries enter the markets of Greece and Turkey to sell their products, in which they have a comparative advantage.

Clearing arrangements based on bilateral trade of equal exports and imports give each participant country the opportunity to sell goods that cannot easily be disposed of in other free markets. This is important for Greece and Turkey, which can sell to east European countries such agricultural products as lemons, oranges, raisins, grapes, olive oil, cotton, and tobacco, as well as bauxite, iron sheets, raw leather, and similar raw materials, for which demand in west European countries is not satisfactory. Such clearings are being abolished in Greece, first, because of its entrance into the European Economic Community, and second, because Eastern planned economies do not seem to want such clearings any more. Yugoslavia and the Soviet Union have already stopped using them and have entered into free trade tranactions; Bulgaria abolished clearings with Greece as of January 1981 and contemplates their abolition with other countries. However, Albania and Romania want to remain under the system of clearings, for the time being.

The recent desire of the east European countries to abolish the clearing system and introduce free trade in their transactions would probably work against Greece and Turkey, since they are expected to import industrial goods without a proportional increase in exports of their agricultural goods. This would mean increasing deficits in the balance of trade for these two economies, on top of the already large deficits they have with the advanced market economies, particularly those of the European Common Market. Such trade deficits would have undesirable effects on the international position of the currencies of these two countries, and eventually on their domestic economic conditions in terms of income and employment.

Turkey's currency is already in a very weak position. It has been devalued in recent years, and is expected to experience further devaluations, mainly because of continued pressure on the balance of payments. This is so because of the increasing gap in the trade balance that is not covered by invisible sources (remittances from emigrants to Western countries, tourism, and other similar sources).

Greece also has a great and growing deficit in its balance of trade, mainly with the EEC countries. But surpluses in tourism and shipping services, emigrant remittances and deposits, and investment in foreign currencies cover the trade deficit. However, as the deficit becomes larger, there is a growing pressure for devaluation of the drachma. Such currency devaluations in the Balkans may reach the stage of undercutting other countries by grabbing export markets, a possibility that indicates the need for further cooperation.

Under the system of free trade, each country is free to choose the products it desires. This would lead, most probably, to more pressures on the agricultural sector of Greece and Turkey, which provides the bulk of exports. These countries, therefore, cannot escape the undesirable results that developing countries face: producing and exporting mainly primary products with low income elasticities. Furthermore, abolition of clearings would mean not only a reduction in the quantity of agricultural exports to east European countries (which at times resell them to third countries when they do not use them) but a possible reduction in prices as well.

Under free trade the Eastern buyers may force prices even lower because they hold a monopsonistic position in certain products, while Greece and Turkey operate under competitive conditions with other Mediterranean countries. Perhaps the demand from Eastern countries for bauxite and other metals, as well as cotton and (to a limited extent) light manufacturing products, could increase, but demand for citrus fruits and tobacco might decrease. This would mean prolonged hardship for the producers of such products in Greece and Turkey because it takes time to change from production of citrus fruits to soybeans, for example, for which demand in foreign markets is high. In such a case the budgets of these two countries would have to provide for additional agricultural subsidies to avoid rapid decline in the exports of related products.

And alternative way out of the dilemma of abolishing clearing arrangements and avoiding declines in agricultural exports for Greece and Turkey would be to create trading or export companies similar to those in Japan and (to some extent) in Germany. Established public and semipublic corporations or production and marketing cooperatives in these two countries, as well as private enterprises, can undertake such foreign-trade operations with other Balkan and east European countries. Some of the advantages of such companies might be the following:

1. They involve less bureaucracy and more efficiency than the governmental clearing arrangements.

2. They would promote better understanding and trade coordination with their counterparts in the Eastern planned economies because of their similar structure and organization.

3. They provide an effective way of coordinating policies with the EEC, members of which have already entered into trading agreements with the Comecon countries through such companies.

4. They make possible a more effective bargaining position for trading products in which they specialize. From time to time they can negotiate mutual trading in products that could not be exchanged under free trade conditions. For example they can argue "If you want us to buy such and such machines at those prices, you have to buy such and such of our agricultural products at predetermined prices."

A serious problem for Greece and Turkey in trading with their northern neighbors, as well as with any other planned economy, is the monopsonistic nature of imports by these controlled economies. There is the advantage of stability in such markets, but there is the great disadvantage of abrupt changes in trade policy, mainly because of noneconomic considerations in the bargaining and trading process. As long as trading decisions may ignore the demands of the consumers and arbitrarily change, the flow and the size of exports to one or a group of controlled economies is uncertain. Increase of trade with such countries seems to depend more on the promotion of friendly governmental relations than on marketing and sales promotion.

The total or partial abolition of clearings (where a certain portion of exchanges may be in kind) is expected to increase the economic, and decrease the noneconomic, considerations in foreign trade among these countries. Moreover, free trade and payments in hard currencies would make them first-class customers to each other, instead of keeping them in the unfavorable position where each country tries to dump its unwanted products on the other. Under such conditions the Balkan countries can play a more effective role in promoting trade between EEC and Comecon and, more important, as a bridge between Europe and the Middle East.

The existing big enterprises in Greece and Turkey are mainly family-owned oligopolies. They may enjoy comfortable rates of profit under protection imposed, in many cases, for the support of small companies. These businesses may neglect innovative activities. Under these conditions such "sleeping" firms may face difficult problems when exposed to greater competition as a result of closer cooperation with EEC or Comecon countries.

A large majority of enterprises in these two countries consists of small or middle-size companies. It seems that the middle-size companies are efficient, while the small ones must depend on overworked family members and are in operation solely because of protection. In order to survive foreign competition, it would be advisable that they group themselves into larger economic units. Then, through better organization and production planning, they could achieve economies of scale and lower costs.

Such groups may take the form of holding companies or production cooperatives, depending on the competitive organizations they are expected to face in international markets. An adjustment period of a few years may be required for these small companies to organize and prepare themselves for the expected challenge from northern Balkan and other enterprises. Such companies are mainly in the canning, fats, glass, electrical, cosmetics, rubber, and ceramic industries.

INTERREGIONAL TRADE AND INVESTMENT

Although interregional relations among Balkan countries are not yet ready for a customs union, closer trade ties are possible and desirable. It seems that the fears and suspicions that prevail among these nations, including Albania, which is usually overlooked in regional studies, are political or psychological rather than economic. Economic relations may be considered as the means of breaking such political and psychological barriers, which may be stronger among these nations than between them and other big international competitors. Furthermore, the size of the market is, and must be, a decisive factor in policy considerations for trade and investment expansion.

It should not be overlooked that there may be obstacles to closer cooperation because of fear of future competition resulting from technological transformation and assimilation. Thus, the Greek agro-industrial enterprise Aegean refused to accept a Bulgarian order for machinery used in the processing of raisins. The main reason was the fear that Bulgarian engineers would become familiar with the technology involved.

Expected competition, especially in exported products, is an additional obstacle to closer ties among the Balkans. Already there is strong price and quality competition among Greece, Turkey, and (to some extent) Bulgaria in grapes, wine, and tobacco. It may be suggested that instead of working to establish a customs union, in the very near future it may be better for these countries to work to create a sound basis for economic integration, with emphasis on joint investment; later they can proceed toward economic unification. Joint investment ventures can proceed pari passu with closer trade cooperation in products that are complementary in the Balkan economies.

It seems that developed countries at more or less the same stage of development and with industries enjoying high rates of protection can successfully create customs unions and eventually integrate their economies. The Balkan countries, however, have neither developed nor underdeveloped economies. They can be classified as being at the semideveloped level of the self-sustained stage of growth. Although there are differences in the degree of industrialization, with Greece and Turkey being less industrialized than their northern neighbors, they have roughly the same per capita income (with the exception of Albania and Turkey, which are at a lower level), if allowances are made for cheap housing, free medical protection, and other social services in the planned Balkan economies. Such economic homogeneity may be advantageous for further cooperation. Furthermore, the fact that these countries have had political and territorial differences in the past, mainly over Macedonia, Dobnya and Epirus, has prevented the fullest development of trade among them. The gradual abolition of such differences would show in what products each country has comparative cost advantages, so that greater regional specialization and higher levels of production can be obtained.

In the past almost all Balkan countries have stressed outward trade instead of relying on inward or intra-Balkan trade. The main reasons for such an outward-looking policy include the following:

1. Political and territorial differences and suspicions have prohibited expansion of trade among the Balkan nations.

2. Specialization in the production and export to developed nations of mainly primary products by almost all the Balkan nations has not allowed a satisfactory growth of intra-Balkan transactions.

3. Ideological and structural differences have not permitted mutual investments and joint ventures.

However, a significant degree of differentiation and diversification in the production process has taken place in recent years. As a result there is some degree of specialization in different products and emphasis in different sectors. An obvious difference on a sectoral level is the greater emphasis on industrialization by the northern Balkan planned economies and that on services by the southern market economies of Greece and Turkey. Such differences in specialization offer fertile grounds for further increase in intra-Balkan trade. The fact that Bulgaria, Romania, and to some extent Yugoslavia were for a long time exporting their products primarily to the Comecon planned economies, and Greece and Turkey mainly to Western market economies, suggests that some degree of specialization has been developed. Therefore, complementary trading and joint ventures may be expected to increase in the foreseeable future.

The proposed establishment of an Intra-Balkan Chamber of Commerce and Industry (ICCI) would benefit all the countries involved. It could promote more trade and tourism, solve problems of trariffs and transportation, and arrange the establishment and operation of joint ventures among the member nations. Such joint investment ventures might include the production of bauxite, uranium, copper, and other metals, especially in border areas of Bulgaria, Greece, and Yugoslavia. They may even include atomic power plants like those already operating in Bulgaria. The promotion of more trade and investment among the Balkan countries, in turn, would make their exports more independent than relying on the economic conditions of one or a few countries in the West or in the East. (For the relationship of exports, investment, GDP, and the productivity of labor in the Balkan countries, see Tables 4 and 5 and equation [2] in the Appendix.) This would be particularly important for Greece, Turkey, and Yugoslavia, whose exports depend heavily on the market conditions of West Germany.

The expected abolition of "clearings" or bilateral agreements between Balkan countries and the introduction of multilateral trade would bring about adjustment of production and trade toward complementary commodities, so that greater efficiency, cheaper production, and a healthier basis for long-term trade would be created among the nations of that area. Such trade liberalization would eventually show in which fields and commodities each country has comparative advantages, so that production and intra-Balkan trade could be improved. This would indicate which factors are complementary, where closer cooperation might be fruitful, and whether eventual unification would be preferable as an alternative to free international trade or national isolation and autarky. The establishment of intra-Balkan institutions or cartels in sectors such as transportation, manufacturing, agriculture, tourism, and other services might then be needed to coordinate and promote trade and investment, thereby creating economic ties that would be difficult to break because of political or other differences.

Although the present trade among the Balkan countries is a small proportion (about 6 percent) of their total foreign trade, the trend is positive. As Figure 7.1 shows, all countries considered significantly increased their exports to each other. Exports from Bulgaria and Yugoslavia to Romania and vice versa increased by four times or more during the 1970s. The same thing can be said for the increase of Greek exports to Albania, Bulgaria, and particularly Romania, where a rise of more than six times occurred. Also impressive was the growth of exports from Turkey to Romania (from $4 to $74 million, 1970-78) and its imports from Romania (from $8 to $174 million) and Bulgaria (from $4 to $22 million during 1970-78). Trade between Turkey and Greece, Yugoslavia, and Albania did not increase as significantly as among the other countries.

High rates in growth of trade can be observed among the Balkan countries and the other Comecon countries. Greece, for example, increased its exports to Comecon by more than three times (from 3 to more than 10 billion drachmas) during the 1970s. Lemons, peaches, apricots, grapes, cherries, strawberries, and similar products in their original form or in cans are prominent in Greek exports

FIGURE 7.1

**Exports Among Balkan Countries, 1970–78
(F.O.B., million U.S. dollars)**

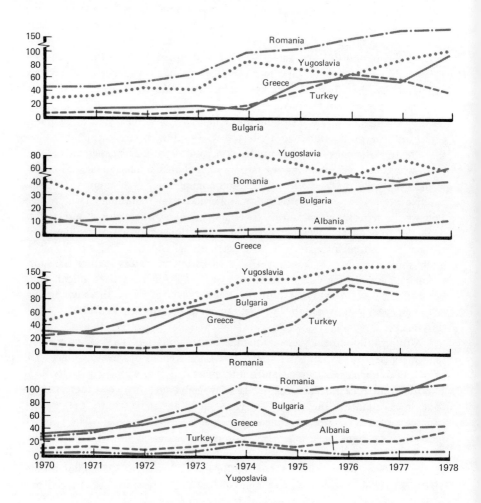

Source: United Nations, *Yearbook of International Trade Statistics*, various issues.

to the east European economies, which absorb about two-thirds of the total exports of these products.

In 1980 Bulgaria signed an agreement with Turkey to export some 50 million kilowatts of electricity per month, with the provision to increase such exports later. Similar agreements were concluded between Bulgaria and Greece on matters of trade, transportation, communications, electricity, and other infrastructural and cultural projects. Bulgaria, along with other Balkan planned economies, produces relatively large amounts of electricity, mainly from hydroelectric projects and atomic reactors. Similar atomic reactors are projected to be established in Turkey (at Mersin) and eventually in Greece.

The centrally planned economies of the northern Balkans realized that the policy of autarky is detrimental to technological modernization and long-term economic development. Opening their borders to more international trade and investment means not only selling more of their products to other countries but also importing new products, new techniques, and new methods of production. On the other hand, the market economies of Greece and Turkey may import from their Balkan neighbors not only cheaper products but also some new methods of collective production. Such methods may include the construction of man-made lakes (useful for irrigation), the planting of new forests, and even the setting up of pilot cities so widespread in Yugoslavia and especially in Bulgaria.

Growth of Foreign Trade

All Balkan countries export mostly primary commodities and import mainly machinery and fuel. As expected, therefore, their terms of trade—the price index of exports over the price index of imports—are deteriorating. For example, for Yugoslavia the terms-of-trade ratio was 98 in 1978 (1970 = 100); for Greece, 93; and for Turkey, as low as 71. As long as they are not expected to export oil, the price of which continues to increase, these nations should try to achieve higher industrialization in order to improve their terms of trade as well as their employment conditions. There seems to be a trend in that direction, but there is still a long way to go. Thus, the percentage share of primary commodity exports (except fuels and metals) declined from 45 in 1960 to 20 in 1977 for Yugoslavia, from 81 to 36 for Greece, from 89 to 67 for Turkey, and from 75 to 34 for Bulgaria. For Romania it was 20, and for Albania, 26 percent in 1977.[1]

The quantitative goals in the Balkan planned economies take precedence over qualitative goals, and products are distributed by the plan rather than sold in the market. A similar problem appears with regard to foreign transactions, where foreign importers or exporters are not competing with domestic enterprises. Thus, disruptions of the plans are avoided. The phenomenon of the "terms of trade" illusion, experienced in market economies with overvalued currencies, also occurs in these planned economies, and their short-run exports may not increase as much as they could without such an illusion.[2]

About 50 percent of the exports of Bulgaria and Romania go to other socialist economies—a significant decline from more than 80 percent in the early 1950s—around 15-25 percent to Western developed countries, and the rest to developing countries.[3] The reverse is true for Greece and Turkey, which export about 10 percent to the centrally planned economies, 20 percent to developing nations, and the rest (more than 55 percent) to the other developed countries.

A large portion of the export earnings of these countries is used to pay their foreign debt, which is about 10 percent of GDP. In 1977, Turkey paid 11 percent of such earnings to service its external debt, Greece paid 10 percent, and Yugoslavia paid 7 percent. As a result the reserves of these countries declined rapidly. In Turkey, for example, they were reduced from $2.12 billion in 1973 to only $0.77 billion in 1977. In Turkey, external public debt increased from $1.9 billion in 1970 to $6.2 billion in 1978. In Greece it increased from $0.9 billion in 1970 to $3.1 billion in 1978, and in Yugoslavia, from $1.2 billion in 1970 to $3.5 billion in 1978.[4]

Centrally planned Balkan economies, like all east European economies, are desperately in need of Western hard currency. This desperation became obvious after the Soviet Union sharply increased its concessionary oil prices and asked its client states to turn to the Middle East for crude oil and gas. The Soviet Union pegs its oil prices to the average prices charged by Kuwait over the most recent five-year period (the Bucharest Formula). This means that oil prices will continue to increase, and trade deficits to grow, for the Balkan countries.

The northern Balkan countries had managed to industrialize themselves before the oil crisis, but now they need more oil to keep the machines running, and to avoid stagnation and even economic decline. Moreover, the relative prices of their exports to the West have started to fall and more hard currency will be needed to pay for imports, particularly from the EEC countries, from which they expect favorable tariff arrangements.

Table 3 of the Appendix shows total imports and exports in U.S. dollars for all Balkan countries. Greece, Turkey, and Yugoslavia had large deficits in their balance of trade, as did Albania; while Bulgaria and Romania had, almost in every year, a balanced account of imports and exports, during the period 1955-79. The average annual growth rate of exports and imports was around 10 percent in 1970-78 for Bulgaria and Romania, and close to 5 percent for Yugoslavia. However, for Turkey it was 8 percent for imports and only 2.5 percent for exports, while for Greece it was 6 percent for imports and as high as 13 percent for exports. Thus, there was a considerable improvement from the 1960-70 period, especially in textiles and other manufactured products exported primarily to capital-surplus oil countries.[5] Comparatively speaking, the percentage share of food and other primary commodities in total imports declined significantly from 1960 to 1977, but that of manufacturing increased moderately and that of fuels considerably, particularly for Turkey (from 11 to 26 percent).

There is considerable evidence that sustained economic growth requires a structural transformation toward an increase in the share of industry and a shift away from primary to manufactured exports. There is also evidence that continued emphasis on import substitution ultimately leads to a slowing of growth.[6] During the postwar years Bulgaria, Romania, and Yugoslavia seemed to follow the first growth prescription, emphasizing faster industrialization than Greece and Turkey, while Albania more or less followed an autarkic, balanced-growth approach. In recent years, however, Yugoslavia has pursued an export expansion that has been largely offset by import liberalization, while Turkey has continued to stress an import substitution policy and has maintained high levels of protection.

Depending on the level of industrialization, per capita energy consumption, in kilograms of coal equivalent, was higher in Bulgaria (5,020 in 1978) and Romania (4,042) than in Yugoslavia (2,035), Greece (1,925), Albania (998), and Turkey (793). This use of energy, which increased about five times from 1960 to 1976 for Greece and three times for the other Balkan countries, presents serious problems for the foreign trade sector of all these countries. Thus, Turkey spends about 60 percent of its merchandise export earnings to pay for energy imports, Greece around 50 percent, and Yugoslavia 25 percent. As oil prices continue to increase, growing amounts of export earnings are needed to help pay for energy imports.

The increase in the price of oil and other raw materials during the 1970s imposed a great burden on the Balkan countries, with the exception, perhaps, of Romania (an importer of crude petroleum and an exporter of petroleum products). On the other hand, the slackening in the growth of demand in the West and the inadequate competitiveness of many products, especially those of the planned Balkan economies, led to sharply deteriorating trade balances and growing foreign debts, despite efforts to step up exports to Western markets.

Bulgaria's debt service—the payment of principal and interest on foreign debt—absorbs more than 50 percent of its hard-currency earnings per year. Estimated interest payments in relation to export earnings in trade with developed countries are over 30 percent for Bulgaria and 10-15 percent for Romania.[7] Both Bulgaria and Romania have started an intensive campaign for more economic cooperation with the West, particularly the EEC, in order to obtain hard currency and transfer of technology. However, there are delays in decision making, inflexibility in adopting new technology, and extensive departmentalization in research and innovations.

On other fronts Romania and Yugoslavia, together with other east European countries, have signed trade agreements with Iran and other Middle East nations to provide foodstuffs and industrial products in exchange for petroleum. After the deterioration in economic relations between Iran and the United States and other Western countries, annual trade between Romania and Iran increased by more than 70 percent. Romanian exports of wheat, sugar, meat, eggs, dairy products, chemical fertilizers, machine parts, and services in assembling Romanian tractors at Tabriz, are exchanged for Iranian oil. Similarly, Yugoslav experts are picking up some of the projects abandoned by American and other Western concerns, such as working the largest Iranian copper mine at Sar Cheshneh, in exchange for oil imports.

The growing trade of Yugoslavia with both the EEC (absorbing 26 percent of total exports and accounting for about 40 percent of the Yugoslav imports) and Comecon would help further economic development of the country, probably without disturbing its independent policy.

However, Yugoslavia's independent policy and its alliance with Third World countries present problems in foreign trade for the country. Developing countries absorb only about 15 percent of Yugoslavia's foreign trade, while Western advanced countries absorb about 50 percent and Communist bloc countries some 35 percent. Moreover, imports from Third World countries are in the form of raw material, mainly petroleum. But Yugoslavia needs advanced technological equipment provided by Western industrial economies.

Yugoslav exports cover about two-thirds of its imports, and the trade deficit is covered partially by "invisibles," mainly tourism and remittances from workers in western Europe. The same is true of the trade deficits incurred by Greece and Turkey. Such invisibles are not enough, though, and Yugoslavia's annual balance-of-payments deficit is more than $1 billion.

While the trade balance of Yugoslavia with the Soviet bloc is more or less in equilibrium, that with the EEC countries has deteriorated, especially since British imports of agricultural products have declined rapidly as a result of the EEC farming policy. Before 1970 the EEC absorbed about 40 percent of the Yugoslav exports, but they have dropped to only about 25 percent. This trend might force policy makers of the country to ask for closer economic relations with the EEC and, eventually, full membership.

The adjustment of the domestic economic structure and growth pattern to the long-run worsening of the terms of trade and the reduction of external deficits has become an important policy priority for all Balkan economies, particularly the planned ones. This policy is aimed at the restraint or reduction of imports when exports cannot be expanded. This has hindered economic growth, reduced the supply of consumer and capital goods, and raised prices. As a means of easing import demand, policy makers have set moderate growth targets and projected a reduced pace of investment. A marked decline in economic growth has already taken place in all the Balkan countries because of the unusually low rates of growth in industrial production that used to offset swings in agricultural production.

In order to protect their economies from imported inflation and from domestic cost pressures, the planned Balkan economies maintain fiscal buffers between the external sector and the domestic economy. In addition to central controls over wages and prices, they use implicit taxes and subsidies to maintain price stability for essential consumer goods and services. However, comprehensive price revisions are normally undertaken at intervals of five years, with price increases in most products and price reductions in a few others. Thus, the net effect is an overall modest price increase that, in many cases, is higher than income increases.

Foreign Investment and Multinational Expansion

One of the most important issues of economic development in recent years has been the emergence and growth of big corporate enterprises of an international character. The growth of such giant corporations requires expansion in many nations. Balkan nations cannot be excluded from this economic intercourse.

The rapid expansion of multinational corporations throughout the Balkan nations may create problems of economic and political influence. In this period of extensive ideological prejudice, it is difficult to predict the new trends and the repercussions of such an international corporate expansion in this part of the world. We live in a period of uncertainties, in which the supporters of the centrally planned economies close their eyes when confronted with the real economic gains arising from the market mechanism. At the same time, supporters of free competition cannot see that large parts of production escape the laws of the markets because of the effects created by the formation of giant transnational companies.

The monopolistic or oligopolistic giant corporations usually do not adhere to the competitive market forces of supply and demand. They gradually take away the powers of capitalism and socialism, forming a new system with independent economic units.[8]

In order to counteract the ever-increasing influence of large corporations, what may be needed is some form of regional cooperation among the Balkan governments, acting as a unified power like the EEC, against the growing corporate power. However, such multigovernment and regional policies should try to protect the public and not discourage multinational investment. Technology requires capital concentration and bigness, which in turn require market expansion and suggest a "multicountry" investment policy in the area.

The flows of foreign investment, mainly from industrial countries, provide overhead capital, jobs, and technology for the recipient Balkan countries in exchange for raw materials, as well as returns for the investing countries. In order to have the flow of foreign investment and the accompanying technological transfer continue, favorable conditions, including guarantees against administrative controls and the assurance of profitable opportunities, must prevail.

Not only the market economies of Greece and Turkey, but also the socialist economies of Bulgaria, Romania, and Yugoslavia, offer attractive terms to foreign investors and multinational corporations in return for the introduction of new technology and know-how. Despite criticism that such corporate "beasts" influence and even threaten the economic and political life of the host countries, they are considered, at the same time, agents of technological innovations that provide managerial expertise, capital investment, and employment.[9]

Foreign investment is welcome in all Balkan countries (except, perhaps, in Albania) and plays a vital role in their economies. In particular Greece since 1953 (Law 2687) and Turkey offer many privileges to foreign investors, to the point of being criticized for making their economies too open to foreign economic and political influence. In addition to traditional investments from Western corporations, joint ventures and mutual investments by Middle East countries are appearing in Greece and Turkey. Lebanese entrepreneurs have signed agreements with the Greek government to establish a number of enterprises for the manufacture of agricultural products in the area of Larisa, worth some $23 million.

By 1978, direct foreign investment in Greece amounted to $1.3 billion. Five industries (oil refining, manufacture of petroleum products, chemicals, basic metals, and transportation equipment) absorb 75 percent of total foreign capital (40 percent from the EEC). Foreign investment controls about 30 percent of the total industrial assets and 60 percent of industrial exports. Transactions by 11 large enterprises, in which foreign capital has an average share of 54 percent, account for 94 percent of the trade deficit of Greece. In 1975 there were 227 enterprises in Greece in which foreigners had less than 50 percent of the assets and 65 enterprises with more than 50 percent foreign capital.

A number of foreign enterprises have established themselves in Balkan planned economies for trade and investment. This economic exchange has been intensified during recent years.[10] The socialist Balkan countries are willing to forsake certain controls over incoming foreign investors in return for the hard currency so needed to pay for imported Western equipment and technology. The Intercontinental Hotels Corporation, a subsidiary of Pan American World Airways, operates and continues to build new hotels in east European cities, including Bucharest, Zagreb, and Belgrade. A Japanese consortium, which includes the Nippon Steel Corporation and the Mitsui and Mitsubishi groups, has created trade centers in a number of planned economies, including Bulgaria.

Romania, to some degree following the example of Hungary, has introduced special legislation for joint ventures with the West, especially for investment involving new technology, in which provisions have been made for more protection and less control.

On the other hand, large public enterprises in the Balkan planned economies are making serious efforts to establish new production units, especially units intended to promote their products in Western markets. However, they try to retain the marketing activities of their products. Recently a number of socialist multinationals have started to expand around the world. More than 50 were part of Comecon in 1975. In 1976 some 700 "daughter" companies with more than 10,000 subsidiaries and offices were operating in the West, mainly as joint ventures with capitalists.

For the financing of exports and trade transactions among east and west European countries, a number of joint banks have been established in east European countries. They include the French-Romanian Bank, the French-Yugoslavian Bank, and the International Bank of Central Europe in Budapest, in which planned economies share up to 50 percent.

Although joint investment ventures among the Balkan countries have been limited, a number of joint enterprises and investment projects have been established, primarily on a bilateral basis. Such joint ventures between Bulgaria and Greece include the Chemiport-Bilimport Company, in which Unifert Company of Lebanon participates, for the production of chemical products; the Machine Export Industry (MEVET); the DKW, which cans vegetables and fruits at Almyros (Greece), in which the Bulgarian Plont Export, the Greek Kanaris Company and Uink-Konk of Holland participate; and the Kopelouzos-Balkan Car Impex Company, which manufactures and repairs buses. Four more joint Greek-Bulgarian ventures are in the process of development for the production and trade of fish products, meat products and sausages, and the manufacturing of leather products (DERAS). Moreover, Bulgaria, in cooperation with the Soviet Union, has shown interest in creating an aluminum enterprise in Greece that would be operated by the private sector.

Joint investment ventures can be planned and implemented on hydroelectric dams and irrigation projects, especially in border areas, such as Samoritz-Islaz, near the Danube, and the Iron Gate on the Yugoslavia-Romania border. Other joint investment may include mining enterprises for the extraction and processing of iron, lead, zinc, bauxite, petroleum, and other subsoil resources. Also, bilateral agreements may be concluded for transportation, communications, electricity, banking, tourism, and manufacturing. However, careful feasibility studies are needed to overcome the limited or nonexistent research and the lapses and lacunae of statistical information prevailing in this region.

Since the end of World War II, all Balkan countries have received some form of aid, primarily from the United States and the Soviet Union.[11] Such aid was needed because of economic adversities immediately after the war. However, continuation of aid breeds unhealthy economic dependency. Moreover, aid is often given for political and security reasons, and hidden strings are customarily attached. It would be better for the Balkan, as well as other recipient countries to ask for more trade rather than aid. The transfer of needed technology may take place through trade and investment agreements or joint ventures with multinational corporations and government enterprises, which could stimulate economic development while respecting the economic and political independence of the area.

Loans have been provided by international institutions. In 1980, Romania, Turkey, and Yugoslavia received around $200 million each from the World Bank. Romania was given the loan for the construction of the Danube-Black Sea Canal and for irrigation; Turkey, for structural adjustments; and Yugoslavia, for highways and agricultural credit.

EUROPEAN ECONOMIC COMMUNITY, COMECON, AND THE BALKANS

The European Economic Community

Because of the importance of the European Economic Community (EEC) and the Council of Mutual Economic Assistance (CMEA) or Comecon for the Balkan countries, a deeper review of these two groups is needed. The EEC was established in 1957 at Rome with six members: Belgium, Luxembourg, the Netherlands, France, West Germany, and Italy. They were commonly known as the "Inner Six." Three years later the United Kingdom, Austria, Denmark, Norway, Portugal, Sweden, and Switzerland created the European Free Trade Association (EFTA), the "Outer Seven," at Stockholm. Both groups were formed to gradually reduce their internal tariffs, but the "Outer Seven" permitted the retention of individual external tariffs, including tariff preferences that the United Kingdom had given to Commonwealth nations. Because the EFTA was not as successful as the EEC, the United Kingdom, and Denmark, as well as Ireland joined the EEC in 1973.

Greece and Turkey became associate members of the EEC in 1962 and 1964, respectively, and were allowed to export many of their products to the community free of duty, while retaining their tariffs during a transition period (up to 22 years for Greece). Special arrangements and association agreements have been negotiated or signed with a number of countries in Africa, the Middle East, Asia, and Latin America, as well as Spain and Portugal. Greece became the tenth member of the EEC in 1981; Spain, Portugal, and Turkey are expected to be members in the near future.

The EEC has been successful in almost all fields. Labor, capital, entrepreneurs, and consumers are free to move and compete in the markets of all member nations. Common agricultural, transportation, and other economic policies, uniform external tariffs, and coordinated monetary and fiscal measures are rapidly being advanced. Even political cooperation is being successfully promoted, in spite of differences in languages, cultures, and other areas. Both internal and external trade has increased, primarily because of the reduction in tariffs by high-duty countries during the creation of a common tariff policy.

Moreover, the countries of the EEC have agreed to hold elections for a European Parliament. This political movement is another milestone on the road to closer cooperation and eventual unification. The members of the Parliament (some 410) are elected directly by the people of each member country, instead of being selected from members of national parliaments, as was done before. This process is expected to strengthen the ideals of democracy and the principles of human rights among the members, and indirectly among the countries associated with the Common Market. From an economic point of view, this trend would eliminate dangers from speculation, stabilize the European currencies, and help reduce the possibility of severe recessions and high rates of unemployment.

The first EEC parliamentary elections have already been held, but they were not met with great enthusiasm.

Special trade agreements have recently been enacted between the EEC and some Balkan socialist countries. In March 1980, Romania signed an agreement with the EEC to reduce restrictions and increase mutual trade in industrial and other products. This deviates from the Comecon decision that priority should be given to agreements between Comecon and the EEC.

Although quotation mongers may try to show the opposite, the increasing integration of western Europe, moving toward a United States of Europe, proves that the argument of the inevitability of war among the capitalist powers is weak.[12] The parallel integration process in Comecon, on the other hand, and the increasing cooperation between the two groups indicate that some form of transition, and probably the genesis of a new economic system with elements of both capitalism and socialism, is in the process.

Greece's Accession to the EEC

In order to retain and augment trade with west European countries, Greece has pursued a policy of closer economic ties with the EEC. As a result, an association agreement was signed on July 9, 1961, which became effective November 1, 1962. A transitional period of 22 years was allowed for gradual tariff reduction and preparation for full membership.

With the agreement of May 28, 1979, Greece became the tenth member of the EEC, effective January 1, 1981. Despite the country's full membership, there are provisions for a five-year transitional period for agricultural products in general and a seven-year period for tomatoes and peaches, for which tariffs would be gradually reduced by the EEC. A similar five-year period was provided between the EEC and the new member states of Denmark, Ireland, and the United Kingdom. Another seven-year transitional period is provided for the free movement of Greek workers into EEC countries.

There were, and still are, pro and con arguments concerning Greece's admission to the EEC. Some economists and politicians argue that entry will bring significant economic and political advantages in the foreseeable future. Others feel that EEC membership makes Greece a "provincial backwater," and it may not prove to be as beneficial as others believe; instead, the fascination with the EEC accession may lead to serious hardships, at least with respect to some sensitive and protected industries.

It would seem that the accession of Greece to the EEC would not entail a catastrophe for the country's economy, nor would it provide a panacea for all its problems. From an economic, and especially from a sociopolitical, point of view, there would seem to be no better alternatives in the foreseeable future. Even if Greece remained outside the EEC, most of the economic results, particularly in foreign trade, would occur anyway. By the time of admission, and as a result of association, two-thirds of the imports from the EEC, which count for about half of total imports, were already duty-free.

Therefore, the entry is not expected to be harmful to industries and products for which import tariffs have already been eliminated or are very low. However, for protected small-scale and old-fashioned industries producing such goods as footwear, cloth, leather, and metal products, there would be heavy pressure. Complete elimination of tariffs on imports from the EEC and tariff reduction on imports from non-EEC countries (in harmony with those of the EEC) would probably force a large number of small industries and handicrafts operations to close.[13] An example is the closing of Pitsos Company, producing refrigerators, which was taken over by a German concern.

Given that about 90 percent of the Greek enterprises employ fewer than 10 persons, it is obvious what the admission would mean for such family-owned firms. Many of these protected small enterprises would be wiped out after the accession. Moreover, the high elasticity of imports for their products or close substitutes (around 2) would make things worse. In order to survive EEC competition, such small enterprises should merge with larger ones that are able to apply modern technology of mass production. However, the fact that labor cost is lower (about half) in Greece compared with that of the EEC gives an advantage to these labor-intensive industries over their EEC counterparts.

Nevertheless, the haste in processing Greece's entry into the EEC has generated enthusiasm among many people, and may have stimulated modernization of the Greek economy and some decrease of bureaucratic inertia. Perhaps the intensive competition from the EEC firms may have forced Greek entrepreneurs and middlemen earning high profits to reduce their luxurious and conspicuous consumption in favor of productive investment. But in the near future such EEC competition may prove detrimental to the economy as a whole: unemployment may be expected to increase, emigration of skilled persons to intensify, and the balance of trade to deteriorate.

In the near future there may be greater opportunities for Greece to increase exports to its Balkan neighbors and the Middle East than to the EEC countries. First, EEC duties for Greek industrial products have been eliminated since 1974, and no large market thrust for these products is expected. Second, after the entry, tax advantages and government subsidies to Greek exporters, amounting to some 20 percent or more of their value, would be stopped.[14] Third, agricultural products cannot enter the EEC freely during the transitional period provided by the entry agreement.

Total Greek exports to the EEC (about $2 billion annually in 1980), compared with about $100 million in 1960) are less than half of imports. This means that the EEC should be equally or more interested in keeping Greece in its economic sphere of influence, because it sells far more to Greece than it buys. Moreover, with the incorporation of the sizable Greek merchant fleet, representing 14 percent of world tonnage, the EEC would enhance its maritime power. At the same time, Greece needs the market of the EEC, where it sells about half of its exports.

There seems to be no disagreement between the supporters and the critics of accession that the value of future business transactions of Greece with the EEC is expected to increase the gap in the balance of trade, since imports are expected to increase more than exports. Moreover, an increase in exports would consist mostly of raw materials or semimanufactured products, which would not greatly help to improve labor conditions. There would be some improvement in the balance of payments as a result of incoming investment capital introduced by foreign multinationals, mainly from the EEC. However, the inflow would not be great, because foreign firms generally use host-country sources of financing, making it difficult for local enterprises to use domestic savings for investment. This has been the recent experience of foreign firms investing in developing countries.[15] However, the inflow of capital for speculation and for the purchase of land will be intensified, driving real estate prices still higher.

Nevertheless, the "invisible" sources, especially tourism, shipping, and emigrant remittances, will continue to play their traditional favorable role. But these sources and, even more, deposits from abroad, especially from emigrants, are subject of international political and economic changes—and therefore are unstable and unpredictable.

However, there is nothing wrong with Greece or any other country searching simultaneously for trade expansion and, possibly, other regional associations to the south, the east, or elsewhere. Such trade expansion would make the country a more independent and less subservient partner in the EEC or any other group. This policy would raise its prestige and improve its bargaining position in the future, instead of its remaining a poor satellite of the EEC or an underdeveloped nation. Therefore, Greece should explore the possibility of entering other economic groups or signing trade agreements with other nations, mainly other Mediterranean nations that import large amounts of Greek products. Accession to the EEC should not frustrate efforts for more cooperation among the Balkan and other Mediterranean countries; rather, it should encourage closer economic and sociocultural relations. These pioneering efforts might be instrumental and helpful toward closer cooperation between the EEC and Comecon.

In sector terms, the entry of Greece into the EEC would mean more specialization and expansion in such agricultural lines as peaches, raisins, grapes, lemons, oranges, olives, and tobacco. In general, agriculture would be expected to be in an advantageous position when the EEC subsidies for it are considered. During the transition period Greece will receive $1.8 billion in EEC economic aid. In addition, many Greek farmers will be forced to moderize their production through mechanization, and probably will have to form larger farm units for cheaper production and distribution of their products. This is particularly important for Greek agriculture because of the fragmentation of land into small, inefficient lots (stamps). Similar favorable effects are expected in mining products, particularly bauxite, lignite, and aluminum.

Another sector expected to benefit from the accession is transportation, especially shipping, mainly because of the country's geographical position and its large commercial fleet. The EEC uses oil to cover 55 percent of its energy needs, and 90 percent of it is imported, mainly from the Middle East. Greek ships can transport oil as well as other products to and/or from the EEC.[16] The Greeks, then, can continue to make their fortunes from Homer's "wine-dark sea."

Tourism, already a flourishing sector, would not only keep its importance but expand further, mainly because of Greece's excellent climate and archaeological remains. It may be expected that this sector would continue to play a vital role in covering a large part of the country's balance-of-trade deficit, which was $4.3 billion in 1978.

Most difficulties would occur in the industrial sector, mainly manufacturing. Depending on the degree of tariff protection and subsidization, certain industries may expand, but most of them will be suppressed or wiped out. More important, the establishment of new ones would be difficult. It is not only that most European industries are already more advanced and can produce cheaper and better products, but also that they will continue innovating and modernizing, making it difficult for old or new Greek industries to compete or even to survive.

From a sociopolitical point of view, as an integral part of the EEC, Greece can expect to enjoy more protection and more respect from other countries. Moreover, the social structure of the country may improve, and its democratic institutions may be strengthened, as recent events in other EEC countries indicate.

However, from a demographic point of view, long-run expectations suggest that large numbers of Greeks would emigrate to western Europe and a number of other Europeans would establish themselves in Greece. As an outpost on the European frontier, Greece would become the eastern Mediterranean balcony of the EEC. As long as free movement of population and unrestricted property acquisition are allowed, rich Europeans, primarily Germans who exhibit a strong fondness for Greek touristic and archaeological centers, would settle permanently in the country, a process that has already begun, primarily in the islands. Such an economic "invasion" will be intensified when another EEC candidate, Turkey, with many unemployed or underemployed workers, becomes a full member of the EEC and enjoys the same freedom of movement and settlement in other member countries. Mutatis mutandis, similar results would be expected for other countries entering the EEC, particularly Spain, Portugal, and (probably) Yugoslavia, with which the EEC signed an agreement for closer economic cooperation in April 1980.

The Council of Mutual Economic Assistance

In 1949 the Soviet Union and five east European countries (Bulgaria, Czechoslovakia, Hungary, Poland, and Romania) created the Council of Mutual Economic Assistance (CMEA), or Comecon, as a counterpart to the Organization for European Economic Cooperation (OEEC), now known as the Organization for Economic Cooperation and Development (OECD).

Albania and East Germany joined Comecon in 1949 and 1950, respectively; Yugoslavia became an observer. Mongolia joined in 1962, and Cuba in 1972. At present, cooperation with Albania is weak, if not nonexistent, and Yugoslavia seems to have stronger ties with the EEC than with Comecon. Afghanistan, Angola, Ethiopia, Laos, South Yemen, and Vietnam are in the process of joining Comecon. Nonsocialist countries such as Finland (1973), Iraq, and Mexico (1975) have become associate members of Comecon, and negotiations between Comecon and some Latin American countries are under way.

Initially Comecon was not too effective, mainly because of lack of raw materials and labor. Its longevity and expansion have made it more effective, in recent years, on matters of regional cooperation and economic development. However, transactions between the member nations remain mostly bilateral and, to a limited extent, multilateral. In contrast with the EEC, where market integration is stressed, Comecon emphasizes production integration and long-term economic development.

The main governing bodies of Comecon are the General Assembly, which makes the final decisions and in which all the member nations participate with equal vote; the Executive Committee; a number of permanent committees for different sectors of the economy; and the Secretariat, which deals with day-to-day business and possible areas of cooperation with the EEC.

Other important regional organizations are Intermetall, Interklim, and a number of mixed enterprises such as Haldes, Intrasmash, Agromash, Interatomenergo, Intertestilmash, and similar units for electricity, petroleum, and other products.

To facilitate transactions among the Comecon member nations, the International Bank for Economic Cooperation (IBEC) was created in 1963. This is an organization, parallel with the International Monetary Fund (IMF) in the mainly capitalist countries, which uses the ruble as the basic transferable currency to facilitate clearings among the member nations on a multilateral basis. For further financial cooperation the International Investment Bank (IIB) was created in 1971. The main function of this institution is to help finance investment by the members of Comecon in a fashion similar to the World Bank. IIB has also opened offices in a number of market economies.

Similar bank offices in both socialist and capitalist countries, such as the Anglo-Romanian Leasing and the East-West Leasing (both in London) and the Promolease in Paris, as well as many bank offices and other subsidiaries of west European companies in the Eastern planned economies, create a favorable environment for further East-West cooperation and possible economic convergence, independent of ideological differences. Furthermore, some centrally planned economies participate in both the IMF and the IBEC. Romania, for example, is a member of IBEC and has a special arrangement with IMF, while Yugoslavia is a member of IMF and at the same time is associated with IBEC. IBEC itself has created good relations with the International Clearing Bank of Basel (Switzerland). Also it offered and accepted loans from western European countries in various Eurocurrencies. In addition, it has provided for acceptance of nonsocialist countries as members (Article 43, IBEC Charter).

The mutual needs for raw materials, capital, and technology will probably force greater cooperation among countries with different economic systems, such as those of the EEC and Comecon, and particularly among the Balkans.[17] It is expected that more multinational corporations and joint ventures between EEC and Comecon, as well as between East and West in general, on financial, infrastructural, and other projects will take place. The special drawing rights of IMF or another internationally accepted currency probably will help improve economic and sociopolitical relations in the area.

The trend toward more foreign trade in the centrally planned economies of Comecon, including Bulgaria and Romania, make them not fully immune to stagflation emanating from abroad. In spite of their controlled economies, they are affected by the depreciation of some of their currency reserves. The purchasing power of these reserves, notably dollars, has declined in accordance with their rate of depreciation in terms of more stable currencies or of gold. Under such conditions these countries probably will try to shift to more secure financial funds. In the process they are expected to experience some losses from the depreciated reserves. Thus, Comecon planned economies face problems similar to those of the EEC, and the trend is toward more cooperation between these two groups on related matters.

In light of further trade and investment cooperation between west and east European nations, the question remains: Is Comecon expected to face problems the the EEC similar to those experienced between EFTA and the EEC? It would seem that the trend toward more economic transactions between these two groups of countries does not represent a new movement toward integration, but a policy of gradually abandoning autarky in favor of a more open trade among neighboring nations. The aim is to avoid scarcities and eliminate trade obstacles among these countries with different economic systems.

From the viewpoint of overall trade of the CMEA countries, one should review trade with the West and trade among themselves.[18] Although statistical evidence is insufficient, and it is difficult to make predictions, it seems that East-West relations are expected to work against net trade creation (and may even threaten economic integration) among the CMEA countries. It may be suggested that planned trade quotas, preferred by Eastern planners, make trade easier with the West rather than between CMEA members. There seems to be a trade-off between CMEA integration and East-West relations. However, the need for technological transformation is so great that trade sacrifices among the CMEA countries would be easily accepted. Thus, the economic relations of Bulgaria and Romania with Greece, Turkey, and other EEC members or associate members are expected to improve.

NOTES

1. World Bank, *World Economic Report, 1980* (New York: Oxford University Press, 1980), pp. 125, 127.

2. For further analysis see F. Holzman, "Some Systematic Factors Contributing to the Convertible Currency Shortages of Centrally Planned Economies," *American Economic Review*, Proceedings, May 1979, pp. 76–80.

3. Romania's drive for independence in the 1960s and later led to a proportional increase in trade with Western countries at the expense of that with Comecon. G. Gross, "Rumania: The Fruits of Autonomy," *Problems of Communism*, January-February 1966, pp. 16–27.

4. World Bank, *World Development Report, 1979* (New York: Oxford University Press, 1979), pp. 151, 155; *1980*, p. 139. Turkey's foreign debt, both short- and long-term, passed the $10 billion mark in 1978. Andrew Borowiec, "Turkey Looks to U.S. to Help Resolve Economic Crisis," *New York Times*, January 6, 1979, p. L5.

5. The expected rate of economic growth (g) may be determined by the average propensity to save (s), the expected difference in foreign trade (exports-imports) as a percentage of national income (f), and the capital/output or income ratio (v):

$$g = \frac{s \pm f}{v}$$

Assuming s = 0.15, f = 0.03, and v = 3, the rate of economic growth would be 6 percent of the national income:

$$g = \frac{0.15 + 0.03}{3} = \frac{0.18}{3} = 0.06$$

6. Hollis Chenery presents recent data on semi-industrial countries, in which Turkey and Yugoslavia are included, that support these findings. See his "Interactions Between Industrialization and Exports," *American Economic Review*, Proceedings, May 1980, pp. 381–92.

7. The combined net convertible-currency debt of eastern Europe and the U.S.S.R. has passed the $64 billion mark. United Nations, Department of International Economic and Social Affairs, *World Economic Survey 1979-80* (New York: United Nations, 1980), pp. 53–54.

8. In order to protect the public from excessive corporate power, Professor John K. Galbraith suggests that the boards of directors of large corporations be replaced with public auditors. See his *The Age of Uncertainty* (Boston: Houghton Mifflin, 1977), p. 278.

9. For arguments pro and con, see R. Vernon, *Sovereignty at Bay: The Multinational Spread of U.S. Enterprises* (New York: Basic Books, 1971).

10. Profits from joint ventures are taxed at rates varying from zero percent in Bulgaria to 25 percent in Turkey, 30 percent in Romania, 35 percent in Yugoslavia, and 38.2 percent in Greece (compared with 40 percent in the United Kingdom, 46 percent in the United States, and 50 percent in France and Canada). P. Jonas, *Taxation of Multinationals in Communist Countries* (New York: Praeger, 1978), p. 79.

11. U.S. postwar aid (1948–71) amounted to $2.1 billion for Turkey, $1.1 billion for Greece, and $500 million for Yugoslavia.

12. Although Marx and Engels said that "Working men have no country" and "National differences between peoples are day by day disappearing more and more" (*Communist Manifesto*, ch. 2), they did not predict such trends toward a hybrid system. Veblen's prediction

of perpetual changes of the socioeconomic systems in the thesis-antithesis-synthesis form may prove to be more realistic than that of Marx. Thorstein Veblen, *The Theory of the Leisure Class* (London: Allen and Unwin, 1970) and *The Theory of Business Enterprises* (New York: A. Kelly, 1965).

13. Although imports by Greece from the United States have been gradually reduced to about 5 percent of an estimated $11 billion import bill (because of tariffs higher than those of the EEC), the actual value of American sales to Greece started rising. Many Greek industries, large and small, look across the Atlantic for capital equipment and know-how with which they can improve their competitiveness against their EEC counterparts.

14. For a review of the problems of the Greek industry, see "Greece: Number Ten?" *Economist*, December 16, 1978, p. 60.

15. For related statistics see C. Vaitsos, *Intercountry Income Distribution and Transnational Enterprises* (London: Oxford University Press, 1974).

16. In 1960–80 the world share of the EEC merchant fleet fell from 34 to 18 percent, while the Greek-flag fleet grew tenfold, numbering some 3,800 ships (600 more than the nearest competitor, Britain). John Carr, "New Trade Horizons: Greece Could Strengthen Ties Between East and West," *Europe*, January–February 1981, pp. 10-13.

17. Valuable comparisons between CMEA and EEC are provided by M. Kaser, *Comecon: Integration Problems of the Planned Economies*, 2nd ed. (London: Oxford University Press, 1967), pt. II; N. Bautina, *CMEA Today: From Economic Cooperation to Economic Integration* (Moscow: Progress Publishers, 1975).

18. For new commercial trends among the socialist countries in Europe, see U.S. Congress, Joint Economic Committee, *Reorientation and Commercial Relations of the Economies of Eastern Europe* (Washington, D.C.: U.S. Government Printing Office, 1974).

8

ECONOMIC COOPERATION AND INTEGRATION

POSSIBILITIES OF CONVERGENCE

The main economic goal of each society is prosperity and happiness for all its members. Material and spiritual happiness—"the good life," Socrates called it—includes higher levels of production, security, equal opportunity, dignity, and freedom of expression.[1] Is convergence—that is, a system in which diverse economies adopt similar institutional structures and move toward the middle way—expected to lead to such prosperity and happiness? This question is important for the Balkan countries, where a mosaic of economic systems can be observed.

Both private capitalism and state capitalism are associated with some form of economic and/or political oppression. In the first, inequalities of income and wealth create superiority and economic influence of the "haves" over the "have-nots." In the second, inequalities in political and bureaucratic power create oppression of others by party and governmental officials. In many instances these party and managerial elites seem to confuse the dictatorship of the proletariat with a dictatorship over the proletariat, and are inflexible to social and economic changes.

The effective use of fiscal and monetary policy and the successful management of demand, especially in the market economies of Europe, have contributed to continued progress under capitalism. Similarly, the use of planning in centrally planned economies has made economic growth a permanent feature in the countries under socialism. Through borrowing positive elements from each other, these parallel achievements of capitalism and socialism have led a number of economists and other scientists, in the postwar years, to propose a rapprochement between planned and market economies.[2] Income policies, in the form of price and wage determination or productivity guidelines, tax cuts, investment incentives, and various subsidies introduced by the Balkan market economies to achieve high growth rates and full employment, tend to make these economies more social and less private. On the other hand, a new era of planning, characterized by the introduction of new institutional arrangements and economic reforms giving more freedom to enterprises on matters of prices and managerial decision making, was adopted by the centrally planned Balkan economies, especially during the 1960s. These reforms tend to introduce a Lange-type system of market socialism with rational prices and an efficient allocation of productive resources.[3]

It was thought that detailed economic planning and centralism were responsible for bureaucracy, poor quality, and low labor productivity. As the planned economies moved to higher development levels, the enterprises needed more autonomy on such vital matters as borrowing funds, employment, investment, production, and sales reforms, which meant a movement toward some form of democratic socialism. On the other hand, nationalization, which enhances state capitalism, seems to create serious problems of production efficiency in these countries.

The convergence argument states that capitalistic norms of production and distribution are giving more and more ground to socialistic norms. The capitalist symptoms of inflation and unemployment may be considered similar to the pains of childbirth, the child being regarded as a new social and economic system having more participation and equality, and less discrimination and social distinction. Similarly, socialist norms of production are changing toward more competitive practices, less centralism, and less doctrinal adherence to hard-line theories. Such a parallel movement toward a middle-of-the-road economy seems to support the cosmopolitanism or universalism advocated by the Sophists and Stoics in ancient times.

Despite criticism from conservative elements of both capitalist and socialist countries, who point to the evils of each other's system and talk about inevitable submergence instead of convergence, indications exist that economic and political transformations in the Balkan region point to the gradual reduction of ideological differences and adoption of common policies. From an operational point of view, both systems continue to coexist in the Balkan Peninsula and engage in mutual cooperation instead of mutual extermination. Economic development is gradually reducing the impact of ideological appeals upon the masses. People with full stomachs turn to individual pleasures instead of revolutionary insurrection.

Rapid industrialization and development may weaken ideological and political competition among the systems prevailing in the Balkan countries and cause their economies to progress toward each other in order to form a hybrid society. Thus, the concept of "intermediate regimes," suggested by Michael Kalecki for developing countries, may have particular importance for the Balkan nations.[4]

Technological improvement and economic growth lead to capital concentration and monopolization, particularly in Greece and Turkey. Large corporations and companies in such market economies exercise pressure upon the consumer, through advertising and other sales promotion techniques, to demand more goods and services and to work harder to pay for them. Similarly, in the controlled

Balkan economies, people are under pressure from the planning framework to meet higher production quotas. This type of material progress directs these economies toward common goals, which may lead to more cooperation and eventual regional integration. In such a case a new system, which might incorporate the obvious advantages of both systems and blend the ideal and the real, might emerge in the area. The Balkan countries seem to be mature enough for such an experience. However, more studies and more researchers are needed before such a program is begun.

Political leadership, like entrepreneurship, has lost its glamour, and has become a routine profession, a job to be performed, with more obligations and worries than satisfactions. Such trends will eliminate possible conflicts and speed up economic (and eventually sociocultural) convergence in the Balkan area.

Some of the major economic changes introduced in the planned Balkan economies, such as emphasis on specialization of management with appropriate remuneration according to productivity, acceptance of interest as a cost factor, use of money values in planning-accounting, and emphasis on international trade and cooperation instead of self-reliance, support some of the arguments of economic convergence. Likewise, major changes have been made in the market economies of Greece and Turkey. They include the use of developmental (not necessarily detailed) planning, the growing importance of governmental activities in regulating these economies (through taxation, expenditures, free education, wage-price controls, and other fiscal and monetary measures), and the deviation from free competition in the private sector, either through capital concentration and monopolization, or through the public sector's operating public utility enterprises. All these changes also tend to support a trend toward economic convergence in the area.[5]

The convergence movement lost its glamour in the 1960s, primarily because too great an emphasis was being placed on its political and ideological aspects, at the expense of its economic advantages. Although economics and politics usually go together and it is difficult to separate them, it becomes more and more obvious, particularly with the spread of multinational corporations and the growth of foreign trade, that economic considerations are gaining importance even at the expense of political power.[6]

Large enterprises, growing in number and size year after year, and subsidiaries of multinational companies that have established themselves in almost all the Balkan countries require some independence from controls and more corporate authority over the market mechanism. Furthermore, the current trends toward further trade cooperation and economic intercourse among the Balkan nations bring them closer together. These trends, together with the spread of multinational corporations, liquidate nationalism and prepare the ground for some form of economic and sociopolitical convergence. Such convergence or synthesis may take place not through a conflict of opposites (thesis-antithesis), as Marx predicted, but through a peaceful economic cooperation in which these economies adopt the best of each other's systems.

A method of this sort was described by Plato in his *Dialogues*, and was adopted by the Scholastics in order to modify and reconcile two opposite arguments into a new view that incorporates elements of both. This kind of economic synthesis may be less painful and more instrumental in leading these countries to higher standards of living with the least possible sacrifice of economic and political freedom. A successful experience of closer cooperation and convergence among the Balkan economies may be followed by other countries with different economic systems, particularly the poor and uncommitted countries, which are suspicious of both capitalism and communism and are searching for a middle-of-the-road system—one that can combine the best elements from these two extreme systems to fit their particular conditions.

It is difficult to expect, in the near future, what the supporters of convergence suggest: an optimum role for government and an optimum combination of the public and private sectors in the Balkan countries. However, it is equally or even more difficult to accept the arguments of extreme apologists of either system that "convergence" is the camouflage (the Trojan horse) for subversion and ideological subordination. On the contrary, there are indications of closer cooperation that in the long run may submerge national and ideological differences among these nations and prepare the ground for common policies of development.[7]

Although dramatic changes are not expected in the near future, recent concurrent trends in the Balkan countries may set a good example for further economic cooperation and eventual convergence among other countries or groups of countries, particularly between the EEC and Comecon. However, we should not ignore the short-run strategies and the long-run goals of the two competing systems (capitalism and socialism), as well as of the "big powers," which affect such concurrent trends and symptoms of convergence. Moreover, the fear and suspicion, so common among Balkan peoples, generated by East-West rivalry and the power struggle, are serious drawbacks to convergence on many occasions. Such fear may be intensified by government-sponsored publications and aggressive nationalistic slogans put forward by political zealots, academic "mercenaries," and military expansionists. In these cases the cooperation would become a disguise, a euphemism for a new form of power struggle, and "convergence" would become a utopian dream. However, as Victor Hugo once said, "Today's utopia is tomorrow's reality."

DIFFICULTIES OF CLOSER COOPERATION

Although there is a large body of literature on economic cooperation and integration among market economies, similar literature on groups of countries with different economic systems, such as those of the Balkans, is severely limited. Externalities, economies of scale, changes in terms of trade, capital imports, and joint ventures among these countries may have received isolated treatment in economic literature, but they have not been successfully woven into an integrated framework.

At present the Balkan countries are slowly moving from the stage of economic isolation to the stage of cooperation on trade and investment. However, it is premature to expect formation of a customs union or economic unification in the near future. A serious problem in such a movement toward economic unification is the membership or association of these countries with larger economic regional groups. Greece has become a full member of the EEC, and Turkey is an associate member. Turkey cooperates with Iran and Pakistan for the purpose of manufacturing certain industrial products. Bulgaria and Romania are members of the Council of Mutual Economic Assistance (CMEA). Yugoslavia is loosely associated with both organizations, and Albania is associated with neither.

In connection with these trends, some serious questions may be asked:

1. Will the member countries be allowed by EEC and CMEA to enter into separate agreements and concessions?

2. Given that the Balkan countries are at roughly the same stage of development, somewhere between the self-sustained and the drive-to-maturity stages, would it be better to pursue stronger economic ties among themselves rather than with the more advanced economies of either the EEC or the CMEA?

3. Is it possible that their stronger ties or unification with richer countries might transform them into poor brothers or less developed partners in a dualistic regional framework? Or is it necessary, for their long-run development, to attach their economies to the rich countries with large markets and improved technology?

One should be cautious in arguing for the creation of a customs union among the Balkan countries at the present time. If we review similar cases of regional integration, we will be disappointed. More than 25 different regional arrangements have been made in the past, but the majority of them, mainly among developing nations, lie in the cemetery of defunct or aborted agreements. Only in the relatively more developed countries has it been possible for such schemes to survive. Even the coherence of the Balkan countries as a group has been challenged from time to time. At times Turkey is excluded as an Asian country, and at times Romania is considered a central European country. Sometimes all the countries that border the Danube are referred to as Danubian lands. At other times the whole Balkan Peninsula is thought to be part of southeastern Europe.

In the early postwar years, Soviet domination of economic and political matters in eastern Europe, including those of the socialist Balkan countries, was associated with economic exploitation in the form of buying cheap raw materials and selling back manufactured goods at high prices. However, the political costs of such economic exploitation ultimately became obvious, and in the early 1960s Russia started to reverse the trend by sacrificing economic gains in favor of political stability and friendship. As a result the terms of trade began to favor the east European countries while Russia even accepted losses from intrabloc trade. Transactions among these countries have become more profitable, and decentralization (along with reforms) was followed by closer ties with Western countries, including Greece and Turkey. On the other hand, west and east European countries were not as interested in maintaining economic warfare as were Russia and the United States. This trend has led to the reduction of trade restrictions and further economic cooperation.[8]

The main difficulty impeding closer cooperation in the Balkan Peninsula, which has persisted for many years, arises from the differences and disputes involving national minorities and borders. Such differences and disputes have made the Balkan people suspicious of each other. For years ideology has been—and still is—used to keep such disputes from breaking into open conflicts. Recently, though, the need for economic and cultural cooperation has been used to overcome such disputes in all Balkan countries. In any case, one cannot deny that there is something new in the air. All countries in the area are moving toward greater autonomy. Economic development and educational improvement have made the Balkan peoples less violent, more moderate, and more independent, as each nation tries to demonstrate the superiority of its own system.

Because of the geopolitical importance of the Balkan countries, the big powers always want to exercise their influence upon them. The contacts of the northern Balkan countries with the West were primarily on a government-to-government basis, and always with an eye on Moscow. However, there seems to be some relaxation of the control and influence exercised by Moscow. The Kremlin seems to be more concerned about riots by workers over low wages and high food prices than about a growing Western influence in the area. To avoid outbreaks of unrest caused by economic problems, Moscow allows the Balkan planned countries and eastern Europe in general to turn westward for trade.

Although the Soviet hegemony still prevails in eastern Europe, there are indications that the power of the "polar bear" erodes even as it grows. Yugoslavia, tiny Albania, and Romania are hardly docile followers of Soviet policy. However, an objective integration may iron out suspicions and become more effective by working within the framework of future closer ties between the west and east European economic communities.

Perhaps the main question that could bother European nations in the foreseeable future would be how to obtain closer cooperation and eventual convergence of the market and planned economies in the Balkans. However, national, cultural, and ideological differences should not be disregarded. It takes a long time for such differences to disappear and for institutions to change. One could recall the Ptolemaic system, prevailing for 14 centuries in European astronomy, which placed Earth at the center of the universe. Only after Copernicus placed Earth in orbit around the sun (1543) could many planetary problems be solved with a simplified set of equations. Unfortunately, no simplified system in economics, similar to that of Copernicus in astronomy, has been invented to solve the complexities of modern economic problems on a national or international scale.

The removal of impediments to capital movements arising, among other things, from lingering nationalism, and the problems of tax harmonization and currency devaluation that ensue because of different rates of inflation in different countries, are some of the difficulties of integration not only of the Balkans but also of the EEC and the Comecon countries. Intrabloc and common pricing, as well as planning harmonization between these groups, is even more difficult, if not impossible.

In addition to being partners of the EEC or Comecon, Balkan countries can play a leading role in improving their economic status by creating a customs union or even an economic common market among themselves. There is nothing wrong with the idea of promoting, as far as possible, the creation of a Balkan Economic Community (BEC) and eventually a broader Eastern Mediterranean Economic Community (EMEC).[9] There are indications that the Balkan countries have started to play an important role in promoting closer cooperation among themselves and in expanding trade with almost all the countries of the eastern Mediterranean and the Middle East.

The success of such efforts would make the Balkan Peninsula an important economic and cultural center, a vital link between western Europe and the Middle East. Such a connection would be beneficial to all countries involved because of the expected future development of trade, shipping, tourism, and industry. Trade with Arab countries increased dramatically in the 1970s, and a number of engineering and joint investment agreements have been implemented or negotiated. Moreover, a number of conferences dealing with sociocultural development and environmental protection have been held.

Proposals (mainly by Professor Robert Mandell) for the creation of a Mediterranean Economic Community seem to be less practical than the creation of EMEC.[10] First, because of the relatively large area covered (Gibraltar to Suez), and second, because this area is, or is expected to be, covered under the umbrella of the EEC.

At present the idea of the BEC (and even more the EMEC) seems to be a remote dream. However, an exploration in that direction may help discover common ground for trade expansion and further economic cooperation. It is not necessary to start with impressive and impractical agreements, which may disappoint the countries concerned, but, rather, with cautious trial and error. The worst that could happen would be a return to present conditions So why not try?

From a political point of view, the creation of a Balkan Economic Community presents serious difficulties. But from a geographical and economic point of view, these countries are in an advantageous position; while under the umbrella of advanced groups (EEC or Comecon), they may remain less developed partners of the rich. The examples of southern Italy and Ireland, which remain the least developed regions of the EEC, support this argument.

In the long run it seems proper for any country to join other countries for joint ventures and more trade. In the short run, though, poor countries that join rich partners may face problems concerning infant or protected industries, employment, and economic subordination. Even transitional periods of adjustment, such as that of Greece in the EEC (22 years) do not seem to accomplish much, since economic conditions in the rich countries continue to improve, perhaps more than in the poor countries, and the gap between rich and poor partners remains constant or increases. Improvement in education and technical training, which will create or develop the skills needed to increase productivity and make products more competitive, requires long periods of time and large amounts of investment in human infrastructure that are impossible for the Balkan countries.

The creation of the BEC would probably benefit both the EEC and Comecon, because it would show the strong and weak elements of trade cooperation and eventual economic unification of countries or groups having different economic systems and political philosophies. Such a pioneering effort might break new ground for greater economic cooperation and the eventual convergence of market and planned economies.

The creation of an economic community among the Balkan and/or among the eastern Mediterranean countries seems to be wishful thinking for the time being. In the Balkan Peninsula the influence of the United States and the Soviet Union is very strong and evident, and it may hinder future efforts toward cooperation.[11] Yugoslavia, and to some extent Greece and Romania, may be more interested, and independent enough to promote establishment of such economic communities.

However, it would still be beneficial for two or more countries, such as Greece and Yugoslavia, to enter into closer cooperative agreements and leave the door open for others to join later. The same thing can be suggested for all the countries in the Mediterranean basin. Perhaps a settlement of differences between Cyprus and Turkey, as well as between Israel and neighboring Arab countries, would create the atmosphere in which such agreements could be effective. Closer economic cooperation among these countries could eventually weaken the antagonism between the two superpowers in the area and bring relaxation of tension and reduction of armaments—as was the case, to some extent, with the EEC—and could bring lasting peace and prosperity to the Mediterranean basin. It seems that in the long run it is better to have half of a loaf coming from within than a whole loaf enforced from outside.

NOTES

1. Respect for such human rights was emphasized in the international conferences at Helsinki (1975) and Belgrade (1977). For additional comments see E. Laszlo and J. Kurtzman, eds., *Eastern Europe and the New International Economic Order* (New York: Pergamon Press, 1980).

2. For such proposals see A. Maddison, *Economic Growth in the West* (New York: Twentieth Century Fund, 1964), pp. 18–19; J. Ellul, *The Technological Society* (New York:

Vintage Books, 1967), p. 78; R. Campbell, "Economic Reform in the U.S.S.R.," *American Economic Review*, May 1968, p. 547.

3. Oskar Lange and Fred Taylor, *On the Economic Theory of Socialism* (Minneapolis: University of Minneapolis Press, 1938); Ching-yu Hsu, *Co-wealthism and the New Age* (New York: Vantage Press, 1975), ch. 9.

4. Aristotle recommended a middle way with respect to property acquisition. Although he supported private property, suggesting that "common ownership means common neglect," he seemed to favor a limit to acquisition of wealth, justified by the anxiety about livelihood. The pursuit of wealth in excess of this limit can be considered a corruption or an unnatural form of acquisition. See Ernest Barker, *The Political Thought of Plato and Aristotle* (New York: Dover Publications, 1959), pp. 390–405. For a review of related literature, see T. Lewis, "Acquisition and Anxiety: Aristotle's Case Against the Market," *Canadian Journal of Economics*, February 1978, pp. 69–90.

5. For a detailed comparison of changes in the two systems, see Jan Tinbergen, "Do Communist and Free Economies Show a Convergence Pattern?" *Soviet Studies* 12, no. 4 (April 1961): 333–41.

6. For the pessimistic views about the rapid convergence of the two systems that John Galbraith and Arthur Schlesinger, Jr., expressed at a discussion we had during the International Conference on the Future of Democracy held at Athens in October 1977, see N. Gianaris, *Economic Development: Thought and Problems* (North Quincy, Mass.: Christopher Publishing House, 1978), p. 260. For similar doubts by M. Mihajlov, a Yugoslav writer, see his article in *New York Times*, July 26, 1971, p. 25.

7. For a related discussion see N. Gianaris, "Trends in Economic Relations in Balkan Countries," *Spoudai*, October–December 1977, pp. 849–64.

8. Trade between western Europe and the eastern bloc yielded some $16 billion earnings in 1978.

9. A similar economic organization was in operation around the fifth century B.C. See A. Zimmern, *The Greek Commonwealth* (London: Oxford University Press, 1961).

10. For related comments see Nicholas Gianaris, "Oikonomike Synergasia ton Valkanikon Horon kai e Tase Synergasmou ton Systematon" (Economic Cooperation of the Balkan Countries and the Trends of Convergence of the Systems), *Oikonomikos Tahydromos* (Athens), November 24, 1977, pp. 15-16; and Nicholas Gianaris, "Valkanike Synergasia" (Balkan Cooperation), *Ta Nea* (Athens), December 28, 1978.

11. Some difficulties of Balkan integration are presented in E. Pournarakis, "Development Integration in the Balkans," *Balkan Studies* 19, no. 2 (1978): 285-312.

APPENDIX

TABLE A.1

Gross Domestic Product, Balkan Countries, 1955-77
(constant 1975 prices in billions of national currencies)

Year	Albania	Bulgaria	Greece	Romania	Turkey	Yugoslavia
1955	3.1	2.8	193.0	68.0	166.0	131.0
1956	n.a.	2.7	209.0	62.0	172.0	126.0
1957	n.a.	3.2	223.0	72.0	185.0	154.0
1958	n.a.	3.5	233.0	75.0	194.0	159.0
1959	n.a.	4.2	242.0	85.0	203.0	185.0
1960	4.3	4.5	253.0	95.0	208.0	190.0
1961	4.7	4.7	280.0	103.0	212.0	202.0
1962	4.9	5.2	284.0	108.0	225.0	211.0
1963	5.4	5.7	313.0	118.0	246.0	237.0
1964	5.7	6.2	339.0	132.0	256.0	264.0
1965	6.5	6.6	371.0	146.0	263.0	267.0
1966	7.4	7.3	394.0	159.0	294.0	290.0
1967	8.2	7.9	415.0	171.0	307.0	299.0
1968	8.5	8.6	443.0	183.0	328.0	311.0
1969	9.1	9.3	487.0	196.0	345.0	343.0
1970	9.7	10.5	525.0	212.0	362.0	363.0
1971	10.8	10.4	563.0	238.0	395.0	396.0
1972	11.7	11.2	613.0	262.0	421.0	413.0
1973	12.9	12.1	658.0	290.0	439.0	434.0
1974	n.a.	13.1	634.0	326.0	477.0	472.0
1975	13.4	14.3	674.0	362.0	519.0	489.0
1976	n.a.	15.1	714.0	400.0	563.0	507.0
1977	n.a.	16.1	739.0	432.0	588.0	551.0

n.a. = not available.

Notes: For Albania (1966 prices) and Bulgaria (current prices), NMP; for Romania, national income instead of GDP.

Sources: United Nations, *Yearbook of National Accounts Statistics*, various years; OECD, *National Accounts*, various years.

TABLE A.2

**Regression Analysis of Gross Domestic Product on Investment:
Balkan Countries, 1958–77
(GDP = a + bINV)**

	a	b	F	$\bar{R}^2$	D–W
Albania	442.51 (1.28)	4.00 (23.25)	541	0.973	1.57
Bulgaria	1,264.60 (4.22)	2.61 (28.15)	792	0.977	0.85
Greece	68.90 (3.84)	3.58 (20.06)	403	0.937	0.58
Romania	66.62 (10.30)	5.90 (80.57)	6,492	0.997	1.73
Turkey	86.50 (8.47)	4.23 (24.44)	597	0.960	0.30
Yugoslavia	22.59 (2.25)	2.88 (32.63)	1,065	0.982	0.87

Notes: For Albania (1966 prices) and Bulgaria (current prices), NMP; for Romania, national income instead of GDP. Figures in parentheses represent t-values.

Sources: United Nations, *Yearbook of National Accounts Statistics*, various years; OECD, *National Accounts*, various years.

In Table A.2 statistical regressions are used to reveal the relationship between GDP and investment. For Albania, 16 net observations were available (in 1955–77); for Bulgaria and Yugoslavia, 20 observations (1958–77); for Greece, 28 (19 (1950–77); for Romania, 18 (1960–77); and for Turkey, 26 (1952–77).

Romania had the highest regression coefficient (5.9), followed by Turkey, Albania, and Greece. Thus, an increase of investment by 1 unit, during the period considered, was related to 5.9 units of increase in output or production in Romania, 4.2 units in Turkey, 4.0 in Albania, 3.6 in Greece, 2.9 in Yugoslavia, and only 2.6 in Bulgaria. These numerical values, which measure the slope of change in output (ΔQ) over change in investment (ΔI), $\Delta Q/\Delta I$, do not show the productivity of investment, because other factors in addition to investment, primarily labor, contribute to the increment of production. However, if the contribution of the other factors is about the same, then this relationship of change in output to change in investment gives an indication of the efficiency of investment in each country. It is worth mentioning that this slope, $\Delta Q/\Delta I$, is not the inverse of the incremental capital output ratio (ICOR), $\Delta K/\Delta Q$, in which the

TABLE A.3

Total Imports and Exports of the Balkan Countries, 1955–79
(F.O.B.; million current U.S. dollars)

	Albania		Bulgaria		Greece		Romania		Turkey		Yugoslavia	
	Imp.	Exp.	Imp.	Exp.	Imp.	Exp.	Imp.	Exp.	Imp.	Exp.	Imp.	Exp.
1955	43	13	250	236	382	183	462	422	497	313	441	257
1956	39	19	251	302	464	190	402	455	407	305	474	323
1957	53	29	332	370	524	220	492	422	397	345	661	395
1958	79	29	366	373	565	232	482	468	315	247	685	441
1959	85	34	579	467	567	204	502	522	470	354	687	477
1960	81	49	633	571	702	203	648	717	468	320	826	566
1961	72	49	666	663	714	223	815	792	509	346	910	569
1962	65	41	785	773	701	250	941	818	622	381	888	690
1963	71	48	933	834	714	290	1,022	915	691	368	1,056	790
1964	98	60	1,062	980	885	309	1,168	1,000	541	410	1,323	893
1965	108	69	1,178	1,176	1,134	328	1,077	1,101	576	463	1,288	1,091
1966	119	73	1,478	1,305	1,224	406	1,213	1,186	724	490	1,575	1,220
1967	130	79	1,572	1,459	1,186	495	1,546	1,395	691	522	1,707	1,252
1968	—	—	1,782	1,615	1,394	468	1,609	1,469	770	496	1,797	1,264
1969	—	—	1,749	1,794	1,594	554	1,740	1,633	754	537	2,134	1,474

1970	1,831	2,004	1,958	642	1,960	1,851	894	588	2,874	1,679
1971	2,120	2,182	2,098	662	2,103	2,101	1,087	677	3,297	1,836
1972	2,567	2,627	2,346	871	2,616	2,599	1,508	885	3,233	2,237
1973	3,266	3,301	3,477	1,456	3,468	3,699	2,049	1,317	4,783	3,020
1974	4,326	3,836	4,385	2,030	5,144	4,874	3,720	1,538	7,520	3,805
1975	5,408	4,691	5,321	2,286	5,342	5,341	4,640	1,401	7,697	4,072
1976	5,626	5,382	6,051	2,558	6,095	6,137	4,993	1,960	7,367	4,896
1977	6,393	6,351	6,852	2,756	7,018	7,021	5,694	1,753	9,634	4,896
1978	7,736	7,560	7,655	3,375	9,086	8,237	4,479	2,288	9,988	5,671
1979	8,512	8,780	9,641	3,856	10,915	9,723	4,946	2,261	12,862	6,491

Note: National currencies were converted into dollars at each year's rate. In 1979 they were 115.6 U.S. cents per lev; 2.673 cents per drachma; 22.37 cents per leu; 2.771 cents per lira for imports and 2.985 cents per lira for exports; and 5.4795 cents per dinar.

Source: United Nations, *Yearbook of International Trade Statistics*, various years.

numerator shows changes in total capital or cumulative investments. It simply shows changes in output over changes in investment—the trend of these variables over time.

For all the countries considered, the regression fit was very good ($\bar{R}^2 >$ 0.937). However, the Durbin-Watson (D-W) statistic was higher than the critical value (at 5 percent level of significance) only in Albania and Romania; in the other countries it was somewhat low, indicating the existence of serial correlation, and the results should be interpreted with caution.

A regression analysis of the average labor productivity (Q/L) on investment (INV) is presented below for the countries for which statistical data are available (1958–77):

(1) $Q/L = a + b \, INV$

where *a* is the constant and *b* is the regression coefficient.

	a	b	T-Statistic	$\bar{R}^2$
Bulgaria	2,238.70	0.36	21.41	0.960
Romania	8.84	0.56	34.21	0.987
Yugoslavia	439.16	0.40	10.97	0.869

As the regressions derived from equation (1) indicate, a 1-unit change in investment is associated with a change of 0.36 unit of labor productivity in Bulgaria, 0.40 unit in Yugoslavia, and 0.56 unit in Romania. Thus, investment in Romania is associated with higher rates of labor productivity than in Yugoslavia and Bulgaria.

In all these cases the T-statistics and the corrected coefficients of determination ($\bar{R}^2$) were high enough to indicate a good fit of the regression equations.

A multiple regression analysis for the Yugoslav economy indicates that "exports" (EXP) is a better explanatory variable for labor productivity than is investment. Inflation (INF) is negatively related to labor productivity.

The results of the regression for which the years 1958–76 were used, are as follows:

(2) $Q/L = 0.55 + 0.37 \, EXP - 0.23 \, INF + 0.20 \, INV$ $\bar{R}^2 = 0.958$
         (0.58)   (−0.01)   (0.22)   D-W = 1.38

The figures in parentheses represent the t-values.

As equation (2) demonstrates, when exports change by 1 percent, labor productivity changes by 0.37 percent; the same change in investment explains 0.20 percent of labor productivity. Moreover, when inflation increases by 1 percent, labor productivity declines by 0.23 percent. It seems proper, therefore, for Yugoslavia to emphasize an increase in exports because of the increased labor productivity, which would permit higher remuneration of workers.

The D-W statistic in equation (2) was higher than the critical value, indicating no significant serial correlation.

Table A.4 indicates that each change of 1 unit in exports is related to about 1 unit of change in investment in Bulgaria, Greece, and Yugoslavia; 3 units in Turkey; and 4 units in Albania and Romania. In all cases $\bar{R}^2$ was high enough to indicate a very good fit for the regressions. However, the D-W statistic was mostly lower than the critical value (at 5 percent level of significance), indicating serial correlation.

The multiple regression analysis presented in Table A.5 indicates that for Greece and Turkey "exports" is a better explanatory variable of changes in GDP than is investment, while the opposite is true for Bulgaria, Romania, and Yugoslavia. It would seem, therefore, that postwar economic growth of the socialist Balkan economies, with the exception of Albania (where only nine net observations of exports were available), was based primarily on an increase in capital formation or investment, and not so much on an increase in exports, as was the case in the market economies of Greece and Turkey, where the export regression coefficients were relatively high (2.9 and 8.2, respectively).

TABLE A.4

**Regression of Investment on Exports:
Balkan Countries, 1958–77
(INV = a + bEXP)**

	a	b	F	$\bar{R}^2$	D–W
Albania	154.13 (1.90)	4.26 (15.20)	231	0.966	1.98
Bulgaria	1,074.70 (5.05)	0.81 (10.60)	112	0.854	0.41
Greece	27.66 (4.27)	1.26 (11.63)	135	0.833	0.30
Romania	19.10 (5.49)	4.39 (20.60)	424	0.961	0.42
Turkey	−6.79 (−2.00)	3.14 (19.02)	362	0.935	0.64
Yugoslavia	53.15 (10.20)	0.93 (12.52)	156	0.891	0.85

Notes: For Albania (1966 prices) and Bulgaria (current prices), NMP; for Romania, national income instead of GDP. Figures in parentheses are t-values.

Sources: United Nations, *Yearbook of National Accounts Statistics*, various years; OECD, *National Accounts*, various years.

TABLE A.5

Multiple Regression Analysis of Gross Domestic Product on Investment and Exports: Balkan Countries, 1958-77 (GDP = a + b$_1$ INV + b$_2$ EXP)

	a	b$_1$	b$_2$	F	$\bar{R}^2$	D-W
Albania	1,395.50 (1.88)	1.37 (0.49)	8.78 (0.72)	25	0.855	1.52
Bulgaria	1,930.40 (10.66)	1.76 (13.65)	0.80 (7.10)	1,510	0.994	1.62
Greece	100.21 (13.39)	1.66 (9.56)	2.89 (12.04)	1,388	0.990	1.18
Romania	66.64 (7.11)	5.90 (16.87)	0.004 (0.002)	3,043	0.997	1.73
Turkey	60.37 (7.15)	1.78 (3.76)	8.25 (5.41)	665	0.981	0.70
Yugoslavia	69.67 (10.04)	1.88 (15.61)	1.04 (8.77)	2,815	0.997	2.55

Notes: For Albania (1966 prices) and Bulgaria (current prices), NMP; for Romania, national income instead of GDP. For Albania, 9 observations; for Greece, 1950-77. Figures in parentheses are t-values.

Sources: Tables A.1 and A.3.

Table A.5 shows that in all the countries considered, the regression fit was very good. The corrected coefficient of determination, $\bar{R}^2$, was more than 0.980 for all countries. However, for Albania, where variations were relatively large, the data would hardly give reliable projections. The D-W statistic was higher than the critical value (1.1 at 5 percent level of significance) for Albania, Bulgaria, Romania, and Yugoslavia. For Greece and Turkey, however, it fell in the inconclusive range or was low enough to signify the existence of serial correlation and thus make the projections doubtful.

NAME INDEX

SUBJECT INDEX

Achaeans, 4, 10, 11
Adrianople, 13, 23, 123
Aegean islands, 10, 24, 36
Africa, 48, 49, 81
agriculture, 13, 31, 34, 50, 73,
    100, 110, 112, 120, 124–25,
    126, 128, 131, 157
aid, foreign, 153
Albania, 4, 7, 16, 17, 19, 30, 38,
    39, 42, 47, 48, 57, 59, 65–
    66, 69, 79, 81–83, 86–88, 89–
    90, 92, 93, 99, 100, 103, 110,
    111, 115, 117, 120, 126, 129,
    140, 143–44, 147, 152, 154,
    168, 173
  energy consumption, 149
  member of Comecon, 159
  regressions, sectoral, 173–74,
    177, 178
  sectoral allocation of invest-
    ment, 125
  trade, 140, 147, 149
  transportation, 124
Albanian League, 30
allocation of productive resources,
    163, 164
Ankara, Turkey, 37, 45, 50, 60
Armenia, 17, 23
Asia Minor, 10, 12, 17, 21, 24, 25,
    37, 43, 116
Athens, 11, 18, 20, 40, 50, 51,
    60, 88, 112–13, 120
Austria, 18, 19, 21, 23, 24, 25, 49,
    118, 122–23, 154

balance of payments, 44, 45, 141,
    157
balanced growth, 109, 149
Balkan Conference, 50, 51
Balkan Entente, 42, 50
Balkan wars, 49
Belgrade, 79, 116, 152
Berlin, Treaty of, 23, 34
Bessarabia, 13, 19, 21, 25, 26, 27,
    41, 42, 43
birth rate, 26, 82
Black Sea, 11, 14, 16, 19, 20, 24,
    50, 79–80, 120, 121
Bosnia and Herzegovina, 22, 23,
    46, 48, 72, 74
Braila, Romania, 22
"brain drain," 84
Bucharest, 21, 22, 24–26, 33, 50,
    148, 152
Bucharest, Treaty of, 24
Bukovina, 13, 18, 25, 41, 42
Bulgaria, 4, 7, 32, 33–36, 37, 41,
    42, 43, 46–48, 49–51, 57,
    59, 60, 62, 63, 66, 68, 69,
    79–81, 82, 83, 84, 86, 87,
    89–90, 93, 101, 103–104,
    110, 114–15, 117, 120, 121,
    122, 129–40, 143, 145,
    151–53
  energy consumption in, 149
  exports, 148, 158, 160
  member of Comecon, 158, 167
  sectoral ICORs, 126
  statistical regressions for, 173–76,
    177–78
  transportation, 122, 123

per capita income (*see* income per capita)

Peloponnesus, 10, 15

petroleum, 22, 42, 64, 114, 149, 153

Phanariots, 19, 40

Philike Hetairia (Society of Friends), 20

planning, imperative, 59

planning, indicative, 59, 73

pollution, 9, 40

population density, 82, 83, 102
    growth, 83, 89
    rural surplus, 26
    urban, 27, 88, 89

productivity, 41, 75, 77, 92-98, 115, 120, 139, 140, 170
    labor, 26, 71, 98-101, 102-103, 164, 170, 176
    capital, 103-104

reforms, agricultural, 112

reforms, economic, 45, 70

regional pluralism, 111

regressions, statistical, 173-76, 177-78

Rhodes, 39

Rhodope Mountains, 22

Romania, 4, 6, 7, 13, 18-20, 21, 22-23, 24-27, 32, 36, 37, 40-43, 49-51, 57, 59-60, 62, 63, 65-66, 68-69, 71-80, 82-84, 86, 87-88, 89, 90, 92, 93, 97-98, 100-101, 103-104, 120, 124-25, 126, 129-31, 137, 139-40, 144, 149, 151, 152-53, 155, 167, 168, 170
    education, 42
    energy consumption, 149
    exports, 147, 148
    member of Comecon, 159-60, 167
    national income, 172

regressions, statistical, 173-76, 177-78

sectoral ICORs, 216

sectoral investment, 124-25

transportation, 121-22, 123

Romans, 4, 13-14, 16

Russia, 17, 19, 21, 23, 24-25, 27, 33, 36-37, 41, 42-43, 48, 49, 73, 79, 81, 167

Salonika, 13, 20, 23-25, 43, 50, 60, 79, 82, 116, 120, 121-22, 123-24

savings, 40, 94

sectoral allocation of investment, 124-25

sectoral pluralism, 110-11

self-management, 72

Serbia, 19-20, 22-23, 24-25, 35, 47, 48, 49, 72, 74

Sèvres, Treaty of, 37, 43

Slavs, 13, 14-16, 17, 20, 41, 46, 81

Slovenia, 48, 73-74

Smyrna, 20, 37, 79

Sofia, 13

South Africa, 32

Soviet Union, 41, 45, 47, 71, 76, 98, 110, 128, 140, 148, 153, 158, 170

Spahis, 18

state capitalism, 63

Struma (Strimon) River, 79

subsoil resources, 80

Syria, 10, 43, 122

tariffs, 46, 50, 97-98, 145, 154, 156

taxation, 25, 46, 57, 165

tax incentives, 94-95

tax system, 34, 98

technological improvement, 99, 111, 164

ABOUT THE AUTHOR

NICHOLAS V. GIANARIS earned the B.A. at the Graduate School of Economics and Business of Athens, the LL.B. at the University of Athens, and the M.A. and Ph.D. in economics at New York University. He has taught in the United States and abroad. At present he is associate professor and economics program coordinator at Fordham University, Lincoln Center, New York.

Dr. Gianaris is a member of the American Economic Association, Royal Economic Society (U.K.), Economic History Association, and American Association of University Professors. Listed in *American Men of Science* and similar volumes, he has also received the N.Y.U. Founders Award for scholarly achievements.

He has contributed a number of articles to both American and international economics publications and has presented panel papers at symposia on southeastern Europe. Parts of his previous book, *Economic Development: Thought and Problems* (1978), were translated into French and Spanish by the International Monetary Fund for use in the IMF Institute's courses on financial analysis and policy.